RECEIVING LOVE

RECEIVING LOVE

Transform Your Relationship
by Letting Yourself Be Loved

Harville Hendrix, Ph.D.

and

Helen LaKelly Hunt, Ph.D.

**SIMON &
SCHUSTER**

LONDON • SYDNEY • NEW YORK • TORONTO

First published in Great Britain by Simon & Schuster UK Ltd, 2005
A Viacom Company

Copyright © 2004 by Harville Hendrix and Helen LaKelly Hunt

The right of Harville Hendrix and Helen LaKelly Hunt to be identified as authors
of this work has been asserted in accordance with sections 77 and 78 of the
Copyright, Designs and Patents Act, 1988.

3 5 7 9 10 8 6 4 2

Simon & Schuster UK Ltd
Africa House
64–78 Kingsway
London WC2B 6AH

www.simonsays.co.uk

Simon & Schuster Australia
Sydney

A CIP catalogue record for this book is available from the British Library

ISBN 0-7432-6364-2
EAN 9780743263641

Printed and bound in Great Britain by
Mackays of Chatham Plc, Chatham, Kent

Acknowledgments

Every book is the result of a partnership with many persons and sources.

We want to especially thank the many couples whose lives and work are reflected in these pages. Were it not for their vulnerability and courage, this book would never have been conceived, much less written. These include couples who shared their lives in therapy and those who contributed their insights on the healing process in response to our research inquiry and telephone-bridge conversations.

We also want to thank the many Imago Relationship therapists who contributed their experience of working with couples around the issue of receiving, contributed their wisdom, and helped conduct the research that led to our conclusions.

Sanam Hoon, our assistant, deserves special appreciation for her tireless and splendid management of the couples' research project, and for collating all the interviews into useful information.

Our office staff deserves special appreciation for handling the details of our lives so that we would have the time to complete this book. They include Michell, Sally, Rich, Nedra, and our house-keeper, Eileen.

In addition, we want to thank the people in our lives who have helped us personally learn to receive. The Imago community of wise and loving Imago therapists saw ways that both of us have given, but in a patient and loving way they also helped us experience new levels of receiving love. We acknowledge and honor each one in the Imago community.

Deep thanks goes to Barney Karpfinger, our agent and friend, who has been our support and manager through the whole project.

We want to thank Tracy Behar, our editor at Atria Books, and her colleagues, Suzanne O'Neill, Judith Curr, and Wendy Walker, for their availability and support. We could not have brought this project to completion without them.

Finally, we extend affectionate thanks to the Rev. Dr. Jim Forbes, pastor of The Riverside Church in New York City. Not only did he officiate at our personal recommitment ceremony, he has hosted several Imago Relationship Therapy workshops for couples at the church. We think it is fitting to end these acknowledgments with the poem he wrote about the core dilemma which is at the heart of this book:

Receiving and Giving

I'm a novice when it comes to receiving.
Giving has become my expertise.
But giving alone without getting
Becomes soon a fatal disease

If the intake valve is not opened
There's no way to maintain a supply.
There comes a point in the cycle of life
When the out-going stream runs dry.

Straining out love from a vacuum
Is like drinking from the heart of a stone.
Try as we may, at the end of the day,
We're exhausted, frustrated, alone.

"Better to give than receive," we are taught.
Yet another truth I've learned just by living:
Only the soul with the grace to receive,
Excels in the fine art of giving.

The Rev. Dr. James A. Forbes, Jr.
Senior Pastor, The Riverside Church, NYC
Copyright 1995, New York City

A Special Appreciation

Jean Coppock Staeheli has been our writer and friend for many years. We want to express a special appreciation for her tireless work in bringing this project to fruition. From many random notes, conversations, and case illustrations, she has used her considerable writing talents to bring order out of chaos. We owe her a debt of gratitude for her perseverance during these months and her patience with us as we attempted to make sense out of the material. Thank you, Jean.

Dedication

This book is dedicated to the Board of Imago Relationships International, Inc., a nonprofit organization created and run by Imago therapists committed to providing service to Imago therapists worldwide, and dedicated to the mission of transforming the world one couple at a time: Sara Boxnboim, Ronald Clark, Dan Glaser, Suzette Loh, Michael Borash, Maureen Brine, Bruce Crapuchettes, April Lorenzen, Karl Leitner, Robert Patterson, Kay Schwarzberg, Virginia Thomas, Pam Monday, Wendy Patterson, Eugene Shelly, Maryrita Wieners.

Contents

RECEIVING LOVE

Introduction

Twenty-six years ago the two of us initiated our own romance with a passionate discussion of the significance of "relationship." We spent a good hour on our first date going back and forth about what Dostoevsky meant when he expressed the idea in *The Brothers Karamazov* that God could be more easily found in human love than in the human mind.[1] Since we had just met, this was more a philosophical discussion than a personal one, but it did help us see from the very beginning that we shared a rather unusual interest. In between talk of our previous marriages and our four children, we both confessed that we were fascinated by how the ordinary experiences of attraction, love, and commitment can reveal profound truths about what it means to be human.

Twenty-six years later we're still excited about the same subject. We've devoted our professional lives to probing the surprises and paradoxes of intimate relationships. Two people who are terribly flawed can create a splendid partnership, while two people who've been given every advantage can create an awful partnership. Why the difference? Since 1991 we've been exploring this question and others in a series of books that describe what we have called Imago Relationship Therapy. The first book, *Getting the Love You Want*[2] showed couples the hidden dynamics operating in all marriages and presented tools for turning negative interactions into opportunities for loving connection. In 1992, Harville wrote *Keeping the Love You Find*[3] for single people who wanted to experience personal growth through relationships outside of marriage, and in 1998, we wrote *Giving the Love that Heals*[4] for parents who wanted to create conscious and nurturing relationships with their children. Our original insights into the patterns of attraction and marital happiness still hold, but we now know more about the hidden stumbling blocks that can sabotage all the good intentions partners bring to each other.

In this book our fascination with relationships has led us back again to the possibilities we see in marriage. Despite the 50 percent–plus divorce rate, we believe that marriage continues to exist as pure potential. We see the form of marriage evolving to accommodate a change from what's best for the individuals to what's best for the relationship itself.[5] We don't believe that marriage cannot work, but rather that our current, self-focused form of marriage isn't working.

There is always hope for turning a relationship between two, isolated individuals into a true partnership. In every union, there is potential for two wounded people to heal and grow because of the quality of their connection. Ongoing interaction with a long-term partner can be an agent of transformation more powerful than any other. We have come to believe that it is the clearest way for transformation to occur. Marriage may look like a gamble, but the rewards—mental and spiritual wholeness—are very high. Our goal has been to figure out how to reduce the gamble and increase the probability of success.

We are more convinced than ever of the power that relationship has to create and recreate who we are throughout life. From the moment of birth, in a beautifully sensitive feedback loop, infants and their parents learn how to connect with each other to ensure that the infant will survive. The child absorbs these early lessons, and they become blueprints for future interpersonal connections. Although these foundational blueprints can certainly be changed, it's not easy to erase those first lines and carefully redraw the improvements. Fortunately, all of us have the capacity to replace those first blueprints when necessary to become better companions and partners, if we want to work at it.

In addition to the importance of family relationships, each person's link with himself or herself determines how relationships are formed with others. Whether a child learns self-acceptance or self-rejection has implications for every aspect of her relationship with those close to her, especially the intimate partners she will have as she gets older. She will approach her partner with acceptance or rejection depending upon the way she feels about herself. If she can use her relationships as a vehicle for self-caring and self-esteem, she will become a better partner to her husband. Positive changes within the relationship will effect positive changes within the self.

In our previous books we have focused on understanding and explaining human nature in relationship to intimate partnership. Our interest in human nature led us to consider a deeper and larger question: "What kind of universe do we live in that would account for the dynamics of intimate partnership that we can observe?" Our overall interest was in understanding more about where we as human beings fit into the larger tapestry of being. The question of the nature of reality, of what *is,* is essentially an ontological question.[6] Our approach to this big question, though, was by way of an everyday observation that everyone makes. Couples fight. We wanted to know *why* couples fight and ended up developing a theory that describes the basic laws of attraction and de-attraction in marriage. As a result, we became very interested in how people could use psychological concepts to understand and change their behavior.

In this book we continue our psychological line of inquiry and broaden it to explore why people have trouble accepting compliments and positive feedback from their partners and others. But, in addition, we infuse our practical discussion of the role of receiving in intimate relationships with one more philosophical question: "How do we know what we know?" This is the central question in epistemology, a branch of philosophy that explores the origin, nature, methods, and limitations of human knowledge.[7] Throughout the book we pay attention to how we absorb, integrate, and make use of what we "know." Although questions about the fundamental "laws" of human behavior belong formally to psychology, and questions about knowing belong formally to the field of epistemology, we will turn these discussions into user-friendly tools that can help us better relate to our partners and change our behavior.

Finally, we are grateful to be writing this book now because new advances in the field of neurobiology are beginning to clarify the biological mechanisms that underlie psychological insights and observations. Many scientists agree that the human mind is the final frontier of knowledge. To follow the trails that are being blazed in brain research is truly exciting. Although the field is new, it is astounding how much we are learning about how significant relationships influence the creation of sensations, thoughts, emotions, and behaviors, and how these different functions are interconnected within the mind and body. In particular, we have been fascinated to learn that close relationships are *the* crucial variable in neuropsychological development.[8] We will bring information from the frontier of neuroscience into our discussions whenever we feel it will clarify or expand your understanding of intimate partnerships.

We share the view of ancient traditions and popular wisdom in believing that everything *is* connected. We may not know we are connected or feel connected, but we cannot *not* be connected. That is our essence. We are One with the Universe. Writing this book has helped us see the complex network of connections in marriage. On the simplest level, two individuals form a connection when they commit to joining their lives together; each partner comes not only connected to the universe, but already connected to his or her past relationships and experiences; and together they create a system of giving and receiving love, which they share with their children if they have them. And this is just the beginning. We will discover many more circles, loops, and interconnected systems as we explore how to create a truly splendid, conscious relationship, where partners receive as well as give.

IMAGO RELATIONSHIP THERAPY 101

Whether you are well versed in Imago Relationship Therapy or are coming to it for the first time, it will be helpful to review a few basic principles.

Our choice of romantic partners is not random. Unconsciously we are drawn to people who share characteristics with one or both of our parents. When people first get this insight into the mystery of romantic attraction, they are surprised: "You mean I was attracted to my husband because he's like my father?" This can come as a shock, especially when the relationship with dear old dad isn't so great. But when they pause to think about it, they can definitely see the similarity between their partner and one or both of their parents, probably the one who was most problematic. They may come to see that their relationship offers a second chance to revisit the same issues they dealt with in childhood—only, this time, to get it right.

This insight—so fundamental to Imago Relationship Therapy—has led to a deeper understanding of the complexities of attraction and attachment. Sooner or later in every relationship, the initial attraction turns into a power struggle as couples find themselves facing in their spouse the same behaviors and attitudes that drove them crazy in their parents. If the relationship is to evolve from romantic attraction and the consequent power struggle into mature love, the task is to learn to love the difficult parts of your partner, especially those that mirror parts of yourself that you've rejected or hidden, or of which you've lost awareness. When you do begin to love your partner more fully, you begin to heal those places in yourself that were initially wounded in your relationship with your parents.

Although learning to love what bugs you the most is not easy, even distressed couples can learn to do it. After twelve years and the combined experience of more than two thousand Imago therapists, we know that any two people who are willing to look into their past and learn new ways of both containing and expressing their feelings can put their relationship on a better plane. People who make the effort discover a secret: *It turns out that loving your partner is the best way to facilitate your own personal and spiritual growth.*

Most relationships flourish under the influence of these ideas and the therapeutic techniques that accompany them. Couples who've absorbed the insights and made use of the tools we've offered have experienced an amazing renewal. But we became increasingly aware that the Imago Relationship Therapy model was not yet complete. Sometimes people can learn to love their partners, warts and all, *but their partners can't accept it.* Their relationship is thrown out of balance when one or both of them put up barriers to the positive approaches of the other. Unless a positive flow of *giving* and *receiving* is established or *re*established, progress in improving the relationship grinds to a halt. It isn't because these people refuse to do what will be helpful to the relationship; it's that following the steps correctly doesn't always result in a positive transformation.

We didn't understand how important this last step, learning to receive love, was when we wrote *Getting the Love You Want.* We thought that once we taught people to give each other what they needed (which, as any committed couple knows, is challenging enough), we could release them with our blessing to live happily ever after. Who wouldn't be eager to accept the gift of love freely given? We never thought about the fact that the ability to receive love isn't natural and inborn for everyone.

We have since discovered that some lucky souls blossom and heal when they are offered what they need. But most of us have some trouble taking in affection, praise, support, compliments, or gifts from others. For some reason, we are not always able to swallow, digest, and use this food for the soul. We can taste these morsels of love, but we can't digest them as nourishment. Like many people with food allergies, we are left craving the very thing we cannot digest.

Although a reluctance to receive is easy to see in intimate relationships, it's more than a relationship problem. It's an individual problem that shows up everywhere. Notice the next time you deflect a compliment, feel uncomfortable when someone gives you a gift, or feel embarrassed when you are praised. The impulse to step away from positive input is an indication that you have problems receiving. You can use the discussion in this book to help you become more open and receptive, whether you are in a committed relationship or are single.

If you are in a committed relationship, to realize the full potential that exists in your relationship, you will have to deal with this last barrier to getting the love you want. Our previous work has concentrated on the very real difficulties of giving. Now we're going to complete the cycle and focus on the surprising difficulties of receiving.

WHEN THE PROFESSIONAL BECOMES THE PERSONAL

Our recognition that receiving love is a common relationship problem has come slowly through our professional work and our private lives. Over the last decade, Harville's continuing clinical practice and

Helen's academic studies have allowed us to bring new insights to those couples who progressed just fine to a certain point in therapy, but then got stuck. They learned to ask for what they needed, and they learned to give what was required to meet each other's needs. But still the quality of their interaction was the same as if they had *never* learned these skills. No amount of insight or coaching from the therapist helped them to move forward.

We also began to hear from other Imago therapists who felt that some of their couples would make wonderful progress for many months and then, unaccountably, stall out. These clients appeared stubbornly closed to the efforts of their partners and their therapists to draw them toward more positive interactions in the relationship. Gradually, we began to piece together a picture of what was happening. Many of the case examples in this book have been drawn from the extensive interviews Imago therapists have conducted with their clients in an effort to learn more about the resolution of this challenge and others through therapy.

In a neat but painful bit of synchronicity, a major source of insight for this book has turned out to be what was happening in our own marriage. During the years when we were becoming internationally known as relationship experts, we were privately stumbling up against our own difficulties. We knew that while our books and workshops were a lifeline for thousands of other intimate relationships, our own marriage was beginning to sputter and go out. Our hard-won knowledge of how to build a conscious partnership was not enough to protect us from the stresses and strains that were pulling us apart. Not only was this heartbreaking; it was humiliating.

We were finally at the point of divorce. With great sadness we concluded that we could not, in good conscience, tell other people what to do, nor could we present new material to Imago therapists until we had resolved our own problems. We attended the next conference of Imago therapists and told them our marriage was in trouble. They responded to our news with deep, loving support for us as individuals and with the hope that we could find a way to repair our marriage. We left feeling their love and understanding. Their response was a critical factor in our deciding to give our relationship one more year.

We committed to doing everything we could to find out what had gone wrong and how we could repair it. The most important commitments we made from the beginning were to end negativity and move toward amplifying the positive, even though we said many times that we didn't know how to do that. We went back to our Imago Relationship Therapy primer and began to observe how we were interacting. We learned a lot from witnessing how we dealt with our individual issues from childhood and our personal needs. There is one particular moment from that time, however, that stands out as especially instrumental in having helped us understand the subject of this book. One morning, when we were most troubled, we were in our bedroom, and I, Helen, asked Harville, "Do you believe that I love you?"

Harville thought about that for a couple of seconds and said, "No, I don't think you do." I was distraught. I could only respond, "Given all that I do for you and our life together, how could you not know how much I love you?"

But all I, Harville, knew then was that I didn't *feel* loved.

At the same time, there was a rational part of me that knew that my feelings didn't make any sense. Helen had loved my children, she had loved *our* children, she had supported me, and she had supported my work. And here I was turning her generosity into something more self-serving. I was trying to convince myself that there were strings attached to what Helen gave me, that she only did those things because she wanted something back. It was hard for me to admit how much I devalued all of her gifts. Only with time and reflection did I realize that I was not able to recognize genuine love when it was offered.

That morning was our lowest point. How we turned this situation around is really at the heart of the recovery part of this book.

LEARNING TO KNOW MORE COMPLETELY

As we began to work on our marriage, we realized that it would be helpful to reflect upon the premises and beliefs we had brought into our relationship. We began to feel that part of the stressful dynamic we had cocreated was the result of something we had not thought of before. It had to do with how we were relating to Imago Relationship Therapy and each other. We knew a lot about the Imago work. We wrote about it, and spoke about it to others, but we were not integrating it. It was staying at the intellectual level and not getting down to the heart. We were assuming that because we knew the Imago theories intellectually, we were living it. Unfortunately, that was not true.

In studying feminist psychology, Helen came across an idea that proved to be an awakening.[9] It was about the different ways people can know things, and it was called the theory of separate and connected knowing.

The theory of separate and connected knowing states that there are two main ways we know and learn. Separate knowing has a long history in Western academia, starting with the Socratic method. Separate knowing is the kind of linear, goal-oriented knowing most often identified with scientific or empirical methods. In this tradition, the knower is presumed to be separate and detached from the object under consideration. The knower adopts a critical approach to the subject in order to understand it more clearly. His attitude is, "Okay. Prove it. Convince me." When separate knowing is the primary method employed in any given situation, an adversarial and competitive approach toward understanding predominates. The assumption is that any group of randomly chosen people will be able to understand and describe reality in the same, objective way. In other words, what is real and true exists independently of who is doing the observation.

Connected knowing takes place when the knower is aware of employing intuition, emotion, and empathy during the knowing process. The connected knower is not detached and uninvolved. To participate in connected knowing, you must actively affirm the person you are attempting to understand. This affirmation is more than an attempt at sympathetic understanding or the absence of negative evaluation. It is a positive, effortful act that imagines the other person and his or her point of view as fully as possible. The connected knower's attitude is, "Okay. Let me suspend my own critical judgment for a minute and see if I can enter your world and try to feel the truth of what you are saying." An incomplete understanding of connected knowing would lead to the conclusion that connected know-ers can't discern the truth because they muddy the waters with per-sonal feelings, memories, or perceptions. But this isn't right. Con-nected knowing, when done well, uses the knower's intuition, emotion, and empathy as part of the process leading to sound, inde-pendent judgments. Instead of observing the world from a detached, objective position and assuming this position results in an unbiased view of the truth, connected knowing views truth as a process that is evolving and cocreated by those who are participating in it.

Our culture trains us to be separate knowers. The language of objective, rational evaluation and logical thinking has been essential for the evolution of modern society. Science and technology depend upon it. But we haven't had a common language for talking about the contribution made to our maturity and wisdom through what we can sense, feel, and perceive as insight. It's true that connected know-ing has always existed and made significant contributions, but it has always been a poor cousin to rational, logical thought. Fortunately, we are moving from the pejorative designation of connected knowing as "soft thinking" to the recognition that it is an equally valid way of knowing.

Obviously, we need both ways of knowing. People who can use both methods of knowing are open to new points of view and capa-ble of reaching new levels of understanding. They are able to evaluate what they've come to understand, connect it to other things they know, engage in problem solving, and implement actions and solu-tions as a result. A balanced capacity for separate and connected knowing is directly related to the ability to receive love. To receive love, you have to cognitively *know* you are loved (as a separate knower), and you have to *feel* loved in your head, heart, and body (as a connected knower). Knowing it in your head isn't enough.

Most people, however, are not balanced separate and connected knowers. As we were, they are overly reliant on one way of knowing at the expense of the other. Their ability to take in the outside input that could make them whole is limited, so they remain partial selves instead of whole selves. Separate knowers, with few connected knowing skills, tend to be objective, detached, and unable to participate in the experi-ence of other people. Separate knowers have rigid boundaries.

Connected knowers, with few separate knowing skills, have diffuse boundaries and fuse with the experience of others. Connected knowers cannot distinguish their experience from others, and find it difficult to back off and reflect on their situation. Since separate and connected knowers are attracted to each other, when they relate it's like trying to wire two cables together with half of the connecting wires missing. You get a lot of sparks, but the connection just isn't made.

That was certainly true in our case. Helen identified herself as a connected knower, especially when it came to our marriage. She was so embedded in her feelings that she was unable to see our problems clearly, and unable to distance herself enough to take effective action to address them. I, on the other hand, was a separate knower who distanced myself through analysis, and therefore didn't connect to what was happening in my own relationship. Every time Helen approached me as a connected knower, I retreated behind my skills as a separate knower. I distanced myself through analysis, and therefore didn't fully connect to our relationship. The wall between the overly emotional, nonanalytical partner and the emotionally distant, evaluating partner seemed impenetrable.

Fortunately, our commitment to each other was stronger than the wall we had built. Separate and connected knowing proved to be our opening. It gave us a language for understanding what each of us had suppressed. It was the insight we needed to identify and integrate the inner voice of emotion with the outer voice of logic and reason. We now think we were so receptive to the richness of this concept because, in many ways, Imago Relationship Therapy reflects the same insights. Imago Dialogue, in particular, stretches each partner to experience and strengthen his or her joint capacities for both separate and connected knowing.

Once we had the idea of separate and connected knowing, we used Imago Dialogue to explore and integrate separate and connected knowing into our relationship. We worked at balancing the tension between the two and solidifying their complementary natures. After more than twenty years of marriage, we began to "know" things about each other that changed the way we connected. "Knowing" became both a feeling and a thinking process that allowed us to meet each other in the middle of the emotional-cognitive continuum. We helped each other back from the edges of the extreme. I (Helen) became more of a problem solver, and Harville became more attuned to emotional content. We were able to integrate capacities we had lost. This led to greater congruence between our inner and outer lives, and movement toward wholeness and integrity. We moved toward a reconciliation of thought, word, and deed that invited us into an expanded consciousness.

It didn't take long before we saw our personal struggles with separate and connected knowing reflected in the world around us. We began to explore how our private "Aha!" discovery could be made useful to Imago therapists and clients as they labored to improve the quality of their relationships. Imago therapists readily appreciated its power. They saw how they could monitor their own impulses toward separate and connected knowing, and help their clients expand their capacity to be more receptive.[10] Clients could be coached on how to recognize when they were out of balance. Our exploration into these and other applications for separate and connected knowing is just beginning.

MAKING OUR WAY BACK

During our year of repair and healing, we made a steady "three steps forward and one step back" kind of progress. We refreshed our stagnating spiritual lives, became more conscious in our interactions, and spent time listening and talking to each other on a deeper level than we had before. Instead of keeping our Imago Relationship Therapy knowledge at the cognitive level of separate knowing, we worked hard to make it an integral part of our everyday lives. We now have the loving partnership that we have talked about in all of our writings on Imago Relationship Therapy. To paraphrase Gandhi's famous pronouncement on change, we have *become* the kind of partnership we would like to see in the world.

This book is our way of fulfilling our promise to share what we have learned through our own odyssey, as well as through our clinical observation of other couples in crisis. There will be times when we speak openly in the book about our own experience. But, more often, when we draw directly from our own relationship, we will disguise it to protect our privacy (as we always do when we use biographical information from others). Under all our insights, conclusions, and suggestions, however, there is the conviction that comes from having seen it and done it ourselves.

The book is organized into three parts. Part I explores the problem; Part II explores the solution; Part III offers exercises to help couples move through the problem to the solution. Throughout, you'll have the benefit of learning how other couples have struggled, like you, to open their hearts to love. And you'll hear from them directly about the gifts they've received as a result.

SPECIAL NOTE

The couples used in this book are composites drawn from many different individuals. The quotations and psychological dynamics are real, but some of the details of their lives have been changed to protect their identities.

PART I: UNDERSTANDING THE PROBLEM

CHAPTER 1

Nothing's Ever Good Enough

You're never happy with anything I do. I feel like giving up.

When it comes to love relationships, things are often not what they seem. The common wisdom is that romantic relationships would stay happy if people did a better job of *giving* to each other. But that's not what we've discovered. We've found that many people need to do a better job of *receiving* the gifts their partners are already offering. It's surprising how often the compliments, appreciations, and encouragements of a well-intentioned partner make no dent in the armor of an unhappy partner. The compliments are brushed off, the votes of confidence are discounted, and the words of encouragement fall on deaf ears. Why does this happen? And why does this universal but unexplored quirk of human nature carry with it implications for the health of marriage as an institution and the quality of our lives in community with others?

Let's begin with the couple who first inspired our odyssey into the hidden complications of receiving love. After we had been working with George and Mary for several months, George finally understood that Mary wanted more affection. He learned to listen to how she wanted it expressed: gentle tone of voice, looking into her eyes, light kisses on the lips, and a hug twice a day. He worked on it until he got it just right, and then he started giving her these expressions of affection every day as a gift.

What was Mary's reaction? She rejected him. As a separate knower, she had taken in the information that George loved her, but she didn't feel it.

"It's perfect, but you're only doing it because Harville is guiding you." Or, "You never did it before, so I don't believe that you mean it when you do it now." To some degree these objections make sense. Yes, the therapist *did* help, so maybe it doesn't feel completely genuine. The behavior *is* new so there may be some distrust.

But after weeks of this we confessed that her continuing resistance puzzled us. Wasn't George doing exactly what Mary said she wanted? She answered, "Yes, but it doesn't feel right."

We asked Mary to pause and go inside her body for a moment and pay attention to her sensations and feelings: "Take your time and re-create what happens when George shows you affection just the way you want it."

She closed her eyes and waited. Then she said, "I get anxious."

Although there's nothing very startling about this scenario, it was our entrée into a whole new way of understanding why some relationships are stubbornly resistant to healing. At first we didn't realize we were seeing the tip of a problem that had deep roots in the ground of personal identity and relationships. After working with several more couples in crisis, however, we began to wonder whether praise-resistant behaviors in partnerships might be both more common and more significant than we thought.

A Broken "Receiver"

Inside very different relationships we began to notice that the same puzzling barrier to receiving love was leading to frustration and in some cases toward divorce. What is happening when a willing partner is able (sometimes after much coaching) to express caring and admiration, and it isn't received? When one partner is finally able to say and do the right things, why doesn't the relationship *always* get better and the other partner *always* get stronger? Answering these questions will take us deep into the heart of the power that close relationships have to shape and reshape those traits and characteristics that make us distinctly who we are.

In each of the three marriages discussed below, one partner learned how to give appreciation and encouragement to the other, but still ran into resistance. Apparently there was some sort of invisible wall surrounding the intended recipient that made it difficult for gestures of love to penetrate.

Stan and Suzanne

Stan and Suzanne live in the same neighborhood they both grew up in, surrounded by old houses that are occupied by friends, in-laws, and cousins. Stan's quietness and his wiry physique give him an air of competence. It's easy to imagine him managing details and solving problems in his job as a building and grounds supervisor. His capacity to hold facts and figures in his head and coolly analyze problems is matched by Suzanne's capacity to feel the emotions of every single person involved with the problem. When they work together on an issue, they balance each other out. But when they're at odds, Stan's need to stay with the facts and Suzanne's need to stay with the emotions add up to a lot of miscommunication.

Suzanne is short and slight, but her personality is outgoing. She was a stay-at-home mom until their twin sons entered first grade, and then she became an insurance clerk. With all the creative housekeeping she put into it, Suzanne loved staying home. Cooking from scratch, sewing curtains, canning her own vegetables—even though these tasks didn't really *need* to be done the way she did them, she felt good maintaining the domestic standards she'd been raised with.

After twelve years of marriage, Stan and Suzanne entered therapy because she was sure that he was having an affair. Infidelity was the only way she could explain her husband's gradual but steady retreat from their marriage. Despite Stan's heartfelt denials that he was not involved with anyone else, Suzanne could not be convinced. After a difficult year and what Suzanne described as "a mini-breakdown in the supermarket," they decided to get some help.

Suzanne told the therapist: "When we were first dating, Stan followed me around like a puppy. . . . But the truth is that we've had problems ever since we married. We're so different. And we don't know how to talk about what's bothering us. Now, we either fight or avoid each other as much as possible. Stan comes home late during the week, and on the weekend he goes fishing with his brother and his buddies whenever he can. Recently, one of our sons asked me if I was a single mother."

Stan winced when he heard Suzanne say this. It was painful for him to hear how absent he was from his sons' lives. He loved his family. He said he was willing to put in the effort to make things better, but surprisingly, he also said he wasn't sure anything would help. His wife was hard to please. In fact, he confessed that he secretly thought of her as "not good enough" Suzanne. He didn't like thinking that way, but twelve years of marriage had taught him to expect Suzanne's general dissatisfaction with the way everybody did everything. Suzanne was a perfectionist, which was okay, but she was also controlling, which was hard to take. Even though he was considered a master at fixing things at work, he learned not to offer his services around the house. He didn't want to be criticized for choosing *this* color over that or for using one particular material when he should have used another.

Unfortunately, Suzanne was also critical of the gifts people gave her. In the early years of their marriage, Stan would sometimes pick out small presents to bring home. But after a while, he began to tense up for her inevitable response: "The thing wrong with this is . . ." And then she would explain about the wrong color, the wrong size, the extravagance, or some other flaw he hadn't noticed. They would have to find the receipt and return the items to the store where Suzanne usually chose something more to her liking. When she told him, "You shouldn't have," she meant it. And, eventually, he no longer did.

Despite his discouragement, though, Stan was willing to work with the therapist and Suzanne in exploring these issues. Both of them said they wanted to make things better. Over the next few months, they were able to follow the suggestions that are part of Imago Relationship Therapy for creating a conscious partnership. They learned to tell each other what they wanted and needed. They learned how to talk and listen to each other in a way that made them both feel heard and validated. They even took that last, difficult step of trying to fulfill each other's requests.

The most significant request came from Suzanne. She said she needed Stan to be more involved in their marriage and parenting their sons. When she told him how lonely she felt, he agreed to make some changes. He told her he would keep his Saturdays free so he could spend time with the boys. And he asked her if she wanted to set aside one evening a week as a date night for the two of them alone. When he made the offer, she was thrilled. This was exactly what she wanted!

She eagerly anticipated Stan's first at-home Saturday with the boys. As the days passed, though, she got more and more grouchy. By Saturday morning, she was downright anxious. She couldn't pinpoint the problem exactly, but it looked like the closer she got to having her desires fulfilled, the edgier she got.

After a month on Stan's new schedule, the boys were happy, but Suzanne was full of complaints, and Stan was exasperated. She acted as if he still wasn't doing enough or wasn't doing the right thing, and he felt truly burned by her lack of appreciation.

To see why he felt that way, we have to hear what happened when Stan started giving Suzanne what she'd asked for. This conversation took place in the therapist's office:

Therapist:	*So, let's get into a dialogue. Who would like to go first? How did your first week with the new behaviors work out?*
Stan:	*I would like to go first.* (He turns toward the therapist.) *I don't know what to say. I did what I said I would do, and I can't see that it made any difference.* (The therapist redirects him to Suzanne, whom he addresses.) *You're still . . . I don't know . . . unhappy. On Saturday, I didn't go to the game with Bud so I could take the boys to practice.*
Suzanne:	(She repeats what Stan has just said to show him that she has heard and understood.) *So you think I'm still unhappy, even though you canceled your own game so you could be with the boys. Did I get it?* (Stan confirms Suzanne heard him correctly. Then she continues.) *Yes, you made that sacrifice, but you didn't get home from the store in time to check their equipment lists before you took them. I had to interrupt what I was doing and check them at the last minute.*

Stan:	(He repeats what Suzanne has just said. When she confirms he heard her correctly, Stan continues.) *You told me we had to leave at one o'clock and I was home at one.*
Suzanne:	*Well, sort of. But if you'd ever done this before, you'd know that I meant all the preparation had to be done before one.*
Stan:	*Oh, brother!*
Therapist:	(Looks at both of them.) *What about your date together on Wednesday evening?*
Stan:	*Well, we went.*
Therapist:	*How was it? What did you do?*
Stan:	(Turns to his wife.) *Why don't you tell him.*
Suzanne:	*I appreciated the effort, I really did.*
Stan:	*But?*
Suzanne:	*I had suggested that we go to Mario's. It's quiet there and I thought we could talk and relax. But Stan made reservations at that seafood place down on First. It turned out to be crowded and noisy. Frankly, it was irritating. We're not teenagers. I don't know why . . . we go out so seldom . . . why do you have to choose such a scabby place?*
Therapist:	(Turns toward Suzanne.) *It sounds like you were disappointed with the choices Stan made. Is that right?*
Suzanne:	*Yes.*
Therapist:	*Is there more about that? About the effort he made to make the evening special?*
Suzanne:	*I could tell that he tried, but I wished he'd thought about it more.*
Stan:	*And I wish you'd appreciate it more! What's the point of even trying?*

It doesn't take professional training to hear that Suzanne couldn't absorb the positive efforts her husband was making. She could tell, as a separate knower, that Stan was doing things that showed he cared about her and the boys and wanted to be more loving. But she didn't connect to his loving actions in a way that made her feel loved. For his part, Stan heard her say she appreciated his efforts, but it didn't feel as if she did. It felt as if her disapproval canceled out her appreciation. His attempts to make her happy met with a wall of resistance. In this case, it looked as if doing what the dissatisfied partner requested wasn't enough to change the underlying negativity in the relationship.

Stan did not want to live with a critic. None of us wants to. We're usually plenty good at criticizing ourselves without a lot of outside help. In the face of an intimate's continual judgment, frustration boils over into anger. Some partners turn the anger inward and assume their spouse is right: they are incompetent and inadequate. Others turn it outward and attack their spouse for being impossible to please. Thus begins a cycle of attack and counterattack, or attack and withdrawal. Without some deeper understanding of what is fueling this adversarial mentality, the battles get worse. At some point, to make the simplest suggestion seems like taking your life in your hands.

After months of effort, their therapist began to think that Stan and Suzanne simply fell into the category of "difficult" couples whose hidden resistance remains a mystery. But because we'd had similar experiences with other couples, we began to see an underlying pattern.

Al and Rena

When you meet Rena, you are struck by her beauty. She is tall, dark, and exotic, with her handcrafted garments and her unique jewelry. After working as a graphic artist for several years, Rena had gone back to school as a student in conceptual art. Her husband Al is the same height, good-looking, and inclined toward the tailored look his university job demands. Anyone seeing them together would have speculated that this match was going to be either a surprising reconciliation of opposites or a contest of opposing wills. Al's career in higher education had trained him to be an expert in separate knowing, and Rena's artistic personality naturally led her to develop her capacity for connected knowing, sometimes at the expense of her analytic skills.

After four years together, it looked as though what had begun as a grand passion was becoming a grand contest. Both Al and Rena had complaints. Rena felt as if she was being stifled in the marriage: "Al knew who I was when he married me. My art is very important to me. I thought he loved that about me." Then she quoted the Swedish filmmaker, Ingmar Bergman, "I don't create to live; I live to create."

Al acknowledged that he loved his wife's creativity and free spirit, but he needed her to be more "normal," as he put it. In one early session, he turned to her in exasperation to ask, "Why can't we eat dinner together more often? Why does the house have to be such a mess? Why can't you sit down and plan things with me?"

Establishing some order and predictability was especially important to Al because he needed to coordinate visits with the two young children he had from his first marriage. He accused Rena of being uncooperative when it came to accommodating them. If she couldn't welcome his kids with her whole heart, at least she could be around more and *act* like she cared.

After months in therapy, Al and Rena were able to do more verbal negotiation in their relationship. Rena was sympathetic when it came to Al's desire for more organization and predictability in his life. To please him, she told him she would make an effort to be more involved in activities with his kids. And she let him know specifically when and where she would help with the household chores. To fill the cleaning gap, she hired a high school girl to come in and do the heavy housework once a week. Her biggest concession, though, was to cook dinner at home for the two of them more often. When Rena thought about how she had responded to her husband's requests, she gave herself an A+.

Al, however, was not so pleased. He focused on what was still missing. He told the story in terms of what was wrong rather than right. Talking about the three dinners she'd cooked for them last week, he complained that Rena "didn't put her heart into it. She just did it because it was an assignment in therapy." And he was not impressed when she arranged to have the house cleaned: "It feels like she's buying a solution, one that allows her to spend just as much time in her studio as ever." He couldn't shake the feeling that she was going through the motions instead of really shifting her priorities.

When Rena heard this, she threw up her hands and exclaimed, "I give up! What do you want from me? Do you want the blood in my veins?" Although Rena wasn't able to fulfill *all* of Al's requests, she had moved quite a distance in his direction. His negative reaction was exasperating.

Although Al had a point—it would have been terrific if Rena had offered to make these changes without so much prompting—he was refusing to welcome the improvements she *was* making. Both Al and Rena found out what many spouses already know: a flesh and blood partner is not as satisfying as a fantasy lover who anticipates and perfectly meets every desire and every need. Living with the reality that your one-and-only has to creak and stretch to make you happy isn't nearly as gratifying as the dream of a romantic twin. Nevertheless, Rena had been willing to do more of what Al wanted by assuming a more conventional role as helpmate. In return, she expected Al to appreciate the effort she was making and respond by easing up on the criticism.

At some point, we realized we were seeing another example of the same puzzling pattern we had noticed with Stan and Suzanne. Neither Suzanne nor Al responded to their partners' positive efforts as we thought they would. What were we missing? Why were these hard-to-please partners so resistant to positive change? We had to become acquainted with one more couple before we began to get the full picture.

Joshua and Anna

Their family and friends at church considered Joshua and Anna a model couple. Joshua was a good breadwinner, a dedicated father, and a big, take-charge kind of person. He was a lay leader in his congregation and had a special place in his heart for the summer camp they ran for disadvantaged children. During the summer he would take whatever time he could from his home remodeling business, drive his own kids up to the lake, and volunteer as a camp counselor. Anna, too, was devoted to home, family, and her religion. She was a little on the quiet side, but you could always count on her to get things done. Both of them were highly emotional and inclined to see the world through their feelings first. Fundamentally, they were connected knowers. Through time, though, they learned to develop their problem-solving skills—Joshua through his work, and Anna when she eventually returned to nursing school.

Joshua was raised by older parents, part of a small religious community in the Deep South. They brought him up to believe that he had a special role to play in God's plan. When he was seven years old, he fell down some stairs at a construction site, and wasn't expected to recover the use of his legs. When he did, the community called a meeting for praise and thanksgiving and treated him as a special child. Shortly after that, his revered father died, leaving his mother to raise him alone. Joshua's dearest wish was to become as good a man as his father.

Like Joshua, Anna was raised in a devout home; she was also reared by a single mother, but the tenor of her life was entirely different. Instead of being considered special, Anna was brought up with shame. Her mother never got over the guilt she carried from having gotten pregnant out of wedlock. And she never stopped blaming Anna for being the living reminder of her sin and the reason she was ostracized by her family.

Joshua had loved Anna deeply when they married, and he continued to love her fifteen years later. Now, though, he had to admit that his feelings were tinged with exhaustion. He did his best to protect and shelter her, "as a man should." And he did everything he could to convince her that she was a good wife, a loving mother, and a fine person. But he felt he was butting his head against a brick wall.

Anna undercut herself constantly. Several times a week she would say, "I'm no good at that," or "My opinion isn't worth very much," or "Not that I'd know anything about it . . ." But what really drove him crazy was the way she put herself down physically. It was painful to hear how often she referred to herself as fat and homely.

Joshua was more patient than most husbands in his position. He understood that underneath Anna's take-charge persona was an insecure little girl. He wanted her to know how much he loved her, how beautiful she was, and how valuable she was. So he praised her. He encouraged her and told her she was wonderful. He could not believe that his rain of love wouldn't give Anna the nourishment she needed to grow beyond her low self-esteem. When these tactics didn't work, Joshua was at a loss. What else could he do?

Sometimes Anna's sense that things were not going to be okay spilled over onto others. She was often short-tempered with the children and conveyed to them a pessimistic view of the future. He wanted her to be more like his mother: good-natured, confident, and certain that everything happens for the best. Unfortunately, Anna's experiences had not confirmed that rosy view of life. He knew when she was really stressed because she lashed out at him and found fault with whatever he was doing.

The truth is that Anna did not criticize Joshua any more than she criticized herself. Take her garden. Whenever she looked at it, she wanted to cry. Other people told her how gifted she was with growing plants, but when she surveyed her efforts, she despaired. She had a vision in her mind that was always out of reach. When her friends complimented her, she warmed a little because it was pleasant. But mostly, she ignored or disparaged their efforts to compliment her. What did they know?

Anna thought of herself as someone who gave more and worked harder than anyone else. And it was true. She had constructed her life so that it had more demands than any one person could possibly meet. Raising three children while actively volunteering at school and church, plus trying to keep a good house for her husband and doing the payroll for his business kept her stretched emotionally and physically.

Whenever the phone rang, she thought to herself, "Who wants what from me now?" She knew it wasn't very generous, but in the privacy of her own mind, she thought of herself as a martyr to the needs of others—while (*and this is the point*) not getting very much in return. It felt as if giving was the right thing to do, but instead of feeling fulfilled, she felt depleted. Although she would never say it out loud, she secretly thought of herself as Poor Me.

Over time, Joshua became disillusioned with his marriage, and Anna wasn't happy either. As committed Christians, divorce was not an option, so they had to find other ways to fill the void in their marriage. Joshua started consoling himself with extra hours at his business, and Anna became obsessed with returning to school to finish her degree. By the time they entered therapy, he was a workaholic, and she had developed a separate life. When their therapist mused out loud about the possible connection between their marriage problems and their addictive behaviors, they were surprised. They hadn't made the connection.

THE PATTERN

When we cast a sympathetic eye on people like Suzanne, Al, and Anna, who have trouble accepting the good things they are offered, what do we see? We see that they have partners who are willing to reach out to them, but they are not able to accept and profit from these loving gestures. Apparently, they have a "receiving deficiency."[1] But they probably would not volunteer that receiving love is a problem for them. Not only would they not use those words, they wouldn't be able to guess the degree of responsibility they carry for the frustrations they feel in their relationships. This isn't because they are self-centered or dense; it's because they don't know they are putting up barriers that shut out the help and positive feedback they need.[2]

All three of these people felt as if they were running deficits. They believed they were giving more than they were getting. They were unable to see that they were receiving a lot more than they could acknowledge. Although they didn't realize it, their predisposition to be critical of everyone else was just a reflection of how harsh they were with themselves. Their self-criticism manifested itself as criticism of others and made it difficult to be fed by any surrounding goodwill and good opinion.

Yes . . . But

You can tell when people are having trouble receiving love because they say essentially, "*Yes* (I acknowledge what you just said or did) . . . *but* (I can't accept it, I deny it, I trivialize it, I discount it, I don't really need it, or it wasn't good enough). These exact words may not be spoken every time, but this is the underlying sense of what is being said.

The following examples are quite different from each other, but see if you can hear the underlying similarity. It turns out there are a lot of ways to say, "Yes, but . . ."

Robert and Rory have been in a couples support group for several years. Although this has allowed them to explore many aspects of their relationship, they are just beginning to think about their resistance toward fully receiving love from each other. Rory says, "I don't know if I can be completely articulate about this yet, but Robert is a partner who exceeds my expectations. I've never been in a relationship that is as nurturing or loving. But I have a very hard time receiving that. During the day, I have conversations in my mind about what a wonderful husband and father he is, and then he comes home. He walks through the door and something happens. I feel a physical shift happen inside of me, and I either get quiet or I sometimes get irritable or angry or distant." Rory wants to know why she reacts to the man she loves with anxiety and irritability when he comes home at the end of the day.

Dennis and his partner Debra are social workers. But their professional training and experience have not made them immune from the problems we've been discussing. Dennis says: "When Debra acknowledges me in a positive way, such as thanking me for helping around the house or bringing her a cup of tea in the morning, I don't respond. Finally, she started asking me to acknowledge that she had acknowledged me so she could know that I heard her. What I'm finding out is that by not responding, I minimize the impact I have on Debra at some level. It's like I don't want to have that much impact on her. If I don't respond to the positive things Debra says, then I don't have to come to grips with the fact that I'm a person who affects others."

Dennis was able to go further and speculate on why he has a "deflection of receiving." He says, "I don't feel I'm lovable or valuable enough to receive what Debra is giving me. Now I have to figure out why I feel this way."

Debra adds, "Yes, Dennis is very generous at giving and offering to me what he doesn't allow himself. If he says something positive to me, such as how well I interact with his mother or how beautiful I look when we go out, I will accept it because it's wonderful. Then I think, 'Wow, but he never gives that to himself.'"

Christine says she became aware that she has trouble receiving love when she was leading a workshop for single people. She says, "I'd never thought about the possibility that I might have trouble receiving love. But I could see it in the workshop participants—how much they rejected that part of themselves that they were told is needy. They couldn't give credit for the little things their previous partners did for them because they couldn't admit they needed those little gifts. Slowly, over the course of the workshop, I began to realize how much I identified with their difficulty in accepting all those positive gestures."

Christine had another insight, too: "I also became aware of how hard it is to give up deflecting love when there is a part of me that needs to be a victim. You know, when I demand from my partner what I don't have inside myself—like I don't really believe that I'm a generous person—and my partner can't really give that to me. So then I get to be the victim again because he can't give it to me. I find that it's hard for me to give that up." Christine said that once she became aware of the idea that she has trouble receiving as well as giving love, her eyes were opened to a lot of behavior patterns in her life that she hadn't seen before.

These examples, along with the three marriages we've just introduced, give you an idea of how many ways there are to defend yourself against someone else's desire to encourage, help, or love you. But the dynamics underlying this counterproductive impulse are not obvious. Without help, most partners reach a level of awareness that allows them to see their mate's dissatisfaction and their defensiveness. But that's all. They don't know *why* their partner is so touchy, and so judgmental or so self-deprecating. All they know is that it can't have anything to do with *them*. After a while they don't even care what the reason might be. They stop giving.

Unfortunately, this pattern—of rejecting the love your partner is offering until he or she stops offering it—is not uncommon. In fact, for reasons we shall soon see, we believe that barriers to receiving love are developed by us as a result of our early experiences, experiences that are so widespread that they are a part of the human condition. It is not an overstatement to say that every one of us has had firsthand experience in either rejecting the love of others or being rejected when we try to give love to others. And someone who has trouble receiving will also have trouble giving. You can't give back what you haven't taken in. The difficulties are compounded in marriage and other committed relationships because irregularities in one partner will set up reactions in the other.

Couples develop problems with giving and receiving love in tandem. As we shall see in the next chapter, the three couples we've just met have been affected by many complex factors that have worked together to bring them to their present difficulties.

CHAPTER 2

Three Marriages Gone Wrong

Something bad has happened to us.
There's nothing between us anymore.

The three couples we met in the last chapter are more dissatisfied than miserable. Their marriages aren't defined by crises or uncommon losses, but rather by the ordinary gripe and grumble of the battle-weary soldier. These couples still hope for empathy and understanding from each other, and they still make efforts to reach across the divide that separates them. But increasingly, they react to each other by retreating behind imaginary walls or pouncing on each other like predators—not because they don't want to be married anymore, but because they want to protect themselves from further harm. They know you can be hurt more by your loved ones than by anyone else. Over time it has become easier to find fault with the other person than to probe the reasons for their own prickliness.

Why are these couples having problems? And what are those problems? We will not be able to answer these questions until we can get beneath the surface of these marriages. To do that, we not only need more information about who these people are, but we need to sharpen our ability to understand what we are seeing. As we know from the study of physics—what we see and therefore *know*—depends on how we look. So let's start by using a new lens through which to view the concept of "relationship." It will help us understand more about why these relationships are in trouble than we could know otherwise.

AN EXPANDED IDEA OF RELATIONSHIP

We commonly think of a couple as being made up of two individuals who interact with each other over time. Gradually, their interactions fall into certain patterns, which we can then examine to get a more complete picture of how the relationship works.

In Imago Relationship Therapy, we make two major distinctions with regard to these relationship patterns: Some are conscious and others are unconscious. Our goal, through therapy and education, is to help couples make more of their interactions conscious and fewer of them unconscious. People can train themselves to pay attention to the effect they are having on each other, even when tempers are running high. They can choose to say and do things that promote caring and goodwill instead of mindlessly causing pain or intentionally pushing each other's buttons.

It's common for partners to ask, "What do you want from me?" and for them to tell each other, "This is what I'd like you to do differently." One partner makes a change, and that causes a change in the other partner, which in turn influences the first partner, and so on. Improvement or deterioration is accomplished by the omissions and/or commissions each partner makes.

You, Me, and the Between

This common way of thinking about relationships—focusing on each individual—has been very productive. But we want to add another dimension to the discussion. We want to focus on what is *between* the individuals who make up the couple. We want to consider the kind of substance and energy they've created that serves to keep them connected or *dis*connected.

We are indebted to Martin Buber, who first articulated the I-Thou relationship and the Between that connects them in his classic book, *I and Thou.*[1] Although his writing on this subject has been evocative mainly for philosophers and theorists, we have found his ideas to be practical and useful in our work with couples as well. Here is a simple way to summarize how we've used them: Most psychotherapy focuses on the "I" in the I-Thou relationship, but, inspired by Buber, we have found it productive to focus on the *hyphen,* the Between. We became interested in what connects one person to another, and began asking the questions: "What are the factors that attract two people and keep them in a relationship?" "How is each of them changed by their interaction?" "What is the nature of the ties that bind them?" Although Buber did not pursue this line of thinking when he talked about the Between, it has been a rich vein in our investigation of both heterosexual partnerships and same-sex commitments.[2]

What we are suggesting is that the individuals are the first two elements in any relationship. The third element is the Between, which is foundational and, in fact, the source of the two individuals. They arise out of the Between; it creates them. Therefore, partners in a relationship do not create the Between, but they determine its contents by the kind of connection they have. Although it is tempting to conceptualize the Between as an empty space that two people fill up with their experiences and interactions, this is only part of what we mean. The Between may be filled with things we can name, but it is also the generative life force—or the debilitating energy drain—that two people create when they come together. It is energy as well as substance.

Although we don't have ready-made words for this new concept, we can draw on three different metaphors to help us illustrate it. The first is from quantum physics, which has developed the concept that entities that appear to be separate can have a direct effect on each other's essential characteristics. This is true even when we don't understand the mechanism of influence. The most common example of this principle is that a scientist who observes a particle changes some of that particle's characteristics through the actual act of observation. In the same manner, two partners also influence each other in fundamental ways by the way they perceive each other, even when they are entirely separate physically, and even though we don't know exactly how.

Another metaphor comes from Buddhism. The goal of the practice of meditation is to be able to achieve what is called "empty mind."[3] Westerners have trouble understanding the concept of "empty," which to Buddhists does not mean the *absence* of everything, but the *presence* of everything. It's a mystical concept that connotes richness rather than vacancy. In the same way, the Between is dynamic and full, rather than empty and waiting to be filled.

A similar metaphor comes from the Christian tradition of contemplative prayer.[4] The person who practices contemplative prayer does so to achieve a state of mind where the petty concerns of the self are forgotten and the mystery of God, which is all and Everything, can be experienced. The space between the individual and the divine is filled with the presence of the ineffable. The Between that exists between two individuals, too, is essentially mysterious and indefinable.

Mystery is a good term to keep in mind as we continue this discussion. How else can we describe the vortex of creativity within a relationship? We know that the Between is the place where each partner is somehow created in concert with the other, but we don't know exactly how. They create their Between, and in turn, are created by it in some not yet completely knowable way.

On a more practical level, the Between can be a useful concept for helping partners understand the dynamics of their relationship. Although the Between is a spiritual and psychic reality and not a physical reality, it can be useful to talk about it in spatial terms. Regardless of the actual distance that separates them (which could be a couple of inches or thousands of miles), partners feel as if they are close or not close depending on the nature of their Between.

Talking about the Between is a way of talking about the invisible but powerful accumulation of attractions, hopes, fears, experiences, memories, attitudes, and decisions that hold any two people together. The elements of the Between are real, but not tangible. You cannot see what's there, but you guess what's there by the way couples talk to each other and the way they treat each other. If there is distrust in the Between, for example, you know about it because of the suspicions and accusations that are obvious to the observer.

The Between is not static. It is dynamic and constantly evolving, as two people engage each other in fresh experiences. The quality of their connection improves or gets worse depending upon the ideas and feelings they've generated together. Asking couples about their Between can be an effective way to gain insight into the dominant tone of their relationship at any given moment. For example, we often ask, "What does your relationship need in order for you to feel more safe?" or "What can be put into the Between to help you feel more safe?"

Asking about the relationship in this way is less confrontational than targeting a question to one partner or the other. It centers attention on what kind of ties and what kind of energy currently exist that are either bringing them closer or forcing them apart. One partner might respond that he or she wants more love or trust in the Between. This feels less accusatory than saying, "I want you to love me more," or "I wish I could trust you more."

Each couple creates a different Between, with its own content and qualities. For example, the Between in a young woman's relationship with her first boyfriend is different from the Between she creates with the man who becomes her husband, partly because the men themselves are different, and partly because she brings to her marriage elements she had created with her boyfriend and with her caretakers. She carries her past with her.

Ghosts in the Between

People enter relationships with varying degrees of self-awareness. Everyone is aware to some extent of the important people and events that have made them who they are. But most of us do not know the extent to which we continue to be influenced by our previous experiences. We are formed from every important relationship we've ever had. Look into the Between of any marriage, and you will find ghosts from each partner's past. Mothers, fathers, former lovers, best friends, coaches, and special teachers occupy the Between of every marriage and influence the way individuals become partners.

These old ghosts are remnants from both positive and negative experiences—times you were truly loved and times you were hurt, times you were empathically understood and times you were grossly misjudged. All have left their mark.

On some level we understand this without thinking about it. Our common speech shows our awareness that the past inhabits the space between people even if we don't talk specifically about the Between. For example, when we sense that more is going on in a particular interaction than meets the eye, we ask, "Do you think there's something between them?" Or we might say, "They must have a history." What we mean is that we can tell there is sexual energy, mutual dislike, jealousy, or some other emotional thread that weaves these two people together in a particular way. Sometimes the emotion comes from experiences they've each had with *other* people, and sometimes it comes from experiences they've had with each other before this encounter. Whichever it is, we recognize that their Between generates memories and emotions that were created in their past, but are operating in their present.

Sometimes two people who don't know each other drag baggage with them into their first encounter, before they even say, "Hello." A high school girl who has a crush on the cute boy in her English class interjects all kinds of longings and fears into the space between him and her. A man whose wife was unfaithful surrounds a potential girlfriend with all kinds of doubts and mistrust before anything actually happens between them. But not all baggage is negative. Some relationships get a head start because positive associations inhabit their Between. For example, a young college student feels comfortable talking to her professor because he reminds her of her dad. No one comes to relationships empty-handed. There are all kinds of information, prejudice, wishful thinking, and expectations interjected between people before they really get to know each other.

The concept of the Between is most helpful, though, in the examination of relationships that are well established. It invites us to conceptualize what is in the field or ground or space between people and to see *that* as part of the dynamic force that makes them who they are as a couple.

As we shall see, it's often hard for couples themselves to tell what is happening in their Between because they have brought elements into their relationship of which they are not aware. The Between is a complex collection of what is known and unknown. Newlyweds are certainly conscious of many of the desires, fears, and expectations they bring with them into their marriage. They may know that a commitment to monogamy, having a partner who is physically active, and being able to share their feelings with their spouse are important to them. But they also bring important influences and factors integral to their own functioning of which they have no awareness. In this chapter and the chapters that follow, we will explore the unconscious elements we can bring to the Between, and see how these unconscious elements exert great influence on all aspects of our relationships—including whether or not we can receive love.

Let's begin by letting Stan and Suzanne, Al and Rena, and Joshua and Anna tell us more about their marriages. We will initiate our exploration of what is in the Between of each pair by hearing them talk about their conflicts, fears, and disappointments. We'll learn about the fights, slammed doors, and deadly silences first because we want to start with the problems and work backward to the individual wounds that each of them brought to their relationship. The details of their stories are unique, but their underlying problems are universal.

Although most people don't see past the turbulent surface, our purpose is to gain a compassionate understanding of how these good people came to their unhappy passes. We want to know what has happened in their lives to lead them to where they are now. Our ultimate goal, of course, is to arrive at the door that leads to healing.

The material in this chapter was gathered by Imago therapists who interviewed couples after they had spent months or even years in Imago Relationship Therapy. We have drawn on these interviews to construct composite portraits of the people we are using as examples. Their stories are constructed from many different sources and do not accurately represent any single living person. At the time of their interviews, these couples were healthy enough to speak about their conflicts with honesty and insight, something they couldn't have done before therapy. As you read, ask yourself what each partner is adding to the Between he or she has created within the marriage. Specifically, listen for those times the speaker betrays some degree of self-hatred or self-rejection. What we mean is anything that sounds like, "I'm not good enough." As we shall see, self-rejection is directly related to the problems people have in receiving love.

STAN AND SUZANNE: LIVING TOGETHER, BUT EXISTING APART

When we met them in the last chapter, Suzanne had become convinced that Stan was having an affair because, increasingly, he was pulling away from her and their twin sons. It turned out that he was not having an affair, but he *was* taking extra hours at work and spending as many weekends as he could with his fishing buddies. He and Suzanne had never been close, but in the last couple of years, Stan had felt more estranged from his wife than ever. Over the twelve years they had been married, their relationship had progressed from hot fighting to icy coldness.

In therapy Stan attempted to make the changes that Suzanne had requested. He gave up fishing and turned down overtime to be home. Although this is what Suzanne said she wanted, it didn't make her happy. There was always some reason his efforts weren't good enough. Everything Stan did was greeted with, "*Yes* (I acknowledge that you did this great thing), *but* (you didn't do it well enough)." When we left them, Stan was frustrated and discouraged; he wondered whether he would ever do anything well enough to please his difficult wife.

To fully understand what is going on in Stan and Suzanne's relationship, we have to fill in more of their story from the beginning. Stan first saw Suzanne from a distance, standing at her locker on the university campus they both attended. He thought she was beautiful and hoped they would be able to connect. It turned out that he knew her brother, so he was able to finagle an invitation to dinner at her parents' house. From there, he asked her out to coffee.

After several months of hanging out together, Stan decided to risk telling Suzanne how he felt about her. But he got nervous when he imagined telling her face-to-face. He wasn't sure he could get the words out right. So he decided to write his feelings down in a letter. About a week later, when he was giving Suzanne a ride to work, he asked her if she'd gotten the letter. When she nodded, he said, "Well, don't you think it makes sense for us to get married?" Suzanne was taken aback. Whatever she mumbled, it wasn't, "No," so without explicit discussion, they slipped into the assumption that they would be together. Eight months later they got married.

In the months leading up to the wedding and during the wedding itself, they got along fine. But the honeymoon was not a success. Whatever fantasies they had of being transformed into romantic lovers who were entranced by each other's company were not realized. In fact, Suzanne remembers the honeymoon as alarmingly bad: "We fought most of the time. I remember thinking that we were supposed to be in heavenly bliss—sharing everything and having a wonderful romantic time. But we didn't know how to do that. I felt detached, like I wanted to connect and wasn't able to. I ended up feeling, 'Oh well, I'm boring.'"

For many couples, a mediocre honeymoon is not a life sentence to a mediocre marriage. Spouses gradually learn how to laugh, talk, and make love in ways that are satisfying. But for others, the first flush of disappointment *can* turn into permanent disaffection. Unfortunately, in Stan and Suzanne's case the rocky beginning was a foretaste of an unhappy future.

One of the problems was that Stan had grown up thinking that marriage was, in his words, "a waste of time because in order for it to work, a man has to be subservient to the woman and can't have his own attitude and personality." Although he never said this to his wife, there are a thousand ways a lack of confidence in a relationship shows itself to the other partner. It's not surprising that Suzanne found him reluctant and closed in. She didn't know why he was so withdrawn, but she knew that she had married a man who didn't want to share feelings, discuss ideas, or work through problems with her.

It soon became apparent that Stan and Suzanne were mismatched in another way as well. Suzanne wanted more sexual intimacy than Stan could provide. She figured that even if her husband wasn't verbal, he could reassure her through touch, to which she was very responsive. But this second route to closeness didn't turn out to be viable either because sex seemed to be distasteful to Stan.

Their disharmony came to a head several months after the wedding when they had to stay in a hotel to attend a graduation party for their niece. Suzanne went out and bought a sexy negligee at Victoria's Secret and fantasized about the seduction she would stage for their romantic evening. When the time came, however, their love feast was a terrible disappointment. Stan was uncomfortable with her overt sexual behavior, and Suzanne burst out with the accusation that he must be gay.

Because there was so much conflict in the first years of their marriage, it didn't take them long to settle into a ritual way of fighting. As Suzanne says, "The way Stan fights is just to withdraw; that's what he does. He is just quiet and won't engage at all. So I didn't have anybody to fight with because my tendency is to want to get into it and kick it around." Stan agreed that his way of coping with the normal give-and-take of living with another person was to "stay pretty dull and numb to a lot of emotion, good or bad."

Their unhappiness with each other intensified as Suzanne became more aggressive in an attempt to make contact, and Stan shrank into the shadows in an effort to minimize conflict. When Suzanne rushed at him with all her guns blazing, Stan looked for something to hide behind. Often what he found was his newspaper. According to Suzanne, "When Stan wanted to talk to me and I was angry, he put the paper right in front of his face so he couldn't see me. He told me that, when I was angry, I looked just like his mother!"

Stan admits that Suzanne's high emotion, especially her anger, was very hard for him to deal with. "When she was colorful, animated, and loud, I built defenses against it. My natural reaction was to retreat," he says. Every time they tried to discuss something important, there was an explosion, and then the Iron Curtain fell, and they settled into a cold war.

Stan and Suzanne reached a crisis when their twins were born three years after they married. It was their darkest hour. Suzanne was exhausted emotionally and physically, often going night after night without sleep. Although they didn't realize it at the time, she was seriously depressed. Stan, who loved his wife in spite of everything, knew she needed help. He took a month off from work so he could be home with her and their new sons, but he couldn't believe it when Suzanne turned down his offers to help: *No,* she *would get up with the babies again. She had to nurse them anyway. No, it wouldn't work for him to bring them to her in bed. No, she couldn't take a nap now. The house was a mess. If he cleaned the kitchen, she would just have to do it again later herself!* It was painful to realize how completely Suzanne had shut him out.

He couldn't understand why Suzanne rejected the help she so desperately needed. She was undermining his gift of love and his desire to share the burden of their children. "In those first three months after the twins were born, there was such a huge demand on us, and we started to turn on each other because we were each trying to fix our problems in our own way," he says.

Stan's retreat from the relationship took many forms, including working more and spending more time with his male friends away from the house. When he was home, he worked on home improvement projects or hid behind the TV. "I wore a ring but I did my own thing. I did what I wanted. Even though I was married, being alone was safer. Even though we were married, we were living separate lives," he says. Although his "own thing" did not include other women, it did include pursuing his own interests and amusements away from home.

Over time, Suzanne says she came to terms with the fact that "our marriage wasn't a place where we could talk about our feelings." She decided that she needed to look to the outside for that. Although she hadn't been particularly career-minded when she married, she began to turn her attention toward her work as an insurance agent. According to Suzanne, "It seemed that if I needed to talk about something or share my feelings, it had to be outside the relationship. Going outside seemed safer than being married. Marriage seemed to be a burden. Maybe that's not the right word. Maybe 'restrictive' is better. At the end of the workday, it wasn't a fun thing to come home. My fun times tended to be at work." She frowned, ". . . and then there was home."

Although Stan did not know how to draw his wife closer, he was not happy with her emotional defection either. Suzanne admits that their interactions had become a vicious circle: "The more I would play outside and confide outside, the more Stan would know about it and resent it. I had gotten to the point where I saw home as just all obligations and responsibilities."

Stan agrees that they were not a warm and loving couple. Their marriage was characterized by little more than "civil politeness." He says: "I was looking for more appreciation and more love. But the fact is that I had exited and put up a wall. We didn't even look at each other's faces to see what the emotion was. We were together, but we weren't, you know?" When he thought about why he hadn't confronted Suzanne or left the marriage, he said he'd decided to take an empty relationship over an empty house.

Suzanne was the first to crack under the strain. She describes what she calls a mini-breakdown: "I didn't feel like I had anyone to talk to, no emotional support, so I broke down. I was at the grocery store. Everything became a blur." She describes walking down the aisle and not being able to remember what she wanted to put into her cart, not knowing whether to buy bread. "I was bumping into people. I fell apart. I just couldn't make another decision," she says. Somehow she managed to get back to the car and drive home. This incident was frightening enough that Suzanne convinced Stan that they needed to reach out for help. She called a therapist the next day.

Without knowing anything more, we can tell that Stan and Suzanne both brought to their marriage an inability or reluctance to talk. Their Between was filled with self-doubt and the readiness to think that if something was missing, they had no choice but to accept their loss and try to get what they needed outside their relationship. Although there were differences between them—Suzanne was very emotional while Stan was nonresponsive; Suzanne was sexual while Stan was not—both of them contributed to the barriers that existed between them.

AL AND RENA: NO PRINCE AND PRINCESS AFTER ALL

Rena fell in love with Al when she was almost thirty. She had been in love twice before, but those relationships broke up because she always told herself that she didn't want to get married. "Based on my parents' marriage," she said, "I decided that marriage and committed relationships were a trap and I didn't want to be in them." If Prince Charming came along and swept her off her feet, so be it, but she wasn't expecting to find a man superb or exciting enough to spend her whole life with. She knew she could have a perfectly fine life on her own.

Al was a surprise. She saw him sitting in a bar with friends and was immediately attracted to him. There was something about his quiet confidence. When his friends turned out to be people she also knew, they were introduced on the spot. Her sense of his greater maturity and experience was influenced by the fact that he had been married before and had two young children. She was quite taken with his seriousness and his sensitivity. He was struck by her vivacity and the sense of mystery that surrounded her. He loved the way she lived beyond the confines of his narrow, administrative world. As he said, "I had a sense of possibility with Rena. Tremendous possibility. More than I ever felt with anyone else." Rena felt the same way. She felt as if a prince had finally entered her life.

Their courtship was romantic, filled with flowers, midnight suppers on his family's large sailboat, and weekend getaways to bed-and-breakfasts in the country. It was hard for them to care about anything but being together. Rena couldn't stop breathing in the scent of her lover, and everything about Rena was magical to Al. He even kept a grocery list because it was in her handwriting. They gazed into each other's eyes and knew they were soulmates. Their love felt grand, dramatic—something out of Shakespeare perhaps, only without the obstacles. There were no family jealousies or dangerous hostilities to keep them apart. They thought their union must have been ordained by the heavens.

They married a few months after they met and the wedding was perfect, except for one seemingly small thing. Rena was taken aback by how much attention Al gave his son and daughter on *her* special day. A wisp of jealousy clutched her throat when she saw him holding and reassuring his cranky children. She got over it, though, when she thought about how unsettling it must be for them to watch their father pledge himself to a woman they hardly knew.

Al agrees with Rena that the first year of their relationship was intense. As he says, "It was either extremely high or extremely low," as if their two separate selves had been fused together by some overwhelming force of nature. Al laughs when he describes their typical day: "We would wake up, make love, get up, go to work, come home, go out together or stay home and make dinner together, go to bed and talk, make love again, go to sleep, and then do the same thing all over again." Rena confirms that: "It was passion in every form."

Soon enough, though, "every form" began to include passionate disagreements. They loved hard and they fought hard. Rena says, "It was hard to maintain some sort of sanity with all the passion." Their primary struggle was around something quite mundane. They fought over what Rena was eating—or not eating. Rena had an anxiety disorder that she had struggled with since she was a teenager. Al knew about it but had very little understanding of what it would mean to their relationship. He assumed that Rena would begin to relax and take life easy as soon as they settled into life as a happily married couple. He was alarmed when that didn't happen.

Al also discovered that he had to be careful about how he expressed his sexual desire for Rena. She explains: "When someone says I'm beautiful, I have a lot of conflicting feelings about that. It's important to me, and I always want to look good—I work hard to stay thin and attractive—but at the same time, I do not want attention in a sexual way. There's a difference between telling me I'm beautiful and saying something like, 'What a sexy babe!' or something like that. I hate it when I feel sexualized."

After one such misunderstanding, Rena confided to Al that she had been date-raped in high school. He was sickened and enraged by what she told him. He was angry that his wife had had to go through that horror, and angry that *his* sexual relationship with his wife was affected by another man's criminal transgression. When Rena's sexual desire for Al began to wane, he blamed the abuse—and Rena herself. Although he wasn't aware of blaming Rena, he couldn't understand why his love for her wasn't enough to help her heal and move on.

Al's determination to make things okay again took the form of assuming responsibility for Rena's anxiety. "It was very difficult for me at first, wanting to protect and control her. I tried to fix her," he says. Remembering back to that time, Rena agrees: "You were very worried about me and trying to take control of my moods and make it better. That was causing a lot of conflict between us. We fought about my fears a lot."

Rena rebelled against his constant monitoring. She says, "Al had the same kind of behaviors with me that my parents did, particularly around my anxiousness. Like having a certain kind of way he wanted things to be and a certain way he wanted *me* to be."

Al had brought a high degree of egotism and perfectionism into the marriage: "I was raised to think that everybody's supposed to think like me. I thought that our relationship was supposed to be a certain way, was supposed to be perfect." Neither of them could live with his constant need to direct all the traffic between them.

As their romance passed into the daily routine of living, Al and Rena also argued about how much time and dedication she was giving to her work as an art student. She was completely caught up in the exciting possibilities she was discovering in the studio. Somehow, putting dinner on the table precisely at six o'clock every night or making sure the bookcases were dusted just didn't seem as important. When he complained, she told him she didn't know he was such a fuddy-duddy.

Another big issue between them was Al's relationship with his ex-wife and his children. "I was completely unprepared for being with a man who had another family," she says. "Every time I looked at him, it wasn't just *him*—there were three more people standing behind him." She thought he was far too open to their needs and demands, day and night. She says, "He didn't have any boundaries with them. And there was no space for me to express anything about it because whenever I did, we'd have a huge struggle over it. We didn't know how to talk about it."

Rena may have felt that Al was trying to control her thoughts and feelings, but *he* felt that she was trying to take over everything else. She didn't allow him enough leeway to make decisions about his children, including when they could spend time at their home, or how much money he could spend on them.

Often his conflicts with Rena centered on money. She wanted to save for the things they talked about doing together, and Al was inclined to enjoy himself in the moment, especially when it came to making his kids happy. He didn't mind buying on credit, while Rena cringed every time he pulled out the charge cards. Again, they didn't know how to talk about it.

Rena described what their relationship had become: "Typically, we would argue and not really get anything communicated or heard because we would cut each other off and start yelling." She admits that she yelled soonest and loudest: "We were dealing with the classic turtle and orangutan. You've got him hiding and me raging on a daily basis." Al says that after the first year or so, he began to feel as if they were in a competition where there could be only one winner. "I began to feel that I was in some sort of contest and Rena was the opposing team. I was supposed to somehow get what I needed out of her. I just felt more and more stubborn. I decided I would do whatever I needed to do to get what I thought I deserved from her."

His analogy of marriage as a hotly contested match in the semi-finals did not include productive discussion. For a long time, he didn't recognize what a liability not talking was. He says: "I felt there were certain things we didn't *need* to talk about, that they should just be understood. It was shocking to come to the realization that the traditional roles like the ones I grew up with were not going to happen with us. I felt this way even though I tried to have a traditional marriage with my first wife, and it wasn't satisfying at all. There were a lot of unspoken things between me and Rena. I thought she would change her mind about not wanting children and would want them as much as I did. It was hard when I realized there were a lot of other desires I had that I thought she was going to meet. I was disappointed that those desires weren't met."

Rena was also disappointed. "I'd waited so long to get married, and then my prince wasn't there anymore." The strain began to take a toll on both of them. Al confessed that he started thinking about leaving: "I would think, she's not the right one. When she screamed at me, it was like she was kicking my soul."

Al didn't talk openly about divorce, but he felt that his second marriage was "way too much to handle. I was overwhelmed; I wanted to get out, to make my life smaller." Rena, too, began to feel lost. Each of them resented the demands of the other. Rena wanted Al to accept her passion to be an artist and stop demanding that she become Ms. Homemaker. Al wanted Rena to accept his need for involvement with his first family and stop demanding that he do less and spend less for them.

As we saw in the last chapter, when they entered therapy, Rena made a real effort to put more time and effort into their home life. She realized that it must be hard for someone like Al to feel the same excitement about oils and gouache that she felt. But, frankly, she didn't know if she wanted to be with someone whose main priorities were his former family and the smooth running of his domestic life. Rena expressed the pain they were both feeling when she told their therapist, "I guess what was so difficult to understand was how I could hurt so deeply and yet feel so in love."

Al and Rena experienced their love affair as a grand passion. They brought sexual energy and adoration for each other into their Between. They also established between them a strong attraction for each other's opposite traits. Al loved Rena's outside-the-box creativity and Rena loved Al's stability. But the differences that thrilled them in the beginning eventually began to irritate them.

Both of them also brought to their Between an insistence that things be perfect. When it became clear that Al couldn't make Rena perfect and Rena could no longer see Al as the perfect prince, things began to unravel. Neither of them knew how to communicate when real-life disagreements and opposing points of view needed to be negotiated. The suspicion that they had made a mistake began to grow larger between them.

JOSHUA AND ANNA: NO SATISFACTION

When Joshua and Anna talk about their early months together, it's possible to get some clues about the problems that would later multiply in their relationship. Joshua was twenty-six and Anna was twenty when they first met. He was already established in his own contracting business and was reaping some financial reward. In contrast, Anna's mother lectured him to get Anna home before eleven o'clock on their first date, even though she was old enough to stay out past curfew.

Anna had been a student for one year at the local junior college and then had to drop out to work. She was intending to go back in the fall so she could begin taking the courses she would need to become a nurse. But she and Joshua fell in love and married before she could re-enroll. By the time her friends were signing up for classes, Anna was eating saltines and crocheting a blanket for their first baby.

"From our honeymoon on," Anna says, "I felt so inferior and so submissive—like Joshua was my mother hen, and I was under his wing. I just wanted somebody to take care of me." Joshua shares Anna's view of their first months as a married couple: "Our marriage started off in that vein where I was this protector and hero and the Man, and Anna was tucked under my wing. She saw me and I saw myself as her savior from a wretched background." These traditional roles seemed to work for them at first. Joshua says, "We actually did quite well as a team for the first year or so, but it was always around me being dominant and Anna giving in."

Anna was relieved to move from the home of her hypercritical single mother into the home of her powerful, successful protector. But to be taken care of also made her feel guilty. "Joshua seemed so patient that it was unbelievable! I had never encountered anything like that kind of patience in my life, ever. Before our first baby was born, I just stayed home all day and waited for him to come home for dinner. I remember that he was very kind. If I wanted a chocolate milkshake, he got me a milkshake. If I wanted fresh strawberries, he got me strawberries. But my guilt was huge because I wasn't working hard. I was always taught that you're supposed to earn the good things that happen to you. And I wasn't even working!"

Unfortunately, Anna's pregnancy with their first child was quite difficult. In spite of this difficulty, though, they were happy when Anna became pregnant two years later with another child, and the pregnancy and delivery were normal. Two years later, Anna became aware of a little boy who needed foster care and took him in. Anna now had three children at home. It turned out to be more than she and Joshua could handle with any kind of comfort.

Anna says, "We were naïve about taking in one more child. I think I was just too impatient and too ill prepared to take on such a huge responsibility. It was the beginning of too much tension, never enough time, too much to do." Their relationship began to have problems. Joshua says: "Most of our conflicts were around Anna not paying enough attention to me. I felt excluded from the rest of the family and neglected sexually. I tried not to be critical, but I'm sure my unhappiness showed."

To make matters more complex, on top of everything else, Anna had decided she had to go back to school and fulfill her dream of becoming a nurse: "It was becoming clear to me that I wanted to become a professional." While Joshua understood her desire, he thought that if she went back to school, the stress and strain would be too much: "She already was superwoman. She did everything! She cooked all the meals and took care of our three children." But Anna couldn't shake the feeling that being a wife, mother, and homemaker wasn't enough. She should be doing *more,* realizing more of her potential, finding a way to be of service to more people than her family and church community.

Anna admitted that it was hard for her to ask Joshua for help, partly because "he didn't do things in the right way," partly because she didn't want to admit that she needed anything, and partly because they had begun their marriage with the assumption that Anna would be the woman behind the Great Man. Great Men didn't change diapers or do the dishes. Joshua agrees: "My view in the beginning was that I'm the head of the household. I'm the one who represents the family. I'm the spokesperson, while Anna does the supportive work. I've always felt that God had some special work for me to do. I couldn't really do God's work without Anna's help."

Thinking about this period in their lives, Anna says: "I tried to do everything I was supposed to do, and to please him at the same time. I didn't know how to say, 'No.' So I would say, 'Yes,' when I really didn't want to. And then I did too much, and then I was angry and I thought it was my fault." Joshua said he felt excluded from her relationship with the kids, and Anna said *she* felt excluded from *his* relationship with the kids: "I felt he played the kids off me. The more I did, the more Joshua was free to devote time to work. He was so nice and quiet and calm and peaceful, and Mom was always a nervous wreck. He often got the kids to agree with him that Mom was just out of control."

Joshua admits that he didn't like it when Anna was short-tempered with the children. He began comparing his wife to his mother, who had raised him on her own when his dad died. "I wanted Anna to be a much calmer person, like my mother," he says.

He also admits that part of what was happening was that he no longer felt that Anna idolized him as she did in the beginning. "She kicked the pedestal right out from under me, and I fell to the ground. I was very unhappy with her turning into this demanding, pushy woman."

As is true for most other couples, the stumbling blocks in their marriage were kids, sex, and money. Sexual fulfillment was very important to Joshua. Not surprisingly, sex was *not* a priority for Anna: "Sex is fine, but if I am very, very busy, I don't need a lot of sex. It's not a huge thing in my life. What drove me nuts was that I was supposed to read Joshua's mind and initiate sex when and how he wanted it. I may have needed time to make that phone call or read that book or cook that dinner, but what I didn't need was to drop everything and have sex!"

In addition, Joshua and Anna had different opinions about money. Joshua's childhood had prepared him to believe that it was always there when you needed it. Anna's experience was that there was never enough. As she puts it, "With all the money he made, I thought we should be wealthy, but we never saved. We were hugely irresponsible from my perspective, but not from his. He was born into a family that believed the Lord will always provide. So who needs to save? My feeling was that the Lord will provide only if I work my behind off."

When the kids were teenagers, Joshua began to stay at work until late. He would come home from a stressful day of solving problems, managing subcontractors, and mollifying homeowners to find a dinner of cold leftovers, the kids out of the house or sulking in their rooms, and Anna holed up trying to study for a midterm. He coped by zoning out in front of the TV or moving up to his study to do more work. The kids began avoiding him in the evening and knew better than to ask him for help with their homework or for rides back and forth to practice.

For her part, Anna began to feel like she might as well be living by herself. Some nights, when the kids were in bed and Joshua was snoring in front of the TV, she would imagine what it would be like to be free and independent.

In looking back to their beginning, it's easy to see that a large part of what was between Joshua and Anna was her need to be rescued and his need to be the rescuer. Also apparent is Anna's assumption that she was not good enough and Joshua's assumption that he was special. Anna had to work very hard before she felt like she deserved the good things in life while Joshua felt he was born already deserving. Their Between was filled with clearly defined roles, high expectations for both of them, and opposing worldviews. With such demands placed on their relationship, it's no surprise that Joshua and Anna sometimes wondered if they had indeed married the right person.

At one time or another, every one of these six people felt that they had chosen the wrong mate. "If only I had waited longer before getting married, stayed single, only had one child, laid down the law from the beginning, married my high school sweetheart instead." Take your choice! Each of them thought things would be fine if only their spouse shaped up.

In the next chapter we will explore why this assumption is erroneous. Choosing a "better" partner would not have spared them their struggles. We know this because we know how to read the clues they've left behind in their stories. They don't know it, but their relationship problems are really maps that identify the places they themselves have been wounded. Their relationship problems reveal elements of the Between that are hidden but have tremendous power over how they form connections with each other. We will see how the struggles that make them wish for another partner would have become part of *any* Between with *any* other partner they could have chosen.

CHAPTER 3

The Unconscious Connection

*I don't know why I act that way. Sometimes it feels
like both of us are taken over by our evil twins.*

The Between that connects partners to each other is like a slow
stream flowing between two banks. The water in the stream is always
different, yet always constant. If we look down, we can see what lies a
few feet below the surface: plants, stones, ledges, minnows, snails,
and other aquatic beings. But we can't always see to the bottom,
because at a certain depth the light doesn't penetrate, or the surface is
too roiled to see farther. We know that the ecosystem of this stream is
built both from the elements that are easy to observe and those that
are obscured by the shadows.

The Between in every relationship is composed of what you can
see and what you cannot see, of what you know and what you do not
know. There are things partners know about themselves, things they
know about each other, things they don't know about themselves,
and things they don't know about each other. Because so much of our
functioning is unconscious, what we can't see and don't know is just
as important as what we can see and know.

Much of the time we live in the shadows—oblivious, unaware,
and unmindful. We function on "automatic" instead of with full
awareness. We react to situations instead of responding to them. We
keep doing the same damaging or ineffective things we've always
done with the same negative results. We wear ruts into the once fer-

tile soil of our relationships, traveling the same ground over and over until it's almost impossible to forge another path.

All of our negative behavior is an attempt to get something done or prevent something from happening. But the question is, What are we doing and why? Why did we say those particular words, and what did we hope for from that particular action? It's frightening to admit how often we don't know the answer.

That's not to say that all of us are unconscious all of the time. The degree of unconsciousness varies from person to person and from situation to situation. But the unfortunate truth is that in times of conflict, tension, and stress even thoughtful partners can turn into defensive reactionaries. In a second they revert to their lowest level of behavior and say and do things they would never do if they weren't feeling pushed or threatened. Partners tend to be most unconscious in those situations in which they *need* to be most enlightened, cautious, and aware.

Tuning In

In this chapter we will develop a greater conceptual understanding of the dynamics that underlie our unconscious actions in intimate relationships. Basic Imago Relationship Therapy concepts will serve as a lens for sharpening our view of the pitfalls that commonly exist in love relationships. We will identify the patterns that are so universal that they can be considered the basic principles or laws of relationships. Knowing the patterns will demystify behavior that otherwise seems confusing. It may seem that we are wandering from our focus on receiving love, but to understand why the problem of receiving love exists, you have to understand how all the interrelational pieces of a relationship fit together.

The goal of Imago Relationship Therapy is to help people break free from their preset ideas and unconscious reactions by becoming more aware of what they actually think and do. Equally important is being able to assess the *meaning* of what they or their partners are doing. Being conscious means being able to ask and answer questions, such as: "Why do I (or you) do that?" "What is it that I am (or you are) trying to accomplish?" "Is there a better way to get this job done?" Or, to put it in the purest form: "*What is true?*" When you can begin to answer these questions, you can break the grip that habit and conditioning have had on your life. You will be freer to consider a range of personal options, including the option of continuing to do what you're doing *or* to modify, eliminate, or replace your old behavior with something more effective.

There are essentially two tasks involved in becoming more conscious: (1) getting more information about your own and your partner's formative histories, childhood wounds, motivations, dreams, and needs, and (2) learning how to interpret what is happening in your relationship in a systematic and meaningful way. You can accomplish the second task, assessing the significance of what is happening in your relationship, by becoming a better observer of your own life. Imago Relationship Therapy concepts can help you clarify what you're seeing.

The task of becoming conscious can be successfully accomplished by anyone who wants to undertake the effort. Even if you've sleepwalked through all of your relationships up until now, it's not too late to wake up. You can choose to interact with your partner mindfully and with self-control. You can achieve a more profound understanding of the processes at work in your relationship. Every relationship pattern takes two people to shape it, but one person alone *can* stimulate growth in a new direction. Even if your partner slumbers on, your increased alertness can improve your relationship.

The Four Stages of Relationships

What do butterflies and good relationships have in common? Both can be colorful or short-lived—that's true. But we are thinking of something more developmental. Both of them go through different stages of growth. A butterfly has to progress through four distinct stages: egg, caterpillar, chrysalis, and finally to the flying, colorful adult we all recognize. Each of these stages is unique from the others and is absolutely necessary for the one that follows. A good relationship also has four distinct stages: attraction, romance, power struggle, and mature love. As with butterflies, each of these stages is unique from the others and is necessary for the stage that follows. Butterflies don't come into existence unless they've gone through the previous stages, and mature love doesn't come into existence unless the relationship has evolved through attraction, romance, and power struggle.

Butterflies presumably have an easier time of advancing through their stages of growth than humans because there is no volition required for their transformation. They don't have to learn skills and practice good habits to ensure proper development. They know what to do automatically. In contrast, romantic partners have to work together to continue growing. They have to become conscious, set goals, exercise patience, and make good choices if their relationship is to progress to the next level.

Stage 1: Attraction

One of the most important principles of Imago Relationship Therapy is that our choice of mates is guided by unconscious factors that are the same for everyone.[1] What we feel as random attraction is actually more calculated than that, even though we are almost always unaware of the calculations. Our unconscious leads us to an Imago match—a person who offers us the greatest opportunity to heal our childhood wounds.

As the old Chinese saying has it, the greatest opportunity brings with it the biggest danger and challenge.[2] And so it is with choosing a mate. The person we are most attracted to will very likely share some significant traits or characteristics with the parent who gave us the most trouble in childhood. If we follow the attraction through to a committed relationship, we will have the same discord with our mate that we had with our problematic parent. Obviously, we don't put ourselves into this upsetting situation on purpose. We don't intentionally set ourselves up to have a repeat performance of our childhood unhappiness.

Unconsciously, though, we *do* choose the psychological dynamics that are most familiar to us from our youth. What makes it different this time is that we are no longer children. We are adults and have greater personal resources and a better chance of standing up for ourselves than we had before. If we can succeed in working through these problems with our mate, we will get a double reward. We will achieve a happy relationship, *and* we will heal our childhood wounds in the process. The learning and growing we must do to live in harmony with our partner is exactly the learning and growing that's required for repairing the damage of the past. That's what we mean when we say that the purpose of love relationships is to heal childhood wounds.

Let's see how this works in a simple example. Mary falls deeply in love with George. He is well-read, generous, energetic, good-looking, and crazy about her. He also happens to be opinionated, loud, and domineering. Mary's father was also opinionated, loud, and domineering. In the course of growing up, Mary formed her personality within the context of living with her powerful father. In order to get along with him she had to develop traits that fit with his. To keep the peace, she learned to say, "Yes sir," and to keep quiet. She learned to keep her thoughts and feelings to herself. Intensity marked her experiences with her father and made him into a powerfully attracting and repelling force in her life. In effect, her experiences with him trained her to be a match with George.

Stage 2: Romance

If all goes well in a romantic relationship, attraction actually turns into romance. This is the stage we hear about most. Lovers live in a special state of consciousness that is quite selective during this stage. Everything about the beloved is intensified and colorized, while everything about school, family, job, exercise, and so on fades to gray. Romantic love is a psychological and spiritual experience, but to be in love is to understand that we are also products of our biology.

Mary and George felt they were meant to be together. Mary told her friends that she felt at home with George, that being with him felt right. After a few months of exciting dates, weekends away, and quiet evenings in front of the fire, they decided to get married. They talked about the children they wanted to have, their dreams of opening a restaurant together, and the way they would always prefer each other's company above all others.

Much has been written in both fiction and nonfiction about falling in love, and about the chemistry of falling in love. But whether you make it your business to learn the details or not, the important point about the romantic stage of love is that it is intense and ephemeral. Eye gazing, obsessing, daydreaming, and physical desire will change over time into something else. What it *ultimately* changes into is up to the two of you, but as an immediate next step what it changes into is the power struggle.

In this culture we idolize and idealize romance, but, as we will learn, the extent to which we are swept away by romantic love is the extent to which we have been wounded. It is the extent to which we are trying to fill the void in our own being with the being of the one we "love." If we try to possess the essence of our lover and appropriate it to fill our own vacancy, we are ensuring that our relationship will not grow into the mature love that is built on individuation as its foundation.

Stage 3: Power Struggle

This stage is the least fun, but the most fertile. When you and your partner have been together for a while—let's say two to three years—and some of the magic has worn off, your partner begins to annoy you. Things you hadn't noticed before begin to press themselves upon your awareness. You're still in love, but the free ride of romance is now over. You have to get out and walk, and some of the terrain is pretty rocky. You have become aware that you're not always in harmony with your partner and that awareness is disturbing.

Now, the consequences of having made an imago match with a partner who shares traits with your most problematic parent start coming into play. You didn't get some of your basic needs met and your impulses validated the first time around, so you try to get the job done now. However, your partner is not a willing collaborator in this enterprise. In fact, you *chose* him or her, in part, because he or she recreated the same difficulties you had in childhood.

In our previous example, when Mary gets married, she's not a little girl anymore. Now she's a grown woman. At first, Mary loved George's self-confidence and his take-charge personality. Whether or not she was aware that he reminded her of her dad, George made her feel safe. But now, several years later, George makes her feel small and stifled. And that makes her mad. When George starts to hold forth at the top of his lungs, she lets him know that she doesn't like it. She may have had to swallow her anger when her father bullied her, but she doesn't have to keep quiet now. It doesn't take much to trigger her anger at George because she's supersensitive to his particular negative traits. To add to this, George is having his own problems with Mary. Because he also made an imago match, she is triggering unresolved issues from *his* past.

If Mary can learn to communicate her needs and preferences to her husband, and if he can learn to listen, she will have taken a giant step toward healing the wound caused by not having permission to speak up for herself when she was little. She has the chance to build up the skills and the strengths she was not allowed to develop when she lived at home. In an analogy with physical exercise, Mary will be able to strengthen the weak psychological "muscles" she had when she left home, because they are the very ones that are needed to work through her problems with her husband. If she is successful, she will overcome her power struggle with George and they will be able to settle into Stage 4 of their relationship, mature love.

Stage 4: Mature Love

Mature love is the lifetime achievement reward of committed love relationships. In the mature love stage, the relationship continues to flourish from the new processes and interactions that were put in place to meet the demands of the power struggle. The partners have learned how to balance the requirements of closeness and separateness, how to create a sexual life that satisfies them both, how to solve problems effectively together, and how to talk and listen to each other so their differing points of view are understood and honored. In addition, they have used these new ways of interacting to learn more about each other, especially where they have each been wounded and need help to heal. And finally, both partners know how to give love to each other, and how to receive the love that has been offered.

You can see how crucial the power struggle is in stimulating couples to do the work that needs to be done to reach the stage of mature love. But romance and attraction also lend some of their important elements to this stage of a relationship. The partners in mature love have learned or relearned how to infuse their relationship with gifts, compliments, appreciation, surprises, and treats of pleasure. They have re-romanticized their relationship. They look forward to giving gifts to each other, and they are gracious in receiving them from each other. They are refreshed by the attraction they still feel for each other and have learned that in mature love, attraction is based on having a shared past and an ongoing shared present.

A step-by-step guide to doing the things we've just mentioned and a fuller portrait of what a mature, conscious relationship looks like form the substance of Part II of this book.

Unconscious Defenses: Danger—Keep Out!

You will be better able to facilitate the development of your relationship through these four stages when you have some understanding of the common patterns of interaction that can cause problems. One of the most difficult challenges of the power struggle stage is learning to interact fully and openly without barriers. There comes a time when you must communicate more to your partner than complete agreement or high excitement. How do you convey your thoughts on a complex subject when your partner has an opposing view? How do you say what's in your heart when you're not used to speaking frankly and you're afraid you won't be heard? How do you let your partner know that you are worried about, or disappointed about, or disapproving of something he or she has done? How do you disagree?

Since very few people have had the advantage of witnessing healthy interaction in their parents' marriages, they don't know how to address problems or reconcile opposing views when the romance morphs into struggle. All kinds of defensive behavior manifests itself as each partner seeks to stay safe and get their needs met.

People who've experienced a lot of intrusion or neglect in their childhoods have well-developed defenses which we call maximizing and minimizing. If a neglectful parent wounded them, they reacted by exaggerating (maximizing) their feelings to get the attention of their caretakers. If they were wounded in childhood by an intrusive parent, they learned to withdraw and diminish (minimize) their responses in order to protect themselves.[3] Children do what they can to survive. In adulthood, partners repeat the same patterns for the same reasons, and that usually means keeping other people at a distance and enforcing a zone of safety around themselves. Whenever their partner's behavior looks or sounds like the real threats they've experienced in the past, they activate the defenses they used back then. Their defensive arsenal is ready to be deployed at the slightest provocation. An unsuspecting or well-intentioned partner can stumble over a tripwire and never know what they did to set off the attack.

Unfortunately, one partner's defense quickly becomes the source of the other partner's wound. Wounds don't cause damage; defenses cause damage. When defensive partners lash out or retreat in an effort to protect themselves from pain or intrusion, they wound the other partner, who responds with a defense, which, in turn, wounds the partner who was defensive in the first place. A cycle of unconscious wounding and defending gets established that is hard to break.

An interesting aspect of the dynamic is that the defense we use often takes the same form as the problematic behavior of the wounding parent. That makes sense if we remember the imago match. Let's see how this works in the case of George and Mary. At first, Mary responds to George by being quiet and conciliatory. But because she is now an adult, and she is still angry about being the victim of her father's bullying, at some point she begins to talk back to George. During the power struggle, in order to be heard, she starts upping the volume and yelling at him, which is the way her father damaged *her* in the first place. So she is employing a defense that mirrors her father's wounding behavior and is guaranteed to escalate her conflict with her husband.

Instead, if Mary were to walk away when George yelled, ask for a conversation when he cooled down, and then try to find out what was triggering his offensive behavior, she could probably short-circuit the yell/yell-back pattern they've established. In other words, if she jettisoned her defensive reactions in favor of more conscious behavior, they would be able to defuse their explosive dynamic.

But first, Mary has to be aware of what she is doing. Defensive behavior is almost always unconscious. The impulse to protect in a particular way is so automatic that it occurs without conscious intention. We've done the same thing in the past lots of times and, on some level, it's worked. So it remains quickly available as one of our favorite behavioral options. Although defenses come in as many varieties as human beings, here are the two all-star defenses that indicate that someone is acting and reacting in an unconscious manner to protect a deep wound:

I had no choice. This is a way of saying, "I am not responsible for what's happening. I was forced into it." What I am protecting is my sense of self, which depends upon the belief that I cannot and do not make mistakes. If I were to make a bad decision or do something wrong, my sense of self would be shaken so soundly that I might collapse.

It wasn't my fault. "It's someone else's fault. If you hadn't done such-and-such, it wouldn't have happened." Again, it is so unsafe for me to admit vulnerability that I cannot admit it. I will keep the suspicion of weakness out, out, out. (As you can see, this is very close to the denial of responsibility identified above.)

A complicating factor in intimate relationships is that you have two people, each with unconscious defenses, coming together in a situation where the defenses get tangled up with each other. Because of our understanding of the likelihood that each partner has made an imago match, we know that the couple usually has complementary defenses. Tom and Kurt are life partners who illustrate the concept that couples tend to exhibit similar wounds and complementary defenses.

Both Tom and Kurt had very, very critical fathers and intrusive mothers. But each of them reacted to this similar situation in a way that was opposite from the other. Kurt explains, "I wanted to get close and be involved and Tom did not. Especially when it came to his work. Tom didn't want my involvement because his assumption was that I wanted to run his business, or at least work for him or with him. What I really wanted was just to be heard. I felt left out. I wanted to be heard and needed. Tom read that like I was going to come in and take over his life."

Tom continues, "I felt like Kurt was being my father. I didn't see his vulnerability; that he just wanted to share. All I saw was that I was so careful to be autonomous and independent, and I was really worried that I ended up committing to someone who was just like my father."

In this example, Tom and Kurt had similar wounding and complementary defenses. The defense that Tom built against a critical father was to keep his partner at a distance and not let him in. The defense that Kurt adopted as a result of his critical father was to try to move in close and become indispensable.

The deeper the wound, the more defended we become because we have learned that other people can hurt us and scare us. To prevent that, we try to control as much as we can through the use of projections, symbiosis, and minimizing and maximizing.

Projections: The Things I Say About You Say More About Me Than You

The more unconscious we are, the more we think we know about our partner's thoughts, motivations, memories, and feelings—their very essence and identity as a human being. We don't realize how much these projections say about *us,* especially about the traits and impulses we have that are unacceptable, disowned, and lost to our conscious awareness. We essentially assign our partner characteristics we don't allow ourselves to have. We attribute to our partner *something*—a quality, fault, skill, motive, thought, or feeling—that actually originates from us. In a way, we project onto them what we don't or won't know about ourselves.[4]

While projection is often negative, it can also take the form of hero worship or excessive adoration. If we lose an admirable quality in ourselves, we can still have the satisfaction of loving it if we project it onto another person. All is then not totally lost. The same is true with a negative attribution. If we lose a despicable quality in ourselves, we can still have the satisfaction of hating it if we project it onto another person. Projection keeps our missing self alive.

Our romance begins to come to an end when we start to project denied and negative aspects of ourselves onto our lover. The idealization of our partners in romantic love is an assignment to them of positive parts of ourselves that we have disowned. The de-idealization of our partners in the power struggle is an assignment to them of negative parts of ourselves that we have denied.

Whether the projection is positive or negative, it feels as if what we're saying about someone is true. This is because our partner *does* carry in himself or herself some parts that attract our projections. So our projections can look like perception. But much of the time when we talk about how our partner *is,* we are making up a story that has some truth to it. Because projections can feel and sound like gospel, it's hard to distinguish them from accurate observations. One clue that it's a projection rather than an objective assessment is if it's veracity is asserted repeatedly with intense emotion.

Here are some examples of projection from couples we've worked with:

- Cindy is keenly aware of whether she is stacking up well compared to other people, and is quick to accuse her husband of being overly competitive. Cindy is projecting her own competitiveness onto her husband.
- Mark often thinks about having an affair and accuses his partner of being attracted to other men. Mark is projecting his own sexuality onto his partner.
- Darla wishes she hadn't married her husband, and she often tells him she doesn't think he really loves her. Darla is projecting her lack of love onto her husband.
- This example is more complex: Richard was interested in music when he was a kid, but his parents thought music lessons were a waste of time, so he developed a negative attitude about this part of himself. When his wife began taking cello lessons, he wasn't able to be supportive, just as he wasn't able to be supportive of his own impulses toward playing an instrument. Richard projected his self-rejection of his musical impulses onto his wife.

The gay and lesbian couples we've talked to feel that projection is something they need to be especially aware of. To begin with, a gay partner may be carrying more unconscious self-doubt than a straight partner because of cultural disapproval for his or her sexual orientation.

In addition, imagine how easy it would be to project the traits you don't like in yourself onto a same-sex partner who is so much like you.

Projection is an important concept in all intimate relationships. Knowing that intimate partners tend to interpret each other's behavior through the filter of their own, often unconscious, experiences can help alert you to danger. You can recognize what's really going on whenever you are projecting or whenever you are being projected upon by listening for intensity and repetition, and then asking what the allegation might be saying about the one who is making it.

Symbiosis: You and I Are One, and I Am the One

The balance of closeness and separateness changes over the course of a relationship, but the desire for connection never changes. Everyone has a yearning for connection, regardless of his or her ability to maintain it.

Some partners attempt to maintain their relationship by being symbiotic.[5] Symbiosis is the unconscious assumption that other people share your subjective states, thoughts, and feelings. When two people are symbiotic, they have an inability to function on their own as individuals and still be in a relationship. They cannot operate with clear boundaries and be connected. Their connected knowing is so overly emphasized that it has become fused knowing. They think, or act as if they think, that when you love someone and that person loves you back, you must think, feel, and act alike. Symbiosis is operative in both romantic love and the power struggle.

Symbiosis is built on an erroneous assumption that may not be conscious: *Of course, you think the same way about things I do, you have the same feelings I do, you respond to things as I would, you want the same things I do, you have the same taste and preferences I have, and you have the same weaknesses and strengths I have. If your thoughts and feelings oppose mine, or even diverge, then it can't be true love.* For those who are symbiotic, individuation is not an option.

Sometimes the presumption of sameness is explicit: "I know how you feel about this." "We don't want to do that." "You must have felt . . . (however the speaker felt)." And sometimes it's harder to pick up: "That was the best movie we've ever seen." "I know what you're thinking." "You don't want to do that." These comments can be harmless, or they can indicate a serious lack of awareness that you and your partner are different. Symbiotic individuals don't know that it is not appropriate for one person to make assumptions about another, based mostly on what the first person knows about himself or herself. They don't know that it's easier to ask and more respectful to wonder than it is to pronounce "the truth." They don't know that it is possible for two people to be enriched by their individual uniqueness and still stay in intimacy.

You can see how symbiosis is related to projection. Projection is the means by which symbiosis is achieved: *I ascribe to you things that are true about me, and that makes you an extension of me.*

INDICATIONS OF SYMBIOSIS IN RELATIONSHIP

Here are a few key observable indications of symbiosis:

- You get frustrated or irritated when your partner can't read your thoughts.
- You are often disappointed in your partner because he or she doesn't do things right.
- You use criticism as a tool to get your partner to be more like you.
- You are argumentative and dogmatic because there is only one way to think.
- You use guilt or shame in an attempt to get your partner to do things your way.
- You say your partner is like you when he or she does something you like.

The three marriages we've been following have offered plenty of examples of symbiosis. Let's briefly review some of them:

- *Stan said, "A man has to be subservient to the woman and can't have his own attitude and personality."* Stan didn't say, but could have said, "In marriage, the husband and wife have to feel the same way about things." Stan may have become convinced that this was true from watching his parents' marriage, or he may have learned it himself in an early relationship with someone close to him, like his mother. From what he says, we can guess that he hides many parts of himself because he's learned that "it isn't safe to let people close to you know what you're really like."

- *Suzanne said, "If Stan really loved me, he'd know what I wanted."* Suzanne wanted very much to be married to someone who could anticipate her desires before she had to convey them. It soon became clear that Stan wasn't able to perform that role in her life. Then she began to wish he would do what she wanted without argument. She felt that if she explained thoroughly enough, or insisted hard enough, he would give in and see things her way.

- *Al said, "I was raised to think that everybody's supposed to think like me. I thought that our relationship was supposed to be a certain way, was supposed to be perfect."* This is a revealing insight. It's symbiosis in action. In addition, there is the red flag of perfectionism that Al adds to the mix. People are supposed to think like him because he is always right.

- *Al also said, "I felt there were certain things we didn't **need** to talk about . . . I thought she would change her mind about not wanting children. . . ."* Again, in symbiotic relationships, there's no need to talk when there is an assumption that things are as the "I" sees them.

- *Rena "was taken aback by how much attention Al gave his son and daughter on **her** special day."* Rena wanted Al to have the same experience she was having. The children were not important to her during the wedding, so it was an affront to her that they were important to him.

- *Joshua said, "I was this protector and hero and the Man, and Anna was tucked under my wing. . . . I saw myself as her savior. . . . We actually did quite well as a team for the first year or so, but it was always around me being dominant and Anna giving in."* In Joshua and Anna's case, they were one and Joshua was the one.

- *Anna said, "I didn't know how to say, 'No.' So I would say, 'Yes,' when I really didn't want to. And then I did too much, and then I was angry and thought it was my fault."* Anna does not feel she has the right to own her feelings. She must override her needs and preferences in order to do, think, and feel what Joshua wants.

- *Anna also said, "I felt so inferior and so submissive—like Joshua was my mother hen. . . . I just wanted somebody to take care of me."* Anna feels inferior. She cannot take care of herself, and she is willing to subordinate herself to a powerful man in exchange for safety. She became symbiotic with her husband because she thought it was the only way to stay alive.

In a healthy relationship, two people gradually transition from moving within a single orbit to moving in two separate, but overlapping, orbits. They are able to have their own friends, their own interests, their own schedules, and—most important—their own opinions, feelings, and thoughts, while still enjoying and preferring each other's company. They differentiate by strengthening their separate knowing capacities, and they participate emotionally in each other's lives by using their connected knowing skills.

Minimizing and Maximizing, or Hide and Seek

Because a couple is made up of two people, it's easy for polarized, oppositional patterns to get set up in a relationship. One partner pushes or maximizes to get more of what they want and to protect themselves from pain, and the other partner retreats or minimizes to accomplish the same goals. They adopt a separate, and opposing, strategy for maintaining their connection. The result is that they abandon the middle ground and retreat into opposite corners.

This is one of the most common patterns of unconscious interaction and is easy to observe. The maximizer is almost always the first to approach the other. The maximizer floods his or her partner with high energy, plenty of ideas, lots of suggestions, and some drama. This partner wants to discuss and confront problems as he or she defines them. The minimizer rarely initiates, is quiet, nonexpressive, low-energy, and avoidant. The minimizer makes even big things into little things. The minimizer seeks to avoid discussion or confrontation over important issues in the relationship. Both the minimizer and the maximizer are afraid, and both of them are angry.

One couple we worked with in therapy illustrates minimizing and maximizing very well. When they came back to therapy after their vacation, we asked, "What was it like?" One of them said, "We had a *great* vacation. We had this *wonderful* experience. We saw all these *beautiful* things." We then turned to the other partner and asked, "How was it for you?" The other partner said, "Oh, it was okay."

In their moderate forms, minimizing and maximizing are natural and neutral patterns. One isn't better than the other. And all people are capable of both to some extent, although one pattern tends to be dominant and the other recessive. For example, a man who is a minimizer with his partner may be a maximizer at work. In the middle of the power struggle, however, partners tend to revert to type and almost always play only one role or the other. Variations of the same drama are re-enacted over and over again in their relationship in different settings. The issues may change but the characters, and their minimizing and maximizing personae, remain the same.

Let's revisit how Stan and Suzanne polarized during their power struggle. Suzanne said, "The way Stan fights is just to withdraw; that's what he does. He is just quiet and won't engage at all. So I didn't have anybody to fight with because my tendency is to want to give into it and kick it around." Stan agreed that his way of coping with the normal give-and-take of living with another person was to "stay pretty dull and numb to a lot of emotion, good or bad."

Later, Suzanne said, "When we fought, Stan looked for something to hide behind. Often what he found was his newspaper." Stan told Suzanne that she looked just like his mother when she was angry. What Stan has learned to do when a woman is angry is to hide. He doesn't engage or respond, but runs for cover.

In another example, during the time Beth and Fran were working out their problems with alcohol and drug addiction, they also began to see a pattern in their arguments. In this relationship, Beth was the minimizer and Fran was the maximizer. Beth told us, "My experience was that Fran fought, and then she wanted to work it through. My thought during a fight was always, 'You want to break up? Fine, we'll break up.'" Not surprisingly Fran told us, "Well, the way Beth fights is to withdraw."

Al also demonstrates a minimizing tendency when he talks about what it was like to fight with Rena about his kids: "I think my tendency is to just kind of ride out things and pull the covers over my head, and think, 'Tomorrow I will wake up and it won't be a nightmare anymore.' I always think, 'Rena's making more of this than she needs to.'"

As a maximizer, Rena was a perfect match for Al. She felt she had to press Al hard to get her point across at all. She was afraid he wouldn't hear or wouldn't respond if she didn't tell him over and over again how she felt and what she wanted. As she said, "I'd be complaining about something Al's ex-wife did or didn't do, or something one of the kids did, and I just felt out of control and inadequate."

You can see how the maximizer and the minimizer calibrate with each other. The intensity of the maximizing depends upon the degree of the minimizing, and vice versa. One husband accused his wife of giving him the silent treatment as a punishment. The wife responded, "You come at me yelling and being nasty, and my only defense is to not talk. I don't want to deal with you. You're dangerous. If I don't talk, maybe you'll go away." But from the husband's perspective, he has to escalate the decibel level because he doesn't think he'll be heard otherwise. He says, "You don't listen to me. You don't try to understand what I'm saying. I have to make you understand how I feel." The quieter she gets, the louder he gets. The louder he gets, the quieter she gets.

Neither gets what he or she wanted. The maximizer so overwhelms his partner that there is no chance the minimizer will try to offer love. The minimizer makes the maximizer so mad (because everything has to be dragged out of her) that there is also little chance that she will offer love.[6]

The patterns of engagement that were dominant in the household in which you grew up will influence whether you are more comfortable as a minimizer or a maximizer. In therapy, one of our clients was able to see, "My defense was to retreat internally and not express to my mom that I wanted her love. That was my defense. I made a decision that the only attention I was going to get was when I was working." As soon as he said that, his wife was able to view his minimizing habits with more compassion.

The common unconscious behaviors we've talked about—projection, symbiosis, and minimizing and maximizing—all add their ingredients to the Between. We've talked about the Between primarily in psychological terms, but if we were to talk about it in a spiritual sense, we could say that the Between is the *sacred* space between two people, the sacred river that flows between two banks. Like the Ganges, along with whatever pollution has been dumped into it, the sacred river contains healing waters. The Between holds the possibility that individuals can transcend the flaws in their circumstances, change their character defenses, and receive and give love.

Unfortunately, the sacred potential for connection is often not recognized or honored. The Between can easily become an empty, vacuous dumping ground or a noisy, discordant arena for fighting. As we have seen, instead of being filled with reverence and deep listening, it can be filled with the attacks and defenses of two people at odds with each other.

Where Do You Stand?

We've found it helpful to summarize the characteristics of unconscious behavior in a list. This is an easy way to familiarize yourself with the concept and identify what you want to work on. Unconscious behavior is present when an individual:

1. Uses the word "you" in situations of conflict (symbiosis and projection).
2. Believes that the way he or she perceives things is the real truth and invalidates alternatives as anything from incorrect to delusional (symbiosis).
3. Consistently attributes characteristics and motivations to other people (projection).
4. Feels safer alone or in conversations that are not intense (minimizing).
5. Feels that he or she has to use a lot of words and a lot of emotion to engage the partner (maximizing).

The patterns we have identified as part of unconscious behavior are all interrelated. For example, a man who views the world as an extension of himself (symbiosis) is likely to ascribe his own states, feelings, and thoughts to his wife (projection), and may express himself with great energy and forcefulness (maximizing), all as a defense against his unconscious fears. No matter what form his fears take, at base, he fears that if he can't control things, he will die.

Unconscious behavior, however, is not a character flaw. It grows naturally out of the conditions of childhood. All of us have acted from our unconscious to some extent. Our point isn't that you should be ashamed of functioning unconsciously, but that once you understand what you're doing and why you're doing it, you can begin to grow beyond it. When people realize that there is a reason they do what they do—that human behavior follows a certain course within relationships—it's as if they've been handed a key to their own liberation. They can free themselves from the prison of an unconscious existence.

In the next chapter, we'll go back to the childhoods of our three pairs of partners to explore the roots of all this unconscious behavior. We'll trace it all back to an unrecognized, poorly understood fact of childhood that influences everything we are and everything we do. It not only affects how we mate, but how we parent, and what kind of society we create.

CHAPTER 4

The Childhood Roots
of Self-Rejection

I guess I don't deserve the good things in life. I feel like I'm no good.

The romantic stage of a relationship and the power struggle that follows seem to be coming from very different places. At base, however, there is a single engine driving the excessive adoration of the romantic stage and the unconscious behavior of the power struggle. In fact, all our myriad forms of unconscious behavior—projection, symbiosis, and minimizing and maximizing—are fueled by one state: self-rejection. Every one of us rejects or hates some aspects of ourselves, often without knowing it. *Self-rejection is the most universal and least recognized problem in our lives. It is the source of all our difficulties in giving and receiving love.* And it contributes substantially to the significant social problems we face as a society.

Although we may rebel against this notion, we shall see that the processes that lead to self-rejection are an inevitable part of having been born and reared by our caretakers. All of us are guilty of causing self-rejection in our children, and all of us have experienced it at the hands of our parents. Even those of us who were fortunate enough to be well parented and to be good parents ourselves are not entirely immune. The question isn't *whether* self-rejection is a factor in our lives; it's how much of a factor it is. And, how we can recognize and deal with it. In this chapter, we are going to talk about where self-rejection comes from and how this most private of injuries ends up directing traffic in our intimate relationships.

The Present Is a Window into the Past

The way individuals connect with the people close to them reveals what they've learned from past relationships. The problems they have in establishing and maintaining bonds are informative. On the simplest level these problems demonstrate whether they've learned that relationships are safe and people can be trusted, *or* that being close to others is dangerous and people are likely to end up hurting you. The fights, withdrawals, and hurt feelings are really clues to both partners' psychological histories. They not only demonstrate where they are, but chronicle where they've been.

It's a cognitive shift for most people to understand that almost all negative behavior is the result of psychic injuries that have not healed. Being quick to anger or excessively self-absorbed, for example, is more often a symptom of unhealed wounds than a character defect. When people are mistreated, especially as children, they don't know they've sustained a hit that strongly shapes the way they will connect to friends and other intimates in the future.

It seems as if the past should stay in the past. But the truth is that the past is always with us; it's just a question of how it manifests. Talking with an empathic listener is crucial for figuring that out. Talking helps all of us recognize the hurt, attach meaning to it, and undertake whatever personal changes are advisable. It's very much like when you break a bone; it's important to get the bone reset and give it time to heal, so you don't end up permanently crippled.

Partners can learn to reinterpret the behavior that upsets or disappoints them and use it as a clue to understanding what injury they or their partner might have sustained in the past. Knowing you've been wounded doesn't absolve you from personal responsibility for your actions, but it can reduce the negative effects of guilt as you address the problems. Understanding facilitates change more effectively than passing judgment. Approaching your partner or yourself as someone who has learned through experience to react in certain ways as an attempt to survive allows you (and all of us) to be more tender than harsh. Kindness is an appropriate way of life when everyone is carrying the burden of previous psychological injuries.

SPLITTING

The task of identifying our injuries so that we can address them is made more difficult because we can't always see where we've been hurt, and we usually don't know where our partner has been hurt. We think we understand our partners and ourselves better than we actually do. We make pronouncements and blurt out "truths" about each other based on our own misunderstandings and unconscious assumptions. We don't know that it's the traits, qualities, and characteristics hidden from us that are the most important in understanding the mystery of personality.

Splitting Leads to Self-Rejection

Each of us comes into the world *whole* and able to receive love and nurturing from our parents as naturally as we breathe. We are connected to our social context, to all parts of ourselves, to the universe, and to the Divine. This connection is our essential condition. It is not something that is created or can be destroyed, but we can lose awareness of it when we are in pain and dwell in self-absorption. When our wholeness is supported and not interrupted, we experience joy and, eventually, wonder and Oneness with Everything. But when it's not, our capacity for joy and wonder fade, and we become cut off from parts of the external world and ourselves.

This rupture in our wholeness is called "splitting."[1] It is a "connectional rupture." The consequence is that we lose our awareness of connection because bits and pieces of our selves are split off as we progress through childhood. When we say or do things that other people don't approve of, we learn to hide certain parts of ourselves in order to avoid negative feedback. We are willing to not think or do that particular "unacceptable" thing in exchange for staying safe.

Unfortunately, a child often has the experience of being injured when one or both parents do not support her normal developmental needs and impulses. When we talk about needs, what are we talking about? An important example would be the need to stay connected or attached to the caretaker. Besides all the impulses a child has to make to maintain this attachment, the child also has impulses toward exploring, creating an identity, and becoming competent in the world. When these needs and impulses develop, our caretakers can support them or they can not support them, totally or partially.

If the need is met—the parents attend to it, support it, and help the child be successful at integrating it—then it will become a natural and wholesome part of the child's self. If the need is not met, then the child's frustration will lead to pain. In human beings, including children, our primitive, or "old," brains interpret this pain as a sign of danger. The perception of danger causes fear, and fear results in resistance to whatever is seen as dangerous. When you deal with resistance, you are dealing with some heavy-duty parts of a person's attempt to stay alive. Rather than the old brain saying, "*The way my parents handled my needs* was dangerous," it says, "*My needs* are dangerous. I can't have this need, and I can't tell anybody about it, or I'll die. My parents will kill me." There is heart-stopping anxiety that you're going to be punished severely for wanting what you're wanting. It's easier to gag yourself than risk exposure, humiliation, and death from the people who are supposed to love you.

In this way, the child represses—and, therefore, loses to unconsciousness—parts of herself. Perhaps we can think of it as similar to the way the human brain develops from infancy. The infant is born with many million more neurons than she can use. Gradually, she loses the brain connections she doesn't need and begins to strengthen those that will help her survive and thrive in her particular environment. In a parallel process, the infant soon learns which of her actions are greeted with smiles and which cause frowns or, equally frightening, indifference. Better to stop doing what she's doing than risk these negative responses. The difference between the analogies is that the baby is stronger for losing her excess brain cells, but she is weaker for losing traits, talents, impulses, and capacities that—had she kept them—would have made her a more whole, stronger human being.

But the law of survival holds that when our parents disapprove, we learn to disapprove. The part of us they don't like becomes dangerous to us because they may abandon us, and that feels like death. We bargain away that part to keep their love. In the course of growing up, all of us make a series of small, and almost always unconscious, sacrifices to stay safe. As a result, not all of our inborn traits, tendencies, and talents cross into adulthood with us. Parts of ourselves are left behind on the road to maturity. What is left is a joylessness and emptiness we try to fill with things that can't possibly give us what we're looking for.

The consequences of the split self are personally and socially catastrophic for many people. In a severe case this is what can happen: The child has a desire. The parent says, in effect, "You're always wanting things. You want too much." The child learns that it is dangerous to desire. Her joy for living disappears. There's a hole where her joy and aliveness used to be. But all she knows is that it's imperative to stay in the good graces of those who care for her, no matter what the cost. Her curiosity transforms into obsession, joy fades into flatness, and the world becomes an object to be examined and categorized rather than participated in and loved. Her original joy and wonder are gone. She suffers from low self-esteem, which clouds her effectiveness at work and in her relationships. She longs to feel loved; she yearns to feel fulfilled. Her aim in life is to find happiness through relationships, money, career, drugs, and whatever else will end the pain. But however she tries to fill the void, the result is the same: She's still hollow. She is depressed and engages in behavior that is self-abusive. She works obsessively, is addicted to drugs, and bathes in self-hatred. Or she is angry and engages in violence of all kinds. She lashes out at other people and sometimes she is emotionally and physically destructive.

On a social level, the price we pay for not healing the split self is the highest possible. Families are broken apart, children are harmed, substance abuse is legion, way too many people go to prison, the court system is overwhelmed, and eventually, of course, we pay the ultimate price—we generalize our self-hatred onto others with violent consequences.

All of us have participated, to some extent, in this process of eroding our own wholeness. In the same way that no one gets out of life alive, no one reaches adulthood whole and unblemished. Ask the most beautiful model on earth how she feels about her body, and she will point out some flaw that makes her feel gawky or embarrassed.

Self-rejection is an element of the Between in every relationship. Everyone loses parts of himself or herself over time. The degree of loss varies with individuals. Some people have been seriously injured by abuse or other traumatic conditions and have learned that the only way to survive is to stifle or cut off *large* parts of their innate being. They have not had the luxury of free expression or the pleasure of self-discovery. They have come to their relationships with a severely restricted range of behavioral and emotional options: Don't think. Don't see. Don't feel. Don't be. They have learned that being fully alive is dangerous.

On the other hand, other people have been only minimally injured and haven't had to edit themselves very much to be loved and accepted. They have been encouraged to "be themselves" and have been appreciated for who they are. They have had permission to explore and create and discover their unique melodies in the world. Being in a relationship with such a fortunate individual, who functions with no apparent self-hatred and a high degree of self-acceptance and self-confidence, is very different from having a partner who has gotten the idea that he or she is not worthy, valuable, important, or good. It is also rare.

Unconscious Splitting

The parts of us that are split through the process of parental disapproval or neglect constitute what we call the "missing self." But when vital parts of ourselves have been disgraced, they don't go away completely. Instead, they take up residence in the unconscious, where they continue to have power. We become driven by unconscious needs, desires, and capacities that we aren't fully aware of. We don't realize how much of our behavior is an attempt to fill the emptiness that was once occupied by impulses, talents, interests, attitudes, attributes, inclinations, desires, and expressions that we've cut out of our repertoire.

As young children, we have the experience over and over again of turning away from a part of ourselves by short-circuiting an impulse, stuffing down a feeling, or trying to forget something we knew, in order to keep someone else happy and ourselves safe. We have no way of knowing that we are making our available self smaller and our missing self bigger in each instance. If we are aware at all, we think about these small amputations as allowing us to solve an immediate problem.

Let's take an example from a common, ordinary interaction that most parents have with their children: laughing and having fun. When a parent cannot experience joy herself and reacts with disapproval when others are "too silly," then smiling and laughing become painful to the child. And the child's impulse to laugh becomes dangerous to him or her because it causes disapproval and pain, and the impulse must be got rid of, so it goes out of awareness and becomes a prisoner of the unconscious. But we know that what we put into the unconscious doesn't just die or go away. It stays alive in some way, perhaps as a desire. Because we desire what feels dangerous, we've put ourselves into a bind. The laughter and fun we ask and wish for is forbidden because it exists in our unconscious as something that would cause pain if we expressed it. When our partner offers us something fun, we reject the gift. Maybe we react by shutting down our enjoyment, or by being critical of the invitation our partner has offered. Soon enough, our partner stops trying to engage us in laughing and playing, and then we feel hurt that our desires and needs are not being met.

Conscious Splitting

Not all our splits are unconscious, however. We consciously make some decisions about the parts of ourselves that we want to put on public view. From the building blocks of our whole selves, we construct a "presentational self," one that we calculate will help us succeed in our various roles. Think of the difference between the way a tenured professor conducts a class of select students and how she behaves at home on a Thursday night watching *Survivor* with her husband. Or how a corporate spokesman acts in a press interview as opposed to how he acts on an informal date with his fiancée.

The magnitude of our persona corresponds to the degree of our self-rejection. The more of ourselves we reject and the more pressure we feel to be perfect, the less ambiguity we can tolerate and the more important it is to us that we feel accepted. Therefore, we create our persona, a presentational self that will, we think, get the job done.

If there is too big a difference between our presentational self and internal self, we are living with a serious split. We are not what we seem to be. There is incongruence between our inner and outer selves. The inner self may have values that our outer behavior violates, or the inner self may have vices that the presentational self tries to keep secret. An extreme example might be a televangelist who preaches the sacredness of family values, but who amuses himself with drunken orgies on the side.

The private and public implications of living a life of inner and outer incongruence are obvious in such extreme cases. But even in our own humble instances of splitting, losing or rejecting parts of ourselves has consequences for the way we interact in our love relationships, particularly regarding whether or not we will be able freely to give and receive love. For example, we can say we love but not feel loving and then wonder why our partner does not feel loved. Our presentational self has claimed something our inner self does not feel, and our partner can tell that we don't mean it.

The Personal Consequences of the Split Self

In our view, self-rejection is the fundamental human tragedy. It is the engine which drives the unconscious behavior that makes it difficult or impossible to form long-term, enhancing relationships with other people. Here are some of the consequences that derive from splitting and the self-rejection that follows:

Disconnection. When the child's whole self becomes split and he rejects those parts that are not acceptable, his natural connection to himself is ruptured. He may exhibit signs of self-destructiveness, act as if he doesn't know himself very well, or simply seem uncomfortable in his own skin. His connection to other people is also ruptured, because self-rejection is the fertile ground for unconscious behaviors that make positive connection with other people difficult. Meaningful connection with the larger social context is also difficult, as we shall see, because losing parts of himself has implications for how well and completely he can connect to the diversity of opinions and backgrounds represented in a free society. In addition to feeling disconnected from his social context, he also may feel disconnected from his spiritual core, from the cosmos and from the Divine. Emptiness is attended by loneliness.

Well-developed defenses. The more our whole selves have been split, the more of ourselves we've lost, and the more heavily defended we must become. We have learned from past experience that we would do well to be afraid of other people because they can hurt us. In an effort to stave off future injuries, we attempt to control whatever we can in an effort to stay safe. We've learned we can't rely on other people to make things okay, so we had better manage things ourselves.

Self-absorption. The missing self demands a lot of attention. The more injured we are, the more self-absorbed we are. The degree of self-absorption corresponds to the extent of the injury we've done to ourselves through unconscious self-rejection. The more split off we are from our whole selves, the less likely we are to care genuinely about other people. There is, after all, less of us to do the caring. Our inner resources are fractured and depleted. And when we do offer to give, we give what we *think* the other person wants or what we want him or her to have. We have a hard time seeing our partner's needs and wishes as distinct from our own, and we judge them harshly because we judge ourselves harshly. In our self-absorption, we also compete with our partner because that's the only way we can feel good about ourselves.

Addiction. The self that is missing has left a vacancy. Because we don't know what's missing, we try to fill the void with anything that gives us a high and obliterates the void. There are plenty of possible fillers in this culture, but food, material things, work, and drugs have the advantage of being close to hand and are even accepted addictions when kept to their more moderate forms. Because our void is large, however, our indulgence is large. We don't realize that the degree of our overindulgence reflects the degree of our self-hatred. The high we get only masks it for a little while.

We eat too much. We're like the overweight woman standing in front of an open refrigerator in the popular greeting card who is "looking for love in all the wrong places." More risky behaviors also present themselves, such as drug and alcohol addiction, shoplifting, promiscuous sex, gambling, compulsive shopping and overspending, as well as many others. Or, instead of overindulging, we under-indulge and starve ourselves, denying ourselves the very substance we need to stay alive. Either way, we feel terrible because we've learned that our authentic selves are not acceptable.

What makes it hard to see what we're doing is that these addictions work. The adrenaline flows, and we are satisfied (or diverted) for a few hours before the effect wears off and we have to do it again. But because these substitutes never were what was really missing, they will never ease the pain and fix the empty feeling. Only the rediscovery and recovery of our authentic, whole being can make us feel at peace.

Symbiosis. If we are defensive and controlling, we are not likely to be receptive to input of any kind unless it is symbiotic. We can't tolerate information that does not duplicate the views we already hold. The Otherness of others frightens us. So we engage in projection and become symbiotic with others, which in turn makes us more critical of them. Not only do we not like the traits we've projected onto our partners (because they are the parts of ourselves that we hate or disown), we don't like it when they do things differently from us. So we are critical. When we engage in symbiosis, it's difficult, if not impossible, for our partners to please us.

Projection. Our unconscious need and desire to relate to the parts of ourselves we've lost is so strong that we project these parts onto other people. We make other people up in the missing image of ourselves. Since we have already rejected our missing selves, we will naturally reject the person upon whom we are projecting our missing selves. So, first we make them up, and then we dislike them for being the way we created them in our minds.

Abuse. Self-rejection can become self-hatred, which can become self-abuse. Someone who has learned that he is not acceptable, not lovable, and not worthy can easily engage in behavior that is self-destructive. It can take the form of an addiction, or it can manifest itself in other ways. Obviously, cutting, burning, or starving yourself is self-abuse, but so is refusing to let yourself have what you need or refusing to let other people give you what they want to.

Abuse of others is also a consequence of self-rejection and self-hatred. The possible consequences of self-rejection—behavior that is defensive, critical, symbiotic, and controlling—can easily lead to violence against the self and against other people. The same wound that leads one person to self-abuse might lead another person to abuse others.

After reviewing the consequences of the split self, it is easy to see why we think the psychological process of splitting is at the heart of most of the personal and social misery we see in the world. When we are alienated from our basic natures, cut off from sources of inner strength, and ashamed of our normal desires and needs, we spread our unhappiness around to others. Our personal relationships are tainted by our own self-hatred, and our social attitudes are formed by it. Our private wounds produce ripples of dis-ease all around us.

TRACING SELF-REJECTION BACK TO CHILDHOOD

To understand where self-rejection comes from, we have to look into the past. Most of the significant injuries to our sense of self occurred in the formative years of childhood. We are fortunate to have information about the childhoods of the six partners in the three marriages we've been following. From their interviews, we can learn something about how early wounds have made it difficult for them to deal well with the complex interactions that are required in a committed relationship. We have their memories of what it was like to grow up in their families, what their parents were like, and how they felt about themselves.

As we know, human memory is notoriously unreliable when it comes to recalling facts. But when it comes to matters of the psyche, the way we *feel* about what happened can be as significant as the facts of the case. (See Exercise 8 for help in sorting out how your childhood has influenced your current attitudes and beliefs and your ability to give and receive love.)

Stan and Suzanne

Let's start with Stan and Suzanne and see what can be learned from their childhood experiences about the lack of communication and polarization in their relationship. Why does Stan retreat from sex, from talking to his wife, and from being at home? Why is Suzanne so critical, confrontational, and unappreciative?

Stan: Hard Times

Stan's background has familiar themes—scary and alcoholic father, dependent mother, lack of money, experiencing close relationships as dangerous rather than safe—but his experiences were more extreme than most. This extremity helps us follow the trail from wounding to missing self to defensive behavior more clearly than would be the case if his childhood had been less damaging.

Stan comes from a family of poverty, where there was daily terror over not being able to pay the bills. His father was an alcoholic who was either totally withdrawn or physically violent when he was home. Fortunately, his father was often on the road as a long-haul trucker when Stan was young. His mother and father separated when Stan was ten. At that point, as the oldest male in the household, Stan became the "man" of the house for his mother, younger brother, and two sisters.

After the divorce, Stan's father paid no child support, and his mother gradually went blind and was unable to work. Their family of five barely scraped by on the minimum disability stipend his mother received. As soon as he could, Stan started working to add income to the family. His mother came to rely on him for the kind of material and emotional support a wife expects from her husband. Here is how he now views several critical aspects of his life:

My father. "It was survival of the fittest most of the time. Everyone adapted to their own style, and I just disconnected and detached and went my own way. I had no sense of being connected to or trusting either parent. I was totally shut off emotionally and physically, and would be absent whenever possible.

"When my father was living with us, he had two modes of operation. There was absolute silence where he wasn't speaking to anyone in the house, or he was in an absolute rage, beating people up.

"My father was a yeller so that's one of the hardest things for me to deal with today. When anyone yells, I have a hard time. When I was a boy I would just go up to my room and kind of put my head under the pillows and try to get away.

"No matter how nasty my father got, I would never show that he had hurt me. No matter how hard he hit me, I wouldn't cry. I never backed down because I didn't want to give him the satisfaction he was looking for. I would just totally distance myself from my emotions around being beaten."

School. "I got Cs, Ds, and Fs. I wasn't a very good student. I would refuse to do my work and no one could make me. I started drinking and getting into trouble when I reached high school."

My mother. "After my dad left, my mother was always looking to me for comfort. I *became* her emotions and I was responsible for her emotions. I grew up feeling responsible when she was angry or sad or disappointed, feeling that it was my fault. She started to go blind and couldn't work, so our family of five was living on $351 per month disability. At fifteen I went out and got a job bussing tables so I could support the family. There was a constant state of financial panic in my house. My mother was always storming through the house banging cupboards, complaining there was no money for food, no money for taxes. I grew up with this fear of someone knocking on our door one day and kicking us out of our house."

Work. "I look at who I am today and I obviously made a decision that the only attention I was going to get was when I worked. At some point in my early twenties, I realized I was turning into my old man, the one person I hated most. I had this great training in how to withdraw or get angry. I had been drinking quite a bit. I decided to quit drinking and get responsible. I went to community college and tried to shape up. I decided the best I could do was work and support my family."

Sex. "I remember when I was little I had this Cinderella coloring book. I watched my dad go through the whole book drawing nipples on Cinderella.

"I know that my father had lots of affairs. He was on the road a lot and was gone for great periods of time.

"I don't have any understanding of where it comes from, but my mother is just sickened by sex. The thought of it. Anything sexual. Any type of sexuality, she is disgusted by it."

Marriage. "What evolved was I had this fantasy of being rich and alone. If I'm alone, it's just safer that way. I didn't think marriage worked. When I looked at people who stayed married for a long period of time, the man always had to get weak, and . . . submissive.

"I guess I assumed I would get married to Suzanne, but I never really liked her. I never really wanted to be married in the first place. But I guessed that's what people did—they married by default."

Stan's father was unpredictable and dangerous. His mother was needy and poverty-stricken. It's not hard to see why Stan would fantasize about being alone and rich. In addition, his initial feelings about Suzanne are a frightening basis for marriage.

It's also easy to see why Stan minimizes with Suzanne. He learned from the beginning that the way to get through anything in one piece was to "disconnect, detach," and "try to get away." We can only guess how hard it must be for him when Suzanne starts yelling. As he says, "When anyone yells, I have a hard time."

Although Stan doesn't say this, almost certainly he has suffered grave wounds to his self-esteem. Failing at school was a way of making the external reality conform to how he felt inside. And, refusing to do his homework is analogous to refusing to eat; it's one of the few arenas of life a child can control.

Stan describes a state of symbiosis with his mother that amounts to emotional incest. The role he played in his mother's life was more appropriate for a husband than a son. Instead of protecting and nurturing him as a parent, his mother treated him as if he were an intimate confidant. At the age of ten or twelve, he took on responsibility for a mother who was going blind, three other siblings, and the fact that there was no money.

Stan did not have the opportunity to experience interpersonal relationships as a source of gratification, but he learned early that working was a reliable source of self-esteem. This may be part of the reason he spent a lot of time at work after he got married, especially as his relationship with his wife worsened.

Stan's sexuality was formed under the influence of a father who sexualized everything and a mother who found sex abhorrent. His disgust with his father and his overidentification with his mother resulted in his own deeply ambivalent attitudes toward sex. When confronted with his wife's natural desire for a fully sexual relationship, he retreated in confusion. He had learned to hate the sexual part of himself as a man and to believe that good women felt the same. Unfortunately, neither he nor Suzanne understood the reason for his aversion. What they were left with was Stan's desire to avoid sex and Suzanne's feelings of rejection because of it.

Suzanne: A Peripheral, Invisible Person

Suzanne's father left the family when she was little, and her mother remarried when she was seven. As she says, "My childhood is a blur to me. Since I've worked on it in therapy, I can pick out bits and pieces, but I don't have a nice, neat story like Stan does." She was a deeply feeling child who was repeatedly scolded for being too emotional. In different ways, her parents gave her the message that they didn't want to hear about her authentic feelings or experiences. They could only tolerate what they had already decided they wanted to hear.

How I felt as a child. "I think growing up, I always had this sense in my gut that something wasn't right. I knew I felt sad a lot of the time, and I felt lonely. Everybody worked very, very hard—my parents in particular—to make sure that the façade stayed in place, but I think we were very, very isolated. Whenever I ventured toward, 'Hey, isn't something wrong here?' It was, 'No, everything's fine and wonderful.'

"I was included in the family, but I always felt like an addendum. There was a large gap between my two brothers and me. I always felt like I was looking in from the outside. The basics, like food and clothes, were met. But I was always told that my temperament was a problem. I was always told that I was too emotional, that I reacted to things in the extreme. If I wanted something, I always felt like I had to fight harder to get it.

"One time I set the table in front of my family without being told and I was so proud of myself. I got them to come to the table and look, but they didn't react. I said, 'Don't you think I did a good job?' And they said, 'No, that's what you're expected to do.' And that took the fizz out of wanting to achieve.

"I think the greatest gift somebody could have given me was asking me how I felt about something. Being a child, I can remember feeling the world, feeling the pain, feeling the joy, but it had to be very, very below the surface. What showed on the surface was a monotone, invisible, peripheral person. I tried so hard not to let anything show, to be more like my mother—very stoic and controlled and reserved.

"You learn that you can't be totally honest, that truth and honesty were not safe, and not what people wanted to hear anyway. I thought I was a very boring person because I had nothing to share. I was an invisible person."

My mother. "My mother was the focal point for me in my life. She was a very strong person who didn't show her feelings. She was very much a flat line. There was no joy; there was no sadness. She was always right in the middle. I know now that as a child I yearned to connect with her on a human level, but all I could do was watch her and look at her. I don't remember interacting and having conversations about real things. My mother was a consistent, flat person, and the message was that I was emotional and that was not good."

My stepfather. "My mother was divorced when I was little. Then one day, she remarried. My stepfather and she went to church one day and signed the papers, and they were married. I remember coming out of the church with her, and there was no joy, no nothing. My stepfather was the man of the house now and he expected to be obeyed. He was never wrong and he never praised his children. I tried to keep safe from him because I didn't want to be criticized. I couldn't trust my emotions with him."

My biological father. "I remember one time when my biological father came to visit and I hadn't seen him in a long time. I was maybe fifteen and 5'8" tall. I was so happy to see him, I ran and jumped into his arms, and he said, 'Oh no, you're too old for that.' I was so embarrassed to be criticized for a genuine show of affection. I thought, 'Well, that will never happen again.'"

Even her biological father, whom Suzanne idolized *in absentia*, couldn't accept who she was. She learned that wanting things and needing things were somehow disgraceful. Later, when her twins were born and Suzanne desperately needed help, she couldn't allow Stan to help her. And, unfortunately, her refusal of help drove a bigger wedge between them.

We envision Suzanne as a bright, expressive little girl who was forced to wear a muzzle to keep herself quiet. The parental message was, "Your authentic self is not acceptable. You need to trim your emotions and be more like me." She was not allowed to move, to speak her mind, to ask questions, or to express how she really felt. These are multiple wounds, but they all add up to one very damaging message: "We don't hear you. You are only allowed to be here if you conform to our needs. If you want our attention, you will have to escalate, which is the one thing we can't allow." She re-enacts this dynamic with Stan in her marriage. We can now understand why she was so quick to come to the conclusion on her honeymoon that the reason she and Stan weren't connecting was that she was so worthless, so boring.

Suzanne had learned about criticism from her stepfather, and it became the dominant currency in her relationship with Stan. She may have learned to use criticism to keep other negative emotions, such as feelings of worthlessness, at bay. This technique, however, only served to isolate her from the connection she craved with her husband.

Stan married someone who was critical, angry, and yelling—just like his father. Suzanne married someone who was emotionally flatlined and repressed, traits she had the hardest time with in her mother and stepfather. Although, as a child, Suzanne had learned to deal with her parents' minimizing behaviors by making herself as small and quiet as possible, in her marriage, she began to rebel against these constraints. The more Stan retreated, the more she hollered after him, with all the fury that had built up during her childhood. Her maximizing approach was one part rebellion and one part need. She needed to be heard, respected, and accepted—finally. Unfortunately, her aggressive assaults only drove her husband further away.

Al and Rena

Al and Rena had a wonderful, romantic beginning. After his first marriage failed, Al wasn't sure he wanted to marry again, but he was swept off his feet by Rena. It felt so "right" that he never even considered the possibility that he and Rena should do some serious talking and negotiating before they got married.

Rena also thought she might never marry. Her parents had been overly controlling and she vowed that she would never put herself in a relationship with someone who would try to control her. As we know, that's exactly what she did. She married someone who had the worst traits of both of her problematic parents. On the other hand, Al married someone who had the same traits of artistic expressiveness and imagination that he had had as a child, which had not been supported by his parents.

Our understanding of the imago match helps us see that on an unconscious level both Al and Rena had given themselves the opportunity to resolve the wounds of their childhoods. But when they began therapy, they were deeply in the throes of the power struggle, with Rena attempting to change Al through maximizing tactics, and Al resisting with all his might by minimizing.

Al: Pressure to Conform

Al was well taken care of by parents who were affluent, educated, and well-intentioned toward their children. He grew up in a large house with an older and younger sister. There were woods behind their house, and Al used to spend hours by himself traipsing around, mulling over his thoughts and feelings, and creating fantastic worlds in his imagination. Here is what Al has to say about his early life:

What it was like for me as a child. "I never had any support to be my own person. I wasn't encouraged to be myself. I had to be what my parents wanted. I had to follow their rules. My parents went through a period where they fought a lot. My role was trying to keep us kids in line so we didn't create waves or stress.

"I felt lonely and isolated and had that sort of empty feeling of needing something but not knowing exactly what it was. I was a creative person, and that was something that really encouraged my separatism from my family because I knew I couldn't share that side of myself with them.

"My parents were both capable through body language or even just a facial expression of scoffing at something, of expressing some sort of distaste for me, like I was some sort of annoyance. I interpreted those actions as their general disappointment in me. I felt that anything I might do or attempt to do or feel or think was ridiculous or wrong. I didn't really feel safe with them or feel accepted and validated and recognized as a person, different from them, but still worthy.

"I always felt like I wanted to keep the world at arm's length, just so I could figure out what was going on in me. I didn't want my parents to see me too close because I was questioning my own worth."

My mother. "My mom knew how to take care of us on the practical side, but the whole emotional, intimate side wasn't easy for her. She didn't encourage our individuality. She had a hard time being patient with ideas or thoughts that were contrary to her own. I don't think she was imaginative. She wasn't comforting or nurturing as a mom. No quiet conversations about feelings or shared thoughts. She never took time out to really see me or my sisters. I really missed what I imagined a mom could be in terms of warmth.

"My mother was religious, and she used that wonderful tool of guilt on me, which colored my perceptions and interactions with her. She tried to use a sense of right and wrong to get me to do what she considered the right thing. I felt like I wasn't good enough, and so I was terrified that I was going to be found out and ridiculed and ostracized."

My father. "My father was a distant person that I had tremendous respect for. He was the epitome of being responsible and hardworking. He would come home after his nine-to-five job and take care of the house and yard. Things were always pristine, something we could be proud of. But there wasn't any intimacy or connection. There was one story that he told me about the military, and I remember that as a cherished moment because he actually opened up to me.

"My dad had a pretty set way of looking at the world. It was pretty rigid. A lot of those values I have actually always had in common with him, but there wasn't much room for discussing. My parents didn't do a lot of free, open discussion and that colored my childhood. On the one hand, there was stuff I could count on, but the flip side was that they were very rigid."

My children. "When my first child, my daughter, was born, I found myself treating her in ways that I knew I'd always wanted to be treated. I wasn't capable of really giving that sort of generosity to my ex-wife. But I found it so easy to give with my own children."

Al's sense of himself as a valid person, just as he was, was injured by his parents' dismissal of or annoyance with the traits they didn't appreciate in him. He certainly wasn't abused and neglected, as Stan was, but he definitely perceived his parents' disapproval and their "distaste" for him. Al talks about feeling "lonely and isolated and that sort of empty feeling of needing something but not knowing exactly what it was." People sometimes have an inkling that parts of themselves are missing, leaving behind a hole they attempt to fill with all kinds of things. Because none of their substitutes is what they really need to feel whole again, their emptiness remains, and in the meantime they've added a whole array of additional problems that come with the compensation they reached for, problems such as alcohol and drug addiction, overspending, overeating, workaholism, and gambling. In Al's case, he tried to fill the void with work and by being the best divorced dad there ever was.

Al's mother was a quintessential homemaker in a traditional role. This is what Al was raised to expect from a wife, although he chose Rena, who never pretended to be a conventional homemaker. He turned out to be attracted to a woman who was not able to give him the domestic comfort he was used to and that he said he wanted. Al's mother did not acknowledge and nurture his emotional side, but she did take care of things at home. She also did not value divergent views. She expected and needed her son to be symbiotic with her view of the world. Al's reaction to this pressure to conform was to reveal as little as possible to his parents. It was good training for the minimizing response he developed with Rena.

Al's family taught him how to see the world from a symbiotic worldview. As he said, he thought there were things between himself and Rena that didn't need to be discussed, because she would certainly hold the same opinions and have the same feelings he had. When she didn't, he thought he'd chosen the wrong wife. It didn't occur to him that what needed changing was his assumption that Rena would see the world as he saw it.

We can also detect in Al's story a strain of perfectionism in his dad that Al adopted and applied to his own life. In his marriage, Al carried an idea of what he wanted his wife and his relationship to be like, and when they deviated, he tried to wrestle them back into line. The problem was that Rena did not want to be controlled.

Parents sometimes find themselves able to give freely with their children what is hard to give to another adult. In this case, Al gave his daughter the loving, emotional support he wished he had received from his own parents. However, we can also see a streak of symbiosis running through his relationship with his kids. There was no question in his mind that he knew what they needed, and he wasn't open to different input from Rena. For example, he didn't want to hear it when she disagreed with him about how much money he should be spending on them over and above his child support payments. As such, Al's strong symbiosis with his children and Rena caused great discord in his marriage.

Rena: Rebellious Beauty

Rena's story is one of rebellion against overly controlling parents. Appearances were excessively important to them, at the same time that real needs were neglected. Like many girls in her situation, Rena controlled what she could. She was also deeply affected by her parents' unhappy relationship and decided that a man would have to be perfect before she would consider marrying him.

What my childhood was like. "I think my parents were very insecure with themselves. If they had children who were really brilliant and excelled and were successful in every way, it would make them look good as parents and make them feel better about themselves and their lives. . . . I felt like I could never be good enough. I couldn't get their approval. I really carried around low self-esteem.

"I wasn't the kind of person who was going to be a straight-A student. I was very social and that's where my priorities were. When I was young, I really did try to be the good girl and do what they wanted and be the way they wanted, but when I came into adolescence, I didn't want to do that anymore. I wanted to be my own person and make my own choices. My parents had a lot of expectations for me that never really fit with my own agenda."

My mother. "I was completely enmeshed with my mother, and for a while that was all right, but then it wasn't. She was judgmental. She had a certain idea of the way you should behave or the way you should *be,* and if you weren't that way, she didn't hesitate to let you know it. She was very insecure with herself."

My father. "He was the domineering one of the family. When I was small, I was frightened of him. I remember him being big and angry a lot of the time. When I was older, I fought back. I did kind of have this attitude of, 'Screw you. Leave me alone. Just let me do what I want.' I felt very hurt and angry a lot of the time. And worthless, like I was a total screw-up."

My parents' marriage. "There was a lot of conflict. There were a lot of snide remarks and comments from both of them about 'I don't know why I ever married you.' My dad's favorite thing to do was, every time he went by a church and saw someone getting married, he would say, 'Another one bites the dust!' There were all these covert messages. At the end of the day, my mom would say to my dad, 'Hi dear, how was your day?' Sometimes he would push her away, saying, 'Oh, calm down.' She was just trying to be really affectionate and hug and kiss him on the cheek. And he would get all uncomfortable, as if to say, 'Not with the kids present.'"

My anxiety disorder. "I think I began to feel something was wrong when I was about sixteen, although my parents didn't notice until it started affecting my gymnastics. They were really proud of my gymnastics. I went to my school counselor and talked to her about it, and then she talked to my parents. They got me to a therapist. We tried to do family therapy, but my dad wouldn't cooperate. He didn't believe in therapy. I was okay for my senior year, but then I went off to college and started getting panic attacks. In my junior year, my roommates confronted me, and I went into a university outpatient program where I got right on medication and gradually learned how to take care of myself.

"I think my anxiety developed at a time when I was trying to form my own identity and really feeling disapproved of and unloved. I was so unhappy. I think it was also a cry for help: 'Look! Pay attention, look what you're doing to me!' I think I was really in a huge power struggle with my parents to gain control of my life and be independent and have an identity. I was really angry about the fact that they wouldn't let me do that. I also thought if I was sick, they would nurture me, but that didn't work either. Their response was, 'How could you do this to yourself?' I failed even at that."

My rape. I think the rape was a big part of my problem. When I was fifteen, I liked this boy in my neighborhood. He asked me to come out for a walk with him on a Sunday afternoon. We walked to our local middle school. There was no one there. At first he was nice, but then he got real aggressive, and he ended up shoving me up against the brick wall and raping me. I was devastated, shocked. After that, when he'd see me, he'd say mean things, suggestive things to me in public. When I tried to talk to my mom, she didn't want to hear it. I started to tell her, but she interrupted and went into this tirade about how I shouldn't lead boys on.

"One time when I was dressed up to go out with my girlfriends when I was fifteen, a family friend walked me out to the car and told me I was beautiful and put his tongue in my mouth. I waited until he got into his car and then I ran into the house crying to tell my mom. She told me I must have misunderstood, that he loved me very much, and he was just huggy and kissy with me. I told her it made me uncomfortable and asked her to talk to him. She said she would, but when I asked her in a couple of weeks, she said she didn't. And she never did."

After she left home, Rena decided she was not going to let anyone control her again. When she ended up in a marriage with someone who was a perfectionist, she fought against him and his expectations. Her experience with both of her parents made her feel like an inadequate, bad kid. When she was young, she felt like it was her fault that she wasn't measuring up. When she became a teenager, she was angry at them for not seeing who she really was and insisting that she be something else.

Neither Al nor Rena knew how to talk about the things that worried or upset them. They didn't learn good communication skills by observing their parents' marriages. Al's parents didn't deal with each other on an emotional level, and Rena's parents dealt with each other on the level of negative emotions. Rena's father didn't know how to give and receive affection, but he *did* know how to use nasty comments to denigrate his wife.

Sexual abuse or rape are the most serious wounds a child can sustain. Rena lost her sense that she could feel safe, that her parents could and would protect her, that she was valued and respected for herself, and that she could be honest. She also lost the innocence of childhood. In addition, it was difficult to develop a normal, healthy relationship to sex. These wounds continued to affect Rena in her marriage. In the romantic stage, she was very sexual with Al, but during the power struggle, her sexual desire seemed to evaporate.

Rena still carried a lot of unresolved anger with her into her marriage. It became difficult for Al to offer any suggestions or express any preferences to Rena without getting resentment in return. She was continually re-enacting the drama of her childhood rebellion against her parents with her husband. Pleasing him began to feel like a betrayal of the self. She wouldn't be able to construct a healthy marriage with Al until she stopped projecting negative elements from her past onto their relationship.

Joshua and Anna

Joshua grew up in a fundamentalist Christian family that gave him a sense of entitlement, and Anna grew up with a single mother who was filled with self-hatred and passed it on to her daughter. Joshua grew up with the idea that the man ruled the roost, and Anna believed that she was so inadequate she needed to be ruled.

In essence, Joshua married *his* mother, and Anna married *her* mother. Fortunately, at a certain point, Anna began to want more for herself. But neither she nor Joshua anticipated how much her transition back to school would upset their finely balanced, if dysfunctional, roles. Deciding to pursue her early goal of being a nurse gave her a sense of purpose and made her feel proud. But deep inside she still wasn't sure that she deserved to get what she wanted or that she was worth the effort. She still had to give more and do more than anyone else to gain some sense of okay-ness.

When Joshua and Anna entered therapy, they talked about how they were coping with their lack of connection. Joshua was working too much, and Anna was not functioning as a partner. Both of them were disappointed—in themselves for not meeting the critical standards that had been imposed on them when they were children, and in each other for not being the perfect partners who could provide escape from the pressures and complications of their real lives.

Joshua: A Lot to Live Up to

Joshua's parents were conservative Christians from Alabama. He was an only child. Most of Joshua's memories are of his mother as a single parent. His father was killed in an automobile accident when he was seven, and maybe because he had been killed, everyone who had known his father idolized him as a saint. As Joshua says, "The tradition in our family was that Dad was a wonderful, wonderful man. He was perfect. And he's still with us. He went to be with the Lord, so he's with the Lord overlooking us now."

How I felt as a child. "We saw ourselves as separate from the rest of the world. We had fairly strict boundaries, and we didn't rebel against them. Lots of rules that just seemed normal—no drinking, no smoking, no chewing gum, no TV, no radio, no comics. We saw ourselves as people who were doing God's will, and we prayed for other people that they would be saved. I always had Jesus with me looking over my shoulder. Maybe I could fool Mom, but I couldn't fool Jesus."

Thoughts about marriage. "I was brought up in a male-dominated hierarchy. My mother definitely liked men more than women, and she would look judgmentally at any woman who seemed to be too assertive. 'Well, you can certainly see who wears the pants in that family,' she would say. I always knew that the Lord would lead me to the right choice in a wife. My job was to relax and wait. My wife and I would become missionaries together and live happily ever after. Right. It never occurred to me that there would be conflict in marriage."

Striving for perfection. "I would often pray all night, wanting to become perfect like my father was perfect. I was definitely raised in right and wrong thinking. We were part of the few who were saved on this narrow road to heaven instead of the broad road to hell. Even though I've moved away from my fundamentalist past, and I am nonreligious today, I still tend to think in black and white: you're wrong and I'm right."

Sex. "I didn't have any education around sex. I couldn't talk to anyone in my family about it. At some point, I developed my own theory that I got an erection every time I told a lie. I would feel ashamed every time it happened. I would try to think, 'Now what was the lie that I told?' My church emphasized how important it was to be straight with God, but I didn't get any guidance about how to fit in socially around sexuality."

Joshua says that he accepted their constraints without question. He felt singled out, and as one of the Lord's chosen people he had special privileges and special responsibilities. There was no getting away with anything because Jesus was always looking over his shoulder.

Joshua was trained to be symbiotic in any close relationship he formed. He had no experience of being close to someone who didn't see the world the way he saw it. He needed to find a woman who would buy into his view of male supremacy in order to make his vision of marriage work. Because his father died before he could observe a living marriage, he didn't have the concept that conflict is a natural and inevitable part of marriage, or that relationships change.

Because of the pain and shame he experienced around his adolescent sexuality, Joshua had a particular need to have his sexuality affirmed by his wife. When she expressed different needs from his, her differentiation was threatening to him. If she was too busy or too tired to have sex, he felt rejected and judged as a bad person.

Joshua developed an addiction to overwork and busyness in order to compensate for what was missing in his life. Running his own company and immersing himself in its challenges allowed him to feel, at least for some moments, that he was whole and fully alive. As we've seen, Joshua and Anna did not have a relationship where they could share thoughts, feelings, and responsibilities as equal partners. In addition, Joshua didn't know how to handle Anna's shifting roles, as she attempted to become a more empowered and self-sufficient woman. This compounded his feeling of emptiness and intensified his need for work as a soothing balm. Joshua and Anna could not build the empathic connection that conscious marriages are built on, and the divide between them continued to grow.

Anna: A Tough Beginning

Anna's childhood, like Stan's, was extremely difficult. Although she was not in physical danger, she had to fight for psychological survival. Her mother never moved past the guilt and shame she felt from having had a baby out of wedlock. She never stopped blaming Anna for the fact that she was ostracized by her extended family. Anna was made to feel that her mother's shame and inadequacy actually belonged to her. This is a perfect example of symbiosis and the deadly consequences it can have for children.

What it was like for me as a child. "Not only did I know I didn't have a dad, I knew I couldn't ask about him. I think my mother felt guilty about getting pregnant, so she made me feel guilty about being born. She never forgave herself.

"My mother yelled at me every day. I was always wrong; everything was always my fault. It was my fault I'd made life miserable for her. She had to make me wrong and shame me. She was angry about everything I did. The only thing she didn't yell about was my schoolwork because I was a very good student. But, she was afraid that if she appreciated my grades, I would get conceited. So we never talked about that. Getting good grades was just my duty.

"I also wasn't allowed to look in the mirror because I might get conceited. So in high school I would leave the house without even combing my hair. I was afraid I would get caught looking in the mirror.

"I always asked myself, 'Why couldn't I be an orphan? I would so much rather be an orphan. At least they're happier. It would be so much easier than going through this searing guilt and shaming and humiliation every day.' I know now that it was my mother's self-hatred and self-deprecation that caused her behavior, not me, but that doesn't make my childhood any less painful."

Striving for perfection. "My role in life was to be obedient, not have views of my own, and do what I was told. I coped by being a goody-two-shoes and tried to be as good as possible. My deepest hurt was that I was bad. I knew I was bad. Absolutely, horrendously bad. It felt awful. Protect myself? I wanted to die. I was angry at myself that I was never strong enough to commit suicide. I didn't have the courage. I remember a classmate committed suicide. I just admired her so much for having the courage to do it. I could never do it.

"For a year, I went to a Catholic school, even though my mother was from a fundamentalist background and really didn't trust Catholics. I definitely seriously considered joining a convent, even though I was not Catholic. But my mother would not have allowed it. A couple of times, I went to Mass and hoped my mother would not find out because if she found out I went to Mass—that would be really unforgivable. But basically, I didn't go. I always felt like the oddball out. I never felt like I mixed very well with anybody. There was one kid not going to Mass; that was me.

"I liked thinking of becoming a nun. I thought it would be wonderful to spend the rest of my life trying to expiate my sins and proving to myself and the world that I'm a good person. Whatever it took to prove that I was good, I would perform as many good deeds as I could. I would sacrifice myself."

Marriage. "I thought men were evil and bad. I never thought I'd get married because I was going to take care of my mother the rest of her life because I didn't want to be ungrateful for all the sacrifices she made for me.

"When Joshua formally asked my mother for my hand in marriage, she wrote him a letter telling him that I was a child of shame and advising him not to marry me. So you have Joshua, the miracle baby who had a special mission from God marrying the child of shame."

As we've seen, Anna never stopped trying to do everything perfectly. Eventually, it drove her beyond the point of exhaustion, and still she was not satisfied. Her self-perception, fueled as it was by her mother's continual assertion that she was wicked and would never amount to anything, rested totally on how she performed rather than who she was. It was no wonder that when Joshua showed interest in her and then, wonder of wonders, wanted to marry her, she viewed him as a rescuer who had in effect delivered her from a life of misery. She was more than willing to allow him dominance over her in exchange for deliverance.

When Anna married, she experienced what it was like to be loved for the first time. And, in a perfect fit, Joshua found someone who saw him as the strong, powerful, heroic man he so much wanted to be, but was afraid he wasn't. Both of them had had powerful experiences with symbiotic mothers, and both of them learned that their value as human beings depended upon their performance in their separate, gender-defined roles.

Anna was not aware that Joshua had taken her mother's place as the strong voice who would always be there to tell her what to do. Joshua was not aware of the ambivalent role Anna played in his life. On one hand, Anna was the woman he felt good about guiding and protecting. On the other hand, he compared her to his own strong mother and ended up disappointed in Anna.

It is a tribute to Anna's inner strength that she eventually wanted more for herself than the role of wife and mother. Her need to grow became the push toward change that carried her and Joshua toward a more fulfilling marriage. But before that could happen, they both had to untangle the complicated parental legacy each of them had inherited and understand how their past experiences were driving the dynamics of their marriage.

What we've just learned is that there are reasons people behave the way they do in relationships. Many common forms of unhappiness result from our lack of wholeness. (See Exercises 10 and 11 for help in clarifying which pieces of yourself have been disowned or denied.) Reviewing these stories of childhood allows us to see how an early wound leads to splitting of the self, which leads to self-rejection, which manifests as a defense that is designed to prevent the pain. The defense puts the rejected part out of consciousness, but the individual eventually begins to miss his rejected aspects and ends up with a sense of emptiness. He indulges in compensating behaviors to fill the void. These behaviors can take the form of either self-indulgent or self-denying activities. He becomes self-absorbed and develops symbiotic consciousness. The pain expresses itself in projections, which are evidence of his unwanted self-parts. These unwanted self-parts lead to self-rejection. *And if there is self-rejection, he can't receive love.*

One of the most important defenses people employ to protect themselves from the consequences of the split self is to not let love in. We shall see that this has reverberating consequence for individuals, relationships, and the entire social fabric.

THE SOCIAL IMPLICATIONS OF THE SPLIT SELF

The process of losing pieces of the self is the universal consequence of living in families and societies. Self-rejection and self-hatred are as old as humankind. Splitting on the social level is analogous to splitting in the individual. We can easily see it in the way we as individuals treat those who are different. The same process of finding certain parts of the whole unacceptable or evil, splitting them off, projecting them onto others, and then hating them applies to whole societies, too. Because societies have a stake in the kind of adults they turn out, religion and cultural mores support the splitting of the self along particular lines.

Perhaps the clearest historical example of social splitting comes from the classical Greek city of Sparta. Infant boys who appeared imperfect were thrown from high peaks into the rocky crevasses below. Healthy boys were taken away from their mothers at the age of seven and raised in military barracks under regimes that instilled self-reliance, mental toughness, physical courage, and sacrifice for the good of the state. Homosexual bonds between boys and older men were mandated, just as boys learned from their mentors the skills of combat and war. Boys who were soft, sensitive, afraid, or questioning of authority did not survive.

By contrast, young men who grew up in the strong Quaker families of Nantucket were raised to be pacifist, nonconfrontational, and noncombative. They were instilled with the habits of prayerful waiting upon the Lord, abstinence, and the human brotherhood of all peoples. They were censured for aggression and pleasure seeking, and rewarded for sober industry and being good family men.

At the extreme of any societal ideals, neither the culture nor the individual has the creative advantage of operating from the full range of human potential. Inevitably, despite the advantages to the society in molding people a certain way, there are also negatives. We can see that living in society means that the full human capacity of every individual is compromised. It's true that the process of socialization is meant to ensure that the boy or the girl will "fit in" better, but there is a personal and social price to pay.

In our own Western tradition, the ideal for men has been "rugged individualism." We have devalued vulnerability, sensitivity, and cooperation in boys while promoting a peculiar kind of strong, self-reliant masculinity. A parallel process, of course, has limited the options for girls. In addition, the mainstream split with homosexuals has been so violent that we turned same-sex lovers into a subspecies of the human family. Even today we are still debating whether 10 percent of our population deserves the same rights and privileges as the majority because they are gay. The intensity of this social reaction betrays the degree to which we are split from ourselves on a personal level. Whatever we ostracize in other people provides us with a key to what we fear in ourselves.

Social splits can lead to larger splits in cultural consciousness, like the one that allowed American democracy and slavery to coexist for so long. We were so divided from our own wholeness that our split consciousness allowed us to build an economy on the institution of slavery. We have hated and been afraid of the "darker," sensual aspects of our nature and at the same time hated the part of ourselves that is "substandard." In this way we have projected our split selves onto, and then despised and oppressed, people of color. We have hated and been afraid of the feminine aspect of our nature and consequently oppressed women. We have hated and feared the part of ourselves that is mentally unbalanced and out of control and have mistreated or ignored the mentally ill.

This culture-based perspective helps us see that the loss of our natural wholeness, while socially required, often leads to personal and social dysfunction. It is important for children to be well socialized, but it is also important in a democracy for people to be intact enough to retain a vision that is larger than the prejudices that happen to surround them at any given moment. When the splitting and consequent self-hatred is too drastic, the individual experiences personal pain and the society loses creative energy that could have kept it healthier. In other words, if an individual cannot freely give and receive love, he limits the same capabilities in the society in which he lives.

CHAPTER 5

Rejecting Self/Rejecting Love

You really like this dress? I think it makes me look fat.

Stan was completely baffled when, as a new husband, he paid his wife
Suzanne a compliment: "I told her I thought she had done a good
job on something around the house. She just kind of interrupted me
and started talking about something else. So I asked her if she'd heard
what I'd just said, and she said, 'Compliments don't really mean anything to me.' And she went on talking about whatever." Stan said he
would've been truly depressed if he'd known this was just the start of
an ongoing pattern of not being heard. Although this was a small
incident, it was symbolic of the offer-and-reject dynamic that came
to characterize their relationship.

As we discussed in the last chapter, our inclination to reject love
is born out of the imperfection of our first and most important relationships with our caretakers. As children we learn to latch onto the
safety of our caretakers' approval by letting go of whichever of our
needs or impulses they don't recognize or support. The consequences
of this survival tactic, however, are most clearly seen in the intimate
relationships of our maturity.

Fortunately, many of the early injuries inflicted by parents and
siblings are unintentional—they sting rather than incapacitate. Some
of them even turn out to be strengthening rather than weakening.
For example, one boy who was constantly needled by his family for
being more musical than athletic grew up to become a professional
musician. "After all the ribbing I took, I decided not to disappoint

them," he wryly explained. Obviously, his love of music was not so demeaned that he ended up depriving himself of this joy altogether.

The ultimate effect of such "ribbing" depends on the nature of the assaults and how the one who is injured deals with the wound and its consequences. But in order to deal with it at all, each of us has to recognize the effect that such careless or intentional disrespecting can have on our sense of ourselves. Most of us aren't aware how these isolated incidents, separated in time, link up to form defensive barriers inside us that make true intimacy in committed relationships difficult.

Unless we know the underlying reasons why people reject positive emotion from their partner, the idea that people can't receive the warmth and love they genuinely want makes very little sense. Following the trail from wound to self-rejection to rejection of love helps us understand it. *Not allowing ourselves to be congratulated, celebrated, appreciated, nourished, or loved by people and events outside ourselves is a defense designed to protect us from psychic pain.* Barriers to love are erected in our unconscious as it acts on behalf of our own survival. In fact, a barrier to receiving is often the capstone of all our defenses.

CONNECTING THE DOTS

We've already seen that many of the problems partners have in relationships can be traced back to large and small incidents in their separate childhoods when their natural needs and expressions were ignored, disapproved of, or intruded upon. Because the response to parental disapproval or neglect is to reject in yourself whatever your parent rejected, you grow up to be a partner who carries a measure of self-hatred with you into your relationship. This self-hatred is not benign. It forms the basis of specific problems that are common in intimate relationships.

Following is an outline of how parental rejection leads to self-rejection, which leads to an inability to allow oneself to receive love, and a consequent inability to give love:

1. When we are born, openness and receptivity are our natural state.

2. Sooner or later, our parents or caretakers wound us.

3. The wound occurs when a caretaker does not properly deal with our normal developmental needs and functions. The wound comes in the form of either neglect or invasiveness of some aspects of our natural self.

4. We split off these "dangerous" self-parts because our caretakers do not support them, and these self-parts form what we call the "missing self."

5. Every time we are wounded and split, our conscious self gets smaller, and our unconscious self gets larger. Our available pool of skills and resources is depleted, and our unconscious burden of rejected parts grows heavier. Instead of being able to meet the demands of life with a full complement of emotional and behavioral options, we meet life with a limited number of defensive reactions.

6. We use common defenses, including becoming overly controlling, self-absorbed, and symbiotic, as ways of trying to protect ourselves from further pain. We try to micromanage our environments as a way of keeping ourselves safe, and/or we hold tightly onto what's left of ourselves as a way of protecting against further encroachment.

7. In addition, we try to make the pain of rejection go away by denying our needs (which were the cause of our rejection in the first place) and replacing them with defenses. We resist satisfying our needs in order not to activate the wound. The purpose of our defenses is to put the wound, and the pain it is causing, out of consciousness.

8. Then, we try to fill up the emptiness our defenses cause with things that only add to our unhappiness because they aren't what's really missing and because we embrace them excessively through either self-indulgence or self-denial. We grab onto food, drugs, work, parenting, gambling, spending, starving, or other compensating behaviors, and engage with them in an extreme way.

9. In everything we do, there is the hint or the strain of self-rejection or self-hatred.

10. In order to stay in contact with our rejected self-parts without

having to stay conscious of them, we project them onto our partners.

11. The degree to which we carry self-hatred is the degree to which we can't receive love. It is so painful to become aware—in the form of appreciation or love—of the parts of ourselves we have rejected that we resist and reject the gifts themselves. And sometimes we reject the people who bring us the gifts.

The people around us can often see what our defenses make us blind to. They see that we are attractive, competent, compassionate, or persistent when we cannot own these attributes in ourselves. Even though we have submerged our awareness of these qualities, some of them are still visible to others. So when we receive information from the outside world about the parts of ourselves that we have lost or denied (our missing self), we are forced to experience directly the pain of our loss. We can no longer ignore or slide past the wound and the hole it has left. Others call us into the painful experience of those parts of ourselves we have disowned.

Regardless of whether the input from others is positive or negative, taking it in—receiving it—means having to confront the fact that we are broken human beings. We are not innocent and trusting, ready to meet life with the assurance that we are wholly loved and okay, which is the state into which we are born. We have sustained losses. Experiencing the broken shards of what's left or the void that represents what is missing is painful, and it feels dangerous. After all, the rejected aspects of our being have been the subject of disapproval by the people we depended upon for life. It's safer to block information about our missing selves than to become conscious of our pain. It is easier to go without love than to accept a form of love that reawakens our fears of loss. In fact, to receive love feels far more dangerous than to be without it.

REJECTING LOVE IN COMMITTED RELATIONSHIPS

Marriage and other committed relationships give us the best chance to see the rejection of love in action because there are continuous interactions between the partners that build upon each other through time. If we could keep track of every interaction with notebook and pencil, we could chart the Ping-Pong effect that rebuffs, hurt feelings, and renewed efforts create as they carom off each other. We would soon come to recognize that there are certain patterns or "plays" that are enacted over and over again. (See Exercises 6 and 7 for help in assessing how freely you are able to receive and therefore give love.)

The Many Guises of Non-Receiving

Most couples do not know the large role self-rejection plays in their relationship problems. They haven't seen that it is connected to their difficulties in loving each other. For one thing, self-rejection can be hard to identify for what it is. Many people have an initial resistance to the idea that they have discarded or denied some positive things about themselves. It goes against common sense. Also, self-rejection often masquerades as something else. It can be disguised as hypercriticism of others or dissatisfaction and negativity about life in general. It can also look like perfectionism or shyness or a reluctance to extend oneself by trying new things.

Once you know what to look for, though, self-rejection is easy to spot. Whenever someone is having trouble receiving something positive, you know it's because the would-be gift has hit him or her in a sore spot, in a vulnerable place where that person has tried to deal with a wound by disowning the impulse that triggered it. An individual who is having trouble receiving love will show it by consistently (1) deflecting the positives, and/or (2) absorbing the negatives. Both actions are evidence of the vigor with which the negative self-image is defended. Positives cannot be let in because they run counter to the carefully constructed sense of self that has been achieved. At the same time, negatives are let in without examination because they validate this same negative sense of self.

Deflecting the Positive

Deflecting can take the form of not allowing oneself to *have* the positive or not allowing oneself to *do* the positive. Here are the common ways one or both partners in a relationship might resist the love of the other, and thereby unknowingly expose where they themselves have been wounded.

Rejecting or sloughing off positive comments. The good stuff stops at the gate. When someone compliments them, they say "Oh, that's nothing," or they seem embarrassed or anxious when they are praised. A compliment is handed back before it can hit home.

Rena had good reasons to retreat when her husband commented on her physical beauty. "When someone says I'm beautiful, I have a lot of conflicting feelings about that. . . . I do not want attention in a sexual way," she observed. Sexual abuse is an extreme injury that disrupts the psyche in many different ways. Because Rena had been date-raped when she was young, her sense of being safe and respected was stolen from her. She suffered huge losses. Among other things, she was missing the part of herself that felt comfortable and unself-conscious in her own body. And because her mother paid no attention when Rena tried to tell her what had happened, Rena lost her sense that she would be heard and helped when she had an important concern or problem. It's no wonder that Rena had trouble receiving compliments about her physical attractiveness—they made her feel unsafe and helpless.

In a different kind of example, Teresa was surprised and flustered when her second husband, Robb, told her what a great job she had done preparing their income tax forms. This shouldn't have been a surprise to Teresa, since at work she was considered a good detail person. It took her awhile to understand why she was so reluctant to take in his praise and appreciation. Then she remembered an incident with her first husband that made sense of her reaction. "When Joe and I were first married, I made a big mistake writing out the check for our first month's rent. When we got a notice from the landlord that we hadn't made full payment, Joe said, 'Why are you always so stupid?' He probably could have ripped his tongue out at the time for saying that, but it stuck with me nevertheless. I never felt like I was a competent person around him," she says. Teresa's first husband reinforced her sense of inadequacy, and therefore her inability to accept compliments, by telling her things like, "Fifty percent of marriage is learning how to cook," and "Why do you want to take college classes? You're never going to do anything useful with them."

Refusing gifts or offers of help, or being dissatisfied once you get what you've asked for. For many people it's okay to ask for help, but it's not okay to get it. When the other partner proffers the present that has been requested and yearned for, or the helping hand that is needed, the gift is turned away or turned down.

One way to refuse without saying, "No thanks, I don't want this," is to accept the gift but not appreciate it once you've accepted it. You may even find the love of your dreams and still not be satisfied. In other words, you take the gift, but then complain about it. In an intimate relationship this can take the form of refusing to accept improvements even after a partner has made positive changes at your request.

As we've seen, at the beginning of therapy, Suzanne was not able to accept and appreciate the efforts Stan made to comply with her request that he spend more time at home. Rejecting the changes you've asked for is a common sign that you're having trouble receiving. So is complaining about the good things you've got. For example, Vivian exasperated her friends when she complained about her very nice husband, Jay. Usually, her putdowns were disguised as humor. One afternoon, when Jay stayed home with their young son so she could have lunch with her friends, Vivian made a joke about how real men don't babysit. Her friends were shocked. They wished they had husbands who were considerate enough to take the children so they could get out and have lunch. Apparently, nurturing men were far enough outside Vivian's experience that she felt she had to question their masculinity. She couldn't simply accept that her husband loved her enough to give her this gift.

Deanna's experience provides another example of complaining about the good things you've got. One beautiful spring evening, Deanna and her husband went out for a dressy evening function sponsored by his company. Deanna wore a dress that was over ten years old and a pair of shoes that had definitely seen better days. Driving home afterward, Deanna was in tears over how bad she looked compared to the other women at the party. Her husband was exasperated. He had been through this before. "You've known about this event for months. You could easily have gone out and bought yourself a new outfit. I would have gone shopping with you," he told her.

Later, with her therapist, Deanna was able to locate the root of her "poor me" martyrdom: "My mother would always tell me, 'You don't need that.' I learned that you just go through life never spending any money. I don't think I ever bought anything, ever, that wasn't bargain basement on sale. As a result, I've become a very self-sufficient person, but I have a hard time 'treating' myself, even if I'm offered help to do it."

Not listening. One of the most effective ways of stopping the gift at the entry point is not to hear it. If you don't listen, you can't receive.

Many people have selective hearing. The frequency they can't pick up is the one that transmits positive feedback. Neutral or negative information is received loud and clear, but praise is not. For example, Dan was at his wits' end with his wife, Carla: "She tells me she wants me to be more supportive. I've tried to ask her about her day or sympathize when something goes wrong, but she doesn't listen to me. She gets a certain look in her eye, and I know she's zoned out."

Carla had to admit that Dan was right. She was on his case for not being supportive, but whenever he offered a word of encouragement or appreciation, she tuned him out. "A big moment for me was when I realized that I was acting like my dad," she says. "He used to walk away or grunt at my mother when she was trying to talk to him. And I felt like I couldn't get his attention very often either."

Stewart, like Carla, also has a hard time hearing the positive. Stewart and his wife Katie are a high-profile couple in the art world, mostly because of Katie's reputation as an oil painter. Her paintings are in demand in public buildings all over the world. Stewart, who is a sculptor, feels small by comparison. The audience for his work is much more modest. Even though the invitations to travel, speak, and socialize with other art stars always include both of them, and Katie is careful to use "we" instead of "I" when talking about their life as artists, Stewart feels unworthy. "I get so frustrated with Stewart sometimes. I'll tell him about the magazine that wants to come and film our studios, or I'll be all excited about an invitation we have to be part of the faculty at Oxford, and he'll just sort of walk away in mid-sentence. It's like he is so preoccupied he can't hear the great news I'm sharing," says Katie.

Stewart and Katie sought therapy when their marriage began to unravel. It was painful to for them both to discover how low Stewart's self-esteem had become with regard to his career. "I learned that I was having trouble accepting the good things that were coming into our lives because of Katie. I didn't think I deserved the attention, so I had trouble hearing about it." Working through these issues continues to be an ongoing process for them both.

Excessively adoring your partner. If you demean yourself in relation to a partner you've invested with superhuman qualities, you will have trouble accepting anything that partner has to offer. Your partner is so great and you are so unworthy that you couldn't possibly accept anything from him or her.

In the first years of their relationship, Joan constantly praised and complimented her partner, Kerri. Kerri was sometimes embarrassed by how often Joan told her she was smart or pretty or good at something. Joan came to understand why she did this: "When I was little, I didn't feel good enough, so I would overachieve to try to gain appreciation. So when I got into a relationship with Kerri, I was the one doing all the complimenting. I think I was doing that because it was something I wanted for myself because I didn't get it growing up. And then when Kerri *did* start complimenting me, I didn't hear it. She would have to say, 'This is a compliment, Joan. Did you hear that?'" Joan had idolized her partner and rendered herself insignificant by comparison. Compared to Kerri's shining light, she wasn't worth noticing. Only through therapy was Joan able to unravel the complexity of her own self-denigrating behavior and understand that she was feeding herself by offering to Kerri what she wanted but couldn't accept.

Criticizing, discounting, and devaluing. If you invest your partner with negative attributes, you will have trouble accepting anything your partner has to offer. Anything that comes from a defective partner isn't worth having, right? Criticizing, picking fights, and wanting to be intimate but then saying something that makes him or her uncomfortable—these are all strategies for ensuring that you won't be receiving love. Every time you do it, you reinjure yourself and avoid the possibility of getting the love you want, thus ensuring that your self-rejection remains intact.

For example, Hal's wife surprised him with a CD player for Christmas. She knew he really wanted one. But when he opened the present, he looked disappointed: "Why didn't you ask me what kind to get? This one doesn't have all the options I need. You always go off and buy the first thing you see on sale."

Later, Hal explained why he was *always* critical of gifts. "In my family monetary things, like giving gifts, were a very big deal," he told us. "It was a tit-for-tat kind of thing—if we got a nice gift, we gave a nice gift. If we didn't get a nice gift, my dad would always talk about how cheap those people were. Even to this day, I do the same thing. I have a hard time accepting gifts and the thought behind them because of this."

People who believe their partners are inadequate or defective often display their lack of confidence by trying to control or overly protect them. If you are with someone who, in your opinion, can't manage life well, you may feel you have to do it for them. This puts you firmly in the role of giver or manager, and makes it less likely you'll be in the role of receiver. For example, Tim was very controlling with his partner James. He jumped in to make James' decisions for him in an attempt to protect James from being hurt and making mistakes. The result was that Tim micromanaged the details of their relationship, often in a critical and nagging way. When Tim talked about his early childhood, he revealed that "my mother was hospitalized with clinical depression from the time I was four years old. What I learned was that I couldn't control relationships. I would count on something and then it went away. I made the decision to be responsible, to take charge of things and control life and make order out of life in order to protect myself."

Let's look again at Rena and Al's relationship as another example of one partner trying to control the other. Rena vowed that she would never become involved with anyone who tried to control her the way her parents did. But she did. She says, "It turned out that Al had the same kind of behaviors with me that my parents did . . . like trying to control me and trying to fix me, and having a certain way he wanted me to be." Whether the criticism is voiced or not, it's implied: *You're not capable of running your life as well as I am.* Because Al grew up with the expectation that perfection was possible and it was his duty to achieve it, he tried to control as many things as he could, including his partner. He didn't function as though he believed other people were capable of solving their own problems. Naturally, Rena was hypersensitive to this because of her experience with overly controlling parents. Rena and Al were a perfect imago match.

Depriving yourself and your partner of the things that make life joyful, such as sex, creativity, laughter, or enthusiasm. A lack of joie de vivre often shows itself as depression or aggression. The depressed individual tends to injure herself or engage in self-punishment. The aggressive individual tends to injure others and engage in violence.

Suzanne discovered very early in her marriage that she "wanted more sexual intimacy than Stan could provide." As it turned out, Stan had absorbed real prohibitions from his mother against enjoying sex. Stan's father was a womanizer, and his mother thought both that sex was bad and that men who had sexual desires were evil. She was very vocal about expressing this view around her favored oldest son. As a result, Stan did not allow himself to experience the joys of a full sexual relationship with his wife.

In Anna and Joshua's marriage, a major theme was that sex was tremendously important for Joshua. It was a primary way that he could feel loved and cared for. Anna knew this but had trouble validating him in this way. As she said, "Sex is fine, but what I don't need right now is to drop everything and have sex." The result was that Joshua complained of feeling "neglected sexually." He needed constant reassurance that his sexual self was acceptable. No matter how willing Anna was, he soon needed to be reassured again. The "gift" didn't stick. For Anna's part, life was very serious. She didn't have time for frivolities, and Joshua's need for more frequent sex made her think of a little boy who insists on buying candy when there isn't enough money to buy meat, bread, and milk.

Hearing only criticism and not praise, or hearing praise as criticism. In essence this means that reactions get triggered because of past experiences that have little or nothing to do with what's happening in the present. One reacts rather than listening and responding to what is actually being said.

For example, Janice had worked hard to put together a jazz

orchestra in the high school in which she taught. She had taken a ragtag group of students and turned them into an exciting, polished group of musicians. Finally, it was the night of their debut concert for parents and friends. Her husband, Robert, told us what happened: "It was a wonderful night. The orchestra was fantastic. It also happened to be Janice's birthday. The kids in her group found out about that and arranged to sing 'Happy Birthday' to her after the performance. When the last standing ovation was over, the kids burst into 'Happy Birthday,' and so did the parents. Everyone was cheering and congratulating her. It was fantastic. But backstage afterward, all Janice could talk about was a sarcastic comment one of the students who was not in the orchestra had made. To me, it was trivial. To her, it was the only thing that had happened. It ruined her evening and it certainly ruined mine." Robert was dismayed at his wife's reaction to what should have been one of the greatest nights of her life.

Janice didn't pay much attention to him when Robert mentioned how he perceived her reactions to the evening. But when her student teacher also made a passing comment to the same effect, she thought about it some more. "Actually, I was appalled when I realized there was all this love and appreciation flowing around me," she says, "and I chose to focus on one negative comment from a disaffected kid. It really made me wonder why I had so much trouble taking in the applause and the singing. The only thing I could think of was my mother telling me she thought the only reason women worked was because they had big egos. Maybe that explains why I couldn't just stand on the stage and accept my success."

In another example, Charley knew that Sylvia was hypersensitive about her cooking, so he made special efforts to tell her how delicious the pasta was, or how well she had flavored the meat. Sylvia responded to her husband's kind words with brief smiles, but she came to full attention whenever her antennae picked up the slightest whiff of criticism. One time, Charley said, "Sylvia, you've outdone yourself! This is the best marinara you've every made—by far." Immediately, Sylvia shot back, "What? You don't like my marinara? I thought you liked my sauce." He had to explain that saying *this* was the best didn't mean her previous sauces were no good. They laughed, but only after a couple of tense moments had passed.

Sylvia's father had been a chef and she had learned very early that food was serious business. "There was no such thing as eating for fun at my house. Everything you put in your mouth was fair game for critical comment," she told us. "I guess I'm going to give Charley a break and really *get it* when he tells me something I've cooked is good."

Absorbing the Negative

Partners are also making their self-rejection apparent when they all-too-willingly judge themselves in negative ways. Although absorbing the negative is not the same as putting up barriers to the positive, the two defenses are connected. Besides having the same root cause of self-rejection, an individual who is ready to believe the worst about herself will have a hard time hearing the best. For example, if she thinks she's a screwup, she probably won't embrace the compliment about how organized she is.

Here are the common ways people make it less likely that they'll be able to receive love because they have absorbed a negative view of themselves:

Being openly self-deprecating. It is so common to hear people put themselves down that self-deprecation appears to be socially sanctioned, like having the good manners to say, "thank you." But modesty must be distinguished from self-rejection. The first is simply good taste; the second betrays psychological injury.

Tony couldn't believe that a beautiful girl like Marina would marry him. But she did, just before she graduated with an associate's degree from their local community college. Marina was not bothered by her husband's job, or his lack of a college education. What did bother her, however, was Tony's habit of putting himself down in front of other people. One evening, when they were at a holiday party at the downtown law firm where she worked as a paralegal, Marina was embarrassed to hear Tony tell her boss, "Yeah. I must have caught Marina in a weak moment. I don't know why she'd marry a grease monkey like me."

Tony's self-deprecation was one of the main issues they addressed in therapy. He told the therapist, "I don't know why, but I just can't really believe that I'm good enough for Marina." Somewhere in the past, Tony had had experiences that made it difficult for him to accept the affection and respect of his wife. Tony was missing the part of himself that felt worthy of another person's love and loyalty. Until he found that part again, his marriage to Marina was in jeopardy.

In another example, when Alicia and Jerry began to have problems in their relationship, Alicia jumped to the conclusion that it was her fault. Although they weren't married, they had been living together for two years and had talked about making it permanent. But then, it began to look like Jerry was losing interest in their being together. Alicia blamed her weight, her boring job, and her messiness for his disaffection. It wasn't until after they'd broken up that she learned he had reconnected with an old girlfriend. Alicia assumed the problem was hers, when, in reality, there was nothing she could have done to prevent him from running into his old girlfriend's arms.

Many partners will settle for a poor relationship, rather than none at all. They aren't sure they deserve a good one and would rather tough out a bad relationship than do anything that would risk losing it. One discouraged husband told us that when his relationship with his wife got really bad, all he could do was endure it. By way of explanation he said, "I'd decided to take an empty relationship over an empty house." He was willing to settle for nominal contact instead of the real thing. He thought it was the best he could do.

Having overly high expectations of yourself, or being a perfectionist. One way to keep yourself from enjoying success is to set the bar so high that it's impossible to reach. If you expect yourself to be perfect, there will always be plenty of ways to reinforce your belief that you're not good enough.

Cheryl remembers laughing at one issue of a popular woman's magazine she picked up at the grocery store in 1978. It was the December issue, so the cover was overflowing with "200 ways to decorate your home on a budget," and "25 different kinds of cookies you can make to swap with your friends." But the article that caught her eye was about a woman who had taken in over fifteen foster children to love and support! The whole message seemed to be about doing more, making more, and being more.

Later, Cheryl thought about that magazine often. She wondered whether she had reacted with such disdain because its "do more—be more" message was exactly the one she had allowed her life to be ruled by. She noticed her perfectionism especially at Christmas when she became frantic trying to measure up to some invisible standard, while her husband, Frank, braced himself for an onslaught of crafts and activities. Frank knew one thing: he could never give her a compliment on how beautiful the tree was, or how good the cookies were, because Cheryl was always disappointed in her efforts.

When she and Frank ended up in couples counseling, Cheryl was able to come to terms with the fact that she never felt good enough. She continually tried to "earn" herself some peace by producing proof of her *worth*. If she could just *be* good, maybe someday she would start *feeling* as if she was good. In her mind, her value was absolutely tied to her performance.

In another example, Danny always felt like a loser compared to his more successful father and brothers. His father was a professor at a prestigious university and two of his brothers were in the medical profession. As the odd man out in his family, Danny hadn't enjoyed school that much and had always preferred to work with his hands. He ended up starting his own electrician's business and was quite successful. In his spare time, he makes beautiful furniture out of wood.

No one else thinks Danny is a failure, but he has trouble giving himself credit for what he has achieved. Recently, his wife, Mandy, told him she was tired of him always putting himself down compared to the other men in his family. "Why do you do that?" she asked him. The only thing he could come up with was that feeling bad just felt right. His feelings that he was "less than" were so deeply engrained that they kept him from enjoying his accomplishments, and he didn't know how else to feel.

Willing to put up with abuse. A woman who believes she is nothing but trouble or a man who believes he is worthless will not only put up with abusive behavior from a partner, but may actively participate in the abuse. A gauge of self-rejection in these situations is the degree to which a partner will *not* ask to be treated with dignity and respect.

Stacy's husband openly dated another woman while he was still married to her. However, even after she was confronted with proof of her husband's affair, she held on tightly to him. She was afraid that if she expressed her hurt and disappointment, he wouldn't come back. So she accepted his behavior and never told him how it made her feel. Through this crisis, Stacy came to see how much her childhood experiences had prepared her to think that her worth was dependent upon whether people approved of her or not. If they treated her poorly, she reasoned, she would just have to work all the harder by being "good." That would induce them to treat her better. She said, "When I was growing up, I had to be very diligent about remembering that I was the kid and not the grown-up. I walked very softly around my parents. I was an approval seeker. I did everything I could to please my mom and not be yelled at by my dad. I always wanted people to say, 'Wow. Stacy! You did such a good job on this!' But now I know it's important for me to learn how to confront my husband when he's not treating me well."

In another example, Burt couldn't bring himself to tell his wife, Stella, how often she hurt his feelings. His reluctance was interesting, because he didn't allow himself to be treated poorly in his other relationships. But he let Stella ignore him, trivialize his concerns, discount his feelings, and say negative things about him to their two daughters. The only reason Burt could come up with for his passivity was that his father had allowed the same behavior from his mother. He and his father had both thought of his mother as emotionally fragile. "Whatever the reason, the effect on me is that I allow myself to continue to live with a woman who is not supportive. I've decided I have to get some help so I can tell Stella what I want and what I don't want. If I can't do it for myself, I have to do it for my kids."

What's Between You

It makes a tremendous difference to a relationship how much of the Between is filled with self-acceptance and how much with self-rejection. If you don't think you're worth loving, you can't accept the love your partner has to offer you. You can't believe you're good at something if you "know" you're no good. You can't take in a compliment for your looks if you think you're ugly. You can't accept help if you don't acknowledge that it's okay for you to have needs. And, if you're not aware of a certain aspect of yourself that other people see, you can't accept appreciation for what you don't know you have.

Whether you have consciously rejected a part of yourself or that part has gone underground without your knowing it, the result is the same: When the deliveryman knocks at your door with a gift, you're not home to accept the package. The box may contain the very thing you've always wanted, but if you aren't there to receive it, you'll never have the pleasure of opening the box. You can't accept a gift when you feel so unworthy.

Because there are holes in our perceptions of who we are and our value as individuals, we carry within us certain unconscious assumptions that have the following results: we can't accept ourselves as okay people; we can't accept views or behaviors that are different from the way we see the world; we can't accept help; *and we can't accept love.*

THE PARTNER WHO CAN'T RECEIVE

We've just described how partners make visible their self-rejection and their inability to receive love. To some degree, the nonreceiver is conscious that he isn't being receptive, and he can even tell you why. He can name his reasons. What he isn't aware of, however, is the psychological consequences and benefits to him of his behavior. He doesn't have a clue about why it's so hard for him to get rid of his resistance and instead, begin to be appreciative.

Conscious Reasons

Ask anyone why she's shrugged off a compliment or talked right over someone's effort to convey appreciation, and she can probably tell you why, assuming she can speak honestly. The number one reason is, "I don't want it." But this really is a catchall for one or more of the following:

I don't like the gift. The intended receiver may really find the gift ugly, too personal, too expensive, or inappropriate in some other way. Or the giver's style of giving may be unfamiliar and, therefore, may arouse fear. Maybe the giving is overproduced, and the recipient is uncomfortable being the center of attention. Or maybe the giving is too offhand, and the recipient can't take the gift seriously.

I don't like the giver. The intended receiver can find many reasons to devalue a gift by finding flaws in the giver. Perhaps the giver's behavior is seen as insincere or imperfect in some way. Perhaps, the giver's motivation is seen as questionable, as in, "He's just trying to buy me off." Or perhaps the intended receiver does not hold the giver in high esteem and the gift is consequently not held in high esteem either. To determine whether the giver is guilty as charged or is being slandered by an intended recipient who simply can't receive love, you would have to learn more about both of them.

The gift obligates me to give back. The intended receiver believes that receiving a gift entails an obligation to give one back. This isn't really giving and receiving—it's trading. For some people, having to return the favor challenges their emptiness by making it apparent that they don't have the personal resources to be generous. If you're engaged in trade and you're not getting anything back, you will find that your capacity to give dries up. There just aren't enough resources to give away.

The gift diminishes me. For many people, to receive is to lose power. They believe that you only take something if you are needy, and it's not okay to be needy. Being offered a gift activates defenses against being in a position where you have a need and another person has the power over you to ignore or discount your need.

The gift makes me dependent. This is related to feeling diminished power. If you haven't had the experience of being in a healthy give-and-take relationship where you experience times when you are helping and other times when you are *being* helped with no loss to your self-esteem, the thought of being dependent feels very dangerous.

Underneath all these reasons for not wanting to receive is some measure of fear. Because of past injuries to the self, it feels dangerous to let in a seemingly positive element from the outside that may disrupt the stability of your psyche. Your psychological stability rests on your defenses. To tear down your defenses feels like letting in a whirlwind.

Unconscious Benefits and Consequences

If you ignore or deny your partner's gifts, you don't have to confront the void created by your self-rejection. You don't have to face the consequences of going against your caretakers' injunction that you are unworthy. If you refuse the gifts, you are still under your caretakers' protection. Better to be crippled by the loss of self than abandoned by caretakers who will not love and care for you if you stay whole.

Let's take an example. All children need loving, safe touch. If this need was not met—by caretakers who did not touch or by caretakers who touched harshly or inappropriately—the child will grow up to be an adult who still needs to be touched but *who doesn't have permission to be touched.* The impulse was negated and interpreted by the child to be dangerous. To protect herself, the child put the need into her unconscious and took a negative attitude toward touching. The impulse toward touching now feels dangerous, and danger arouses fear.

Whenever the now-adult thinks, "I would sure love to have my back rubbed," this causes her anxiety. Why? Because the unconscious mind is timeless, and the disapproving caretaker is still there as a memory. To actually receive what she's asked for would be to risk death. But she knows she needs the backrub and she wants it, so she thinks consciously that the reason she's not getting it is because her partner won't give it to her. She asks her partner for it over and over again, and every time he gets enough courage to try to give it to her, she rejects it so she can stay safely in compliance with her caretakers' injunction. In this example, we can see that the defense against receiving love is rooted in the protection of the ego against death.

There are also other psychological benefits that make it hard for the self-rejecting person to start receiving. She thinks: *If I were to let love in, I would:*

- Lose my identity as an unloved person.
- Lose the concept of my partner as unloving.
- Lose my consciousness that I am a victim.
- Lose my feeling that I am entitled to get my needs met because they never are.
- Lose the right to complain and demand.
- Lose the stimulation of anger, despair, and the pathos of hope-lessness.
- Lose the excitement of anticipation that somebody may love me someday.

In other words, I would lose a very powerful identity. This identity serves me in an important way—it stirs my sense of aliveness through pain. To look for love is a tragic journey, with all the excitement and pathos that implies. But to find love is to experience the void, with both the pain and boredom *it* implies.

The Partner Who Is Trying to Give

Pity the poor partner who is committed to someone who cannot receive. Not only does he experience the frustrations of not being received, but ends up with a partner who has certain characteristics that are both the cause and effect of not being able to receive: His spouse is self-absorbed. She has very little to give him, and she can't give to him what she can't receive herself. In addition, she exhibits the propensity for wounding him in the same ways she herself was wounded.

How It Feels

To fully understand the pain of the partner who is not received, we have to remind ourselves of what the opposite feels like. What is it like to know that when you offer help, encouragement, or love to your partner, he or she takes it in and appreciates it? When we allow ourselves to remember or envision such a positive exchange, we feel affirmed, validated, abundant, valuable, generous, and loving. When one partner doesn't accept what is offered, the other one is deprived of these fundamental joys of life.

What we hear most often from frustrated givers is that they feel disempowered and hopeless. One woman told us, "I can't make an impact on my partner. Whatever I do, it's not right or not enough. I want to give up." Someone else, a man this time, said, "I'm married to someone who is a bottomless well. Nothing I put into it fills her up. I feel impotent." Other partners talk of feeling invisible. Some say that, over time, they have lost the sense of themselves as a person who matters; they don't count. This lowered self-esteem gradually seeps into other areas of life, and they find themselves being tentative or submissive at work or with their children.

In addition, they feel rejected. Whenever their offers have been turned down, they feel as if they themselves have been turned away. They don't get to experience the gratitude that is a normal part of giving and receiving. They begin to think there must be something wrong with them. If they were better people, they would be more fully embraced by the people who are supposed to love them.

In this way an injury in the nonreceiver mutates into an injury in the giver. Over time, a partner who is consistently turned down will undergo a process of self-rejection similar to the one that caused the problem in the nonreceiver in the first place. Then you have two people in the relationship who can neither give nor receive, and one of them is very angry. If you don't know that the reason your partner can't receive from you is that he or she has been seriously wounded, you conclude that you are being mistreated out of carelessness or malice. Some people respond to that by staying angry, and some turn the anger inward and become depressed.

GIVING AND RECEIVING ARE PART OF THE SAME SYSTEM

There are many factors that go into creating the complex system of interactions that constitute a committed relationship. But if we isolate just one of those factors—the ease or difficulty with which one or both partners is able to receive love—we can get a general idea of how the whole relationship is affected.

For example, if we are looking for love, we are unlikely to receive it, because we are in the looking rather than the receiving mode. If we demand love, we will not get it because love does not survive when one partner is functioning from such a deprived position. If we expect love, we cannot receive it because doing so would mean altering the consciousness of expectancy to which we are attached.

Relationship Is Not the Same as Connection

Although connection is our essence, and we cannot lose it, one can be in a relationship without experiencing connection. Connection is defenseless relating.[1] To have a strong connection, partners have to open themselves to each other. When they do that, they are able to be vulnerable, silly, and authentic. They can meet each other without defenses. They are willing to share themselves and anxious to learn about the other. They give and receive freely. In order to give, they must be open. This openness and the vulnerability that comes with it makes it possible to receive. When there is true connection in a relationship, giving and receiving are not separate activities, but different places along a continuum of exchanges.

Of course, it is possible to have a relationship without having a connection like this. You can even talk and share without having true intimacy. Partnerships can certainly exist without connection, as most of them do. Since connection depends upon a desire and willingness both to give yourself and to receive the other, not receiving in a relationship is like jamming a stick into the spoke of a bicycle wheel—it stops the action. The wheel no longer turns smoothly on its course, propelling the bicycle forward. If one or both partners can't receive in a relationship, the healthy give-and-take that defines true connection is jammed and breaks down. A lopsided, limping system of interactions takes its place. *But it is not true connection, and it is not true love.*

When the System Is Disrupted, an Opportunity for Healing Grows

As we've seen in our discussion of the imago match, when you commit to a relationship, your partner will usually react to your impulses the same way your parent did. After all, you have committed to someone who shares traits with the parent you had the most difficulty with. As such, you are likely to hear a reprise of: "You think too much." "You feel too much." "You never want to touch me." "I wish you told me more about your feelings." "I wish you could think a logical thought." Since you've experienced these wounds to your self before, your unconscious self-rejection is reinforced in your relationship. This means that both of you have been injured, both of you have rejected parts of yourselves, and both of you will have some degree of trouble receiving love.

You will never find that one partner in a relationship carries unconscious self-rejection and the other is free of it. Everybody has it to some degree. So when we focus on the "partner who has trouble receiving love," we are really talking about both partners, and both are very similar in their ability to let love in. While partners are likely to be wounded in similar ways and have complementary defenses, they are also likely to have experienced differences in the severity of their wounding and in their level of healing. One may be able to give and the other may tend to take, but both have difficulty receiving.

Obviously, the uniqueness of the two individuals involved means that every couple has a characteristic way that gifts of emotional support and material comfort are accepted or declined. Fairly early on, routines are established that are hard to break. They may be unbalanced routines, in the sense that the partners do not give and receive in equal measure, but both individuals have an investment in whatever routine "works." The impulse is toward the stability of the system. Couples are loath to shift familiar interactions to unfamiliar ones because, in the area of relationships at least, what is new is frightening.

However, over the course of time and with constructive information and continuing care, partners can learn to share insights and information with each other that lead to healing. They can do this for each other better than anyone else can. Having our partner's loving and perceptive insights allows us to see those parts of ourselves that are lost to our awareness, where we need to do the most work.

In a neat piece of symmetry, intimate relationships both reveal our lack of wholeness and give us the best opportunity for repairing it. Only in relationship can we find out which parts of ourselves have been lost and how our lost selves have shaped the way we love, work, and play. Our partners hold the key to what has been submerged, discredited, and forgotten in us. In fact, they ask us to bring it back into consciousness; they call us into our wholeness. Even if our capacity to give and receive love has been damaged, we can learn how to experience the joy of giving and receiving. It is never too late. The key is learning how to connect authentically with the one person closest to us.

In the next part of the book, we will find out why there is good reason to believe that even couples with several years of miscommunication and mistrust behind them can heal their individual wounds and create a vital, enhancing relationship. Recent research in neurobiology supports our understanding of the power relationships have to heal the past. And, we follow the stories of Stan and Suzanne, Al and Rena, and Joshua and Anna, as they discover rich veins of connection and compassion in their relationship that they had never experienced before.

PART II: THE SOLUTION

CHAPTER 6

The Science of Relationships

I feel like we've been given a second chance.
It's never too late to put things right.

We have long contended that wounds can heal, self-rejection can be overcome, and relationships can mend. We know this because our clinical experience supports it, and our personal experience confirms it. But we now have an additional source of understanding and hope for couples who want to place their relationships on a better footing. This new information is coming to us from technical advances in neuroscience.[1] What researchers are learning gives us every reason to believe that with conscious effort, couples can learn to replace negative patterns of interaction with positive ones. We know more about how to help people change than we ever have before.

RESETTING THE DEFAULTS

Young women are always counseled, "Don't marry a man thinking you can change him. Either accept him as he is, or don't marry him at all." This is probably good advice. But the fact is that people *do* change, depending on the relationships they're in. Under a mate's tender, loving care a shy person can blossom, an uptight person can learn to relax, and a tightwad can become more generous. The right relationship can help a partner become more curious, expressive, and people-smart, and the wrong one can cause the same person to become withdrawn, rigid, and fearful. This chapter discusses just how important relationship is in determining who we are and who we become. But, to understand why so many people reach adulthood unable to receive love, we have to understand the forces that turn a receptive infant into a fortressed adult.

When we are born, we come to life with a whole array of genetic possibilities. Which of these options get developed depends to a great extent upon the quality of our relationship with our parents. Our parents are our first and most important architects. From the first moment of life, mothers and fathers shape their babies by the way they interact with them. Within the environment of parental stimulation, the child's self begins to take shape, including whether the child will be able to give and receive easily. In effect, parents become artists who use the parent-child relationship as their medium of creativity. Sometimes it's a conscious process, but most often it's not.

There are additional opportunities for revising early patterns and adding new ones, although they aren't as powerful as parental influence. The child, and then the adult, is continually crafted for good or ill by important relationships until his death. School friends, mentors, romantic partners, spouses, children, coworkers, therapists—all have the potential to rearrange some of the initial building blocks laid down in those first years. Each sustained relationship will leave its mark on the way the individual thinks, feels, behaves, and reacts. Relationship is the tool of self-creation and re-creation throughout life.

The awareness that relationships are important is not new, even though Freud himself underestimated their significance. He was so invested in trying to ground psychoanalysis in science that he perceived human beings as primarily biological creatures, beasts with the twin drives of sex and aggression. In the beginning of his clinical life, he based psychoanalysis on separate knowing at the expense of connected knowing. He wanted to make sure his ideas were built on a solid, rational, and respectable footing with a systematic methodology for understanding the human psyche. The effect of focusing on this concern was that he neglected the important but more nebulous influence of connected knowing, both in the conduct of therapy and as a crucial path to understanding for all human beings. Although to our modern eyes his writings do not give appropriate credit to relationship as the creator of personality, he must have known on some level that the primary drive for human beings is to establish interactive ties with others, because since Freud's time writers and clinicians have both increasingly seen relationship as the determinative force in personal development.[2]

What is new is our growing knowledge of *why* and *how* relationships are so formative. Every year we learn more about the biochemistry of relationship and how our brains translate our interactions with others into our physical selves. The fact that there is now cellular evidence for the contention that "relationships make the man (and woman)" gives the concept real heft. Knowing that we leave behind a physical trail of our influence on others and their influence on us should make us more careful in our roles as parents, teachers, lovers, and partners.

We know about the connection between relationship and brain function because of our ability to produce detailed images of the living brain. If the only brain we can examine is a dead one, our options for understanding how human beings think, feel, and behave are limited. Seeing inside the complex brains of live people, however, has allowed neuroscience to become a major field of study.

One of the things neuroscientists have discovered is that human brains can differ significantly from each other. Research that coordinates measurable differences in brain structure with certain kinds of life experiences has led to the conclusion that experience actually builds the brain. We can see evidence that when certain things happen to people during certain critical periods of development, their brains are changed as a result.[3]

We know, for example, that the brains of adults who were abused as children are statistically different from those who were not abused. Those who suffered *significant* trauma while very young remain permanently scarred.[4] We can actually see the structural difference in the parts of their brains responsible for emotion and memory. These internal parts had to adapt to a hostile environment, and that adaptation formed their brains in certain ways. These brain changes enabled them to survive, but they also made it harder for survivors to be as self-aware, self-regulating, or self-confident as those raised in consistently loving homes.

In addition, brain-imaging techniques allow us to see that different parts of the brain become active or dormant depending on what kind of problem solving or what kind of emotion a person is experiencing in the moment. For example, associations between psychiatric symptoms and changes in the relative metabolism of different areas of the brain are being found.[5] Most of this research involves pinpointing the specific circuitry involved in the regulation of anxiety and fear in the aftermath of trauma.

The Brain's Response to Relationship

When a baby is born, she has many million more neurons than she can use. Early experiences and genes shape the way neurons connect to one another in the brain, and thus form specialized circuits responsible for mental processes.[6] This is a kind of biological life insurance. This overabundance of brain cells increases the likelihood that the infant will be able to adapt to, and, therefore, survive in whatever conditions she finds herself. Her brain will never again be as malleable as it is in these first months of life. In fact, each bit of an infant's brain tissue about the size of a grain of rice has 10,000 brain cells. Each of these cells is capable of making anywhere from one to 10,000 connections to other brain cells. When the infant takes her first breath, she is still in the process of wiring up these trillions of connections.

Her experiences will dictate how the wiring of her brain proceeds—which connections will be added to the diagram and which will disappear. Neuroscientists refer to brain development as "experience-dependent," because experience activates certain pathways, strengthening existing neural connections and creating new ones.[7] Neurons and neuronal connections that are not used and do not help her survive wither away in a process called "pruning." The ones that stay are the ones that have been used and reused.

Neurons and synapses can also disappear under conditions of chronic stress. If the baby experiences significant trauma, certain positive connections in the brain do not get made. Sometimes the absence of positive connections is life threatening, as with babies who are deprived of the comfort of their mother's bodies and are consequently unable to develop language skills or form attachments to others. Sometimes the absence of positive connections is not directly life threatening, but it erodes her later chances for joy, fulfillment, and happiness.

If, for example, the baby has the repeated experience of danger when someone gives her something (maybe she is pushed away when she reaches for it, or the object is taken away when she grasps it), the effect on her brain is twofold. The neural connections that link receiving with danger *will get made,* and the connections that would have made receiving safe and natural *will not get made.* In another example, if the baby is "punished" for taking in the world through her emotions and intuition, the neural connections that would have made connected knowing a natural part of her functioning will not have a chance to become established. On a cellular level, these connections appear not to help her survive, so they are not constructed. Given the trillions of hookup possibilities, it seems like a miracle that so much actually gets done right. Even after it has been pruned down to size, the human brain has more connections than there are stars in the universe.

Every time a baby does something or learns something new, the brain cells responsible for that action become strengthened. The stronger a certain set of neuronal connections become, the more likely it is that they will activate in the future. In this way mental, emotional, and physical patterns are established as the baby finds it easier to continue doing whatever it is that she's been doing. She develops habitual responses, like smiling when she sees her mother walk in the door or looking away and crying when she sees her mother walk in. Her biology dictates that whatever she is doing, she will do more of it in the future, and whatever she does not do will be difficult or impossible for her to do in the future. This is what people mean when they say that "experience sculpts the brain."[8]

The most powerful agent of experience for any new baby is her relationship with her parents. Her interactions with them and other caretakers provide the stimulus that literally wires her brain in specific ways. When her parents cuddle her and play with her and comfort her, they are building the neural structures in her brain that participate in the cuddling, playing, and comforting. When she responds by laughing and feeling safe, her brain releases certain chemicals, or neurotransmitters, in her frontal cortex. Serotonin, dopamine, and norepinephrine are stimulated by these positive experiences and go on to activate processes responsible for everything from emotion to memory to bodily function. If her experiences with her caretakers happen to be uncertain or frightening, these neurotransmitters are suppressed, and different ones are released, setting the stage for feelings of anxiety and depression as she grows older.

Reconstruction and Repair

It would be a bleak world indeed if we couldn't restructure some of the negative patterns laid down in childhood. There would be no point in writing this book, whose premise is that you *can* learn to receive love, and you *can* learn to know in a broader, more open way than you've known before. Fortunately, recent new research indicates that the brain is an organ of adaptation, capable of improving its functioning under the right conditions.[9] Even the adult brain, though not as malleable as the infant brain, is known to be plastic. This means that existing neurons are capable of taking on new jobs in order to help the individual adapt to changing circumstances. If you damage the adductor muscles in your thigh, for example, your brain is able to tell your *ab*ductor muscles to take over much of the work your adductors are no longer able to do. Some parts of your brain, such as that responsible for smell, are even able to manufacture entirely new brain cells. This talent for neurogenesis, as it's called, was a surprise to scientists who've only just begun to accumulate the evidence for brain cell regeneration.

The happy conclusion is that our brains are able to adapt, not just physically but also psychologically, to new situations. Some of the early structural and chemical patterns that dispose us to anger, anxiety, self-hatred, and depression can be overridden in favor of new patterns that are healthier. Even abuse survivors can become more peaceful and productive if they are fortunate enough to form trusting relationships later on. Given how imperfect parenting is and how hard life is, we're fortunate to get second, third, and twentieth chances to rearrange our mental furniture.

We can optimize some of these second chances by exposing ourselves to good ideas and trustworthy information. You may believe that listening to your partner is an important way to improve your relationship. But an idea is just an idea until it becomes part of your experience. Change happens when both separate and connected knowing are involved. You have to understand what to do, and then you have to deepen your understanding by letting yourself open to the experience of actually doing it. The parts of the brain involved in cognitive processing and the parts involved in registering emotion must develop patterns of interaction before an abstract idea can become part of your daily living. When you discover by practicing your listening skills that your partner is less defensive and starts listening to *you* when you listen to him, your good idea is suddenly transformed into something you "know" from the inside out. If you do it often enough, your belief that listening is a good idea will be integrated into your behavior, and it will become part of who you are.

When it comes to rebuilding the fundamentals of who we are—like how we react to disapproval, or whether we can talk about our feelings, or how well we tolerate the everyday stresses of life—improvements have to be made in the same medium that spawned the problems. That medium is relationship. *Our problems were created through relationship, and only through relationship can they be corrected.* Let's take an example. Let's say that as a child you were punished for saying how you really felt. You learned to avoid your mother's hurt expression by telling her you liked her tuna surprise when you really didn't. You didn't dare tell your father you thought same-sex marriages were legitimate. And you certainly never shared your fears that your parents might divorce.

But now that you are in a committed relationship, you want to be freer to be your true self. You don't want to keep hiding. To actually undo the damage from the early gag rule, though, you have to experience safety and acceptance in your relationship *now*. Your goal to become more open to receiving is merely a goal until you have a chance to practice being open to receiving in a safe environment. Your goal must move from the cognitive level of "This is what I want to do," to the level of connected knowing where you can say, "This is what it feels like to have the experience of doing what I want to do."

Your new behavior has to be repeated many times because *you are building a new pathway for receiving* in your brain. New behavior can create new patterns, but the connections get strong only if they are used. And they have to be strong enough to counteract the power of your habitual response, which is to keep your mouth shut in order to stay safe.

You won't *know* that it's okay to be your full self instead of an abbreviated, cleaned-up version unless your partner helps you feel good about expressing opinions that may be different from hers, and the two of you end your symbiotic relationship. Your rehabilitation takes place through her reinforcement of your new openness. You have to disagree with her about what she's wearing, or what movie you're going to see, or whether it's a good idea for your son to enlist in the military—and live to tell the tale. Then you'll "know" that it's safe to be yourself. Fortunately, restorative relationships do not have to be with the same people who were responsible for the problem. We don't very often get the chance to work things out with a mean babysitter or coach, or even a parent, but, thankfully, people at a later time can take over the work of psychological repair.

Any nurturing relationship or environment has the potential of stimulating our brains to make positive changes, although exactly which repairs are possible after childhood is still being investigated. As we've said, a loving partner can go a long way to help us develop the neurophysiology of safety rather than insecurity. Environments that are stimulating without being too stressful can help us increase the density of our neural connections and turn us into quick learners. And, supportive friendships can help us reduce the level of stress hormones circulating in our body and brain. We may be sorry that none of these positive relationships and environments played a key role in our early formation, but thank heavens they can play a role now.

Reparative Relationships

The formal therapeutic relationship exists for the purpose of making positive neural changes in the client.[10] Therapists intentionally set out to help their clients reroute old reactions into new responses. Unconscious ways of functioning that were once adaptive but are now destructive get transformed into new ways of thinking, feeling, sensing, and behaving. Over time and with positive reinforcement, these new conscious responses replace the old unconscious reactions. The means of transformation for therapists is the same as it is for parents—the relationship with the therapist or with the parent is the agent of creative change.

However, a relationship doesn't have to be with a therapist to be "therapeutic," in the sense that it is reparative and restorative. All therapeutic relationships, whether they are with caretakers, friends, children, or whomever, have characteristics in common that make them effective. So what are the common characteristics of these corrective relationships? Freud's thought was that the goal of therapy is to make the unconscious conscious. This goal continues to be the guiding light of therapy and therapeutic relationships. The more you learn about your motivations, fears, and knee-jerk reactions, the more you start making sense to yourself. The therapeutic process allows you to deal with your life, not as an impenetrable mystery or a chaotic hodgepodge, but a storyline you can follow. And it allows you to take the abstract ideals of your life that you may know cognitively, and integrate them into connected knowing and living.

You know you are involved in a reparative relationship if you are better able to experience a wider range of emotions and more able to tolerate stress than before. To achieve this healthy emotional resilience, a reparative relationship will spur you to become adept at certain specific skills that your brain has not been stimulated to develop until now. If you are fortunate enough to participate in a relationship like this, even if you've always been emotionally "illiterate," you can learn to:

- Put feelings into words
- Connect experience to meaning
- Identify what triggers anxiety
- Integrate what you're thinking with what you're feeling

All of these skills involve connecting aspects of the self that used to be separate from each other. Consider, for example, the man or woman who is rocked by waves of confusing emotion but can't say what these feelings are and has no idea where they come from. Or, the young person who feels anxious about nearly everything, but has no clue as to what is triggering these feelings. In both cases, the individual needs to know himself or herself more completely in order to heal. And, to know yourself, you must be able to access information on both a separate and connected knowing level, in a balanced way.

Linking information and feelings by using both separate and connected knowing in a balanced way is the key to better functioning on a physiological and a psychological level. If you can't perform these tasks of integration because you haven't had the interpersonal experiences that allow you to learn them, you're in danger of being imprisoned by your own defenses. For example, if you're not sure what's making you angry, then *anything* could be making you angry. If you don't have a way of making meaning from your troubles, then life is reduced to a battleground of random attacks with occasional reprieves. Everything is threatening. The feeling is that you can't let your guard down or you'll be hurt.

The antidote to this kind of isolation and restriction is to have experiences that are connecting and that open your capacity to trust. Reparative relationships accomplish their healing magic by encouraging both partners to:

- Understand and empathize with the other's point of view without judging
- Explore emotions and memories in a way that encourages tolerance and acceptance
- Maintain trust so that new challenges in self-awareness and learning can be undertaken
- Interpret experience in ways that enlarge perspective and promote self-esteem

Experiencing empathy, the freedom to explore, trust, and insight can reset your default reactions to a more curious, tolerant, and confident stance. Because our brains are plastic, consistently positive experiences do stimulate existing neurons to adapt and connect in different pathways. Nurturing relationships help us grow psychologically and neurally in ways that are not possible in nonnurturing relationships. As adults, our most important opportunity for a nurturing relationship comes through committed partnership. It's a breakthrough to realize that *the purpose of committed relationship is not to be happy, but to heal.* And *then* you will be happy!

CREATING THE CHILD'S SELF

The reason for discussing the influence parents have on the neural development of their infants and children is twofold. First, parents with this awareness can shape the relationship with their children from the beginning so as to nurture their strengths and uniqueness. Second, adults who wonder why their relationships are unsatisfying can gain insight into how their childhood wounds are affecting their lives now. Childhood wounds do not go away, but they can become less active when you are aware of them and consciously practice healing alternatives to the poor relationship habits you absorbed when you were young.

Because most people don't have clear memories before the age of five, you can't know for sure how your parents interacted with you when your brain was at its most impressionable. But there is a lot you can surmise based on all the years of memories you *do* have from your family life. You may not know the specific circumstances that shaped your early life, but you can describe your parents' style of relating as you grew up. For example, your mother may have been warm and accepting, but your father might have been a perfectionist. Your father may have encouraged you to try new things, but your mother might have been fearful. Or perhaps it was the other way around.

In addition to memories of your later childhood, you can make some good guesses about how you were parented based on the traits you observe in yourself now. Since the most formative interactions with your parents happened beyond the limits of your memory, you have to deduce what happened *then* by what kind of person you have become. For example, if you react strongly anytime anyone says anything that sounds like negative feedback, it's worth thinking about why you are so threatened. And—more to the point in this discussion—if you react negatively anytime someone gives you *positive* feedback, that too is important to investigate. Drawing a line of understanding from your wound back to the cause of the injury opens the possibility for insight and repair.

The Attuned Parent

In this book the particular wound we are exploring is the difficulty people have in receiving love. This "receiving deficiency" takes various forms, but as we shall see, the root of the problem in every case is the same.

The first act of life is receiving. The first thing the baby does is breathe in and then suck in nourishment. It's the most natural thing in the world. Metaphorically, this is an act of connected knowing, in which life is absorbed through instinct and sensation. If the baby is fortunate enough to have a sensitive and caring parent, the natural rhythm of receiving, and then giving, is set in motion from this first breath. The parent is the pivotal factor in whether or not the ability to take in and give out becomes part of the baby's natural responses, or whether this capacity is ruptured.

If parents are *attuned* to their child, they are sensitive to the child's signals and able to communicate with him in a way that demonstrates their emotional connection with him. They enter into his way of being in the world, the way he sees things. Because of their emotional attunement, the baby is able to "borrow" the more mature brain of his mother or father. He gets in sync with their reactions and learns from them about how to *be* in the world. He uses their brains while his is still developing.

The baby doesn't just use part of his parents' brains; he responds to their *whole* brains, including the parts they are conscious of and pleased to have him absorb, and the parts they aren't so proud of, or are not aware of. They bring to their baby's brain development their unconscious wounds and anxieties, as well as their determined efforts to be good parents. To the extent that he can, the baby tries to do what they do and feel what they feel because pleasing them is the best way to ensure his survival. In this way, the baby's brain wires itself to adapt to his relationship with his parents.

It can be frightening for parents to realize how significant both their conscious and their unconscious functioning is in shaping their children's development. An unconscious parent may not realize how much anger she is carrying. But her baby will feel her anger whether she is aware of it or not. The effect on him is the same as the positive, conscious parenting efforts she makes. Sometimes the best way for an unconscious parent to become more conscious is to observe the effect she's having on her children, who will reflect back to her those traits she's not yet able to see in herself.

Communication between parent and child is no less intense because the child is not verbal. In fact, the first and most important dialogues in the child's life are preverbal. Through cooing, smiling, making faces, singing, and holding, the parent communicates to the baby that his needs will be met and that he is understood.

The parent's most important tool for attunement is the practice of mirroring. The baby smiles and the parent smiles. The baby puckers up to cry, and the parent makes a sad face. The baby sings la-la-la, and the parent sings la-la-la. When a mother mirrors her baby, she is conveying to him that she sees him and that he is fine: "It's okay to be as you are. I am here." In conveying this message, she is, in effect, "holding" his feelings for him by mirroring them. This allows him to relate his experiences to himself and eventually integrate them into his being. This simple act by the parent sets into motion his ability to manage his inner world. He comes to understand that whatever he experiences is a valid part of who he is. This prepares him for the lifelong task of self-discovery.

The High Price of Non-Attunement

Mirroring is so necessary that it even needs to precede the mother's inclination to comfort her baby. Understanding what the baby is feeling must come before reassuring him. Otherwise, the child doesn't have any way of knowing that his feelings are accepted and validated. Feelings that are not mirrored are not integrated. When the mother jumps right into, "It's okay" without mirroring first, the baby doesn't know what to do with his reactions. There is a disconnect between what he is experiencing and the confirmation he is getting from his mother that his experiences are real. Whatever he has just experienced has got be recognized and accepted. If it is not, he has no choice but to escalate the intensity of his feelings or shut them down altogether.

Whenever the parent does not mirror, the child experiences a *split* between himself, his feelings, and what his feelings might mean. If this process of nonacknowledgment and nonvalidation is repeated, the child will not allow himself to recognize what he really feels, so he will not be able to connect what he feels to the things that happen to him. As we discussed earlier, this disintegration and isolation between aspects of the self is exactly the problem reparative relationships must try to remedy later.

This process of splitting and the implications of splitting in adult relationships is central to our story about why people have problems receiving the love they want. You could say that splitting is the main "character" in our drama. Splitting leads to a void, an emptiness, a longing. This void is the source of depression, all forms of self-abuse, and the anger that leads to all types of violence. Every time the child expresses an authentic aspect of himself, and he is not acknowledged or validated—or what he has done is actively disapproved of, discounted, or discouraged—he is less likely to do that particular thing again. Eventually, he will only do it or think it under the cover of secrecy, or he will stop doing it altogether and lose the awareness that it was ever a part of him. His relationship with his parents has effectively edited out a part of his genuine self. In order to survive, he had to let it go. But as we have seen, these parts are never really gone.

A parent can commit two basic sins of nonattunement, and both stem from not mirroring. One is the error of "too much," and the other is the error of "too little." A parent who intrudes into her child's psychic space interferes with his capacity to receive and give love. She imposes *her* feelings and perceptions on him without giving him a chance to discover his own. Equally destructive is the parent who neglects her child and does not recognize, much less nurture, his individuality and personality. Either intrusion or neglect can be abusive. If these errors are occasional, and/or if the parent takes steps to repair them, the damage is minimal. If they are frequent or unpredictably violent, and they are not repaired, the damage is extensive.

All caretakers, even good ones, are nonattuned some of the time. All children experience splitting. All children come to adulthood with childhood wounds. The question is not whether you have been wounded or whether you are fractured or split. The question is whether you can learn what your wounds are and create the kind of loving relationship that will allow you and your partner to become whole. Believe it or not, the same relationship that has caused you grief can become the medium for healing you and your partners' deepest wounds.

CHAPTER 7

Learning to Receive

It's really amazing that loving and accepting all of my partner has made me feel so much better about myself.

It *is* possible to be happy. No matter what your history has been, you have the potential to heal and create the intimate relationship for which you've always yearned. You do not have to stay stuck in that place of desiring what you don't have and not being able to accept what you've always wanted. Healing is possible because our brains are alive to the changes we decide to make in our lives. Our brains respond to evolving circumstances. New neural pathways can be created, and old ones can fall into disuse. If you do something different enough times, you can develop a new attitude, a new habit, or a new ability. Your brain can stop running along those old, familiar negative tracks—the ones that are so automatic it seems as if they equal who you are—and start running along new tracks. Your body and emotions create a partnership with your brain and effect your transformation. Once you were lost and now you are found, just as the hymn promises.

But we can only be evolved in the same context in which we were lost—that is, in relationship. We are born into relationship. Our personalities are formed by relationship. And, we are healed in relationship. Relationship holds both the evidence of our injuries and the means of our salvation. It's the way we become who we are. Through the lights and shadows of our interactions, we can be seen at last.

RELATIONSHIP HEALING

Our yearning for connection and communion is basic to who we are as humans. We feel on a personal level and perceive on a universal level that connection is the essential condition of life. All things are given their reality, their coherence, their form, and their function because of their relation to the whole. Interconnection is the invisible reality that makes all things possible.

In this sense, disconnection—the isolation of the individual—is not real; it's just an illusion. We can *feel* ourselves to be disconnected. We can *experience* ourselves as disconnected. We can perpetuate our own disconnection by rejecting what would be healing. We can be self-absorbed, captivated by our own running commentary, and in love with our opinions instead of listening. We can disconnect by not letting ourselves experience the subjective reality of another person, by not being empathic, or by not letting our partner *in.* We can do any number of things that either cause our feelings of disconnection or that express them. But no matter how disconnected we feel, we are still part of the universal, interwoven tapestry of life. We cannot live in isolation, and we cannot heal alone.

The Mirror of the Other

One of the central myths of our culture is that if you're whole, you don't need anyone else. You can be an island unto yourself, a hero on your own journey. You can conquer alone.

We are saying the *opposite.* We are saying that you cannot be whole without the Other. There is no "I" without "Thou." Through relationship, we are mirrored into existence. The consciousness of who we are and what the world is like arises out of our encounters with other people. We do not become ourselves, except through our relations with parents, siblings, friends, teachers, and others, even those we have learned to consider our enemies. Our identities are the fruit of our engagement with the people close to us. Our selfhood is dependent on them. We can only exercise and enjoy the fullness of our own bodies, minds, and spirits if we develop and experience them in relation to other people.

Just as caretakers evoke or don't evoke the wholeness of a child by helping to create a context for the child, we continue to evolve toward our potential, or not, depending on our context. If the conditions of our lives are conducive to safety, exploration, validation, and competence, we are free to grow into fullness. If the conditions are harsh, we cannot develop the capacities we need until conditions become more favorable.

We are not alone in our dependence on environmental conditions. For us, the relevant conditions are both psychological and physical, but for other creatures they are mostly physical. In the Arctic there is a kind of toad that lies frozen in the tundra until the warmer weather thaws its living tissue, its blood begins to flow, and the creature is brought back to life. In Africa there is another species of toad that lies buried under the burning sand until, once every decade, it rains and the toad climbs out of its sandy sepulcher into the light. In our case, too, we require the right environmental conditions to thrive. Our relationships give us the sun and rain we need to become fully ourselves.

Those who have been traumatized by cataclysmic events, such as war or violence, or by personal events, such as death or betrayal, almost always suffer the symptoms of post-traumatic stress. The trauma is etched into the neural pathways of their brains, and it gets triggered over and over again by everyday occurrences that would not have caused a problem before. Sometimes the pain of past events can be eased when people move into a new environment with new relationships. In this new setting, old pathways gradually become inactive, while new pathways are created. On those occasions when the old pathways *are* activated, the new pathway can also be activated to counterbalance it.[1]

But changing environments isn't always possible or desirable. Another way to develop new neural pathways and facilitate healing is to keep relationships with the same people, but *change the nature* of those relationships. Make the interactions different. One wife told us, "Nothing different has happened inside of me, but the changes in our relationship are making me different." This is the goal of Imago Relationship Therapy: to create the conditions in a relationship that will encourage positive change in the partners. The right environment retrains the brain.

Shifting away from the individuals and toward the relationship is not the way people usually try to solve relationship problems. Almost always, partners focus on what the other person is doing wrong or could do better instead of what they both can do to improve their quality of their Between. When you start envisioning the relationship itself as a living entity, your attitudes change. You start paying attention to what you are contributing, you stop saying negative things, you eliminate criticism, and you start honoring the quality of the invisible forces that hold you together. Every decision you make is considered through the lens of what's best for the relationship.

What You Need to Understand

We want to be honest. The process of changing your relationship is not entirely peaceful. There will be times when you will feel frustrated, and so will your partner. But the payoff for staying the course is getting closer and feeling safer with your partner. If you can hold yourself in relationship long enough, you can dispel your fears and absorb the new understanding and behaviors you need to create neural pathways that are not sensitized to old injuries. You can become knowledgeable, intentional, and capable of other-absorption, or "Thou-ness," and not just of self-absorption and "me-ness." You can start to receive, and therefore be able to give. You will start to mirror the natural rhythm of the universe, which is the oscillation between activity and rest, expansion and contraction, giving and taking.

Learning to Love What You Hate

We know that the reason people can't receive love is because they can't accept positive input for traits, talents, and qualities they've disowned, and they can't receive gifts their parents didn't approve of their having, for whatever reason. In other words, self-rejection and self-hatred block their ability to take in what would be healing.

It's logical to think that the solution would be to start healing by loving yourself. Self-love is worth several billion dollars a year to the economy. Books, videos, audiotapes, and counselors are everywhere encouraging us to be good to ourselves. "Write down personal affirmations, go to a spa, take time out, take a hot bath." This is wonderful advice. And it feels good, at least temporarily. The problem is that conscious self-love, self-care, and self-soothing does not help people start loving the parts of them they've denied, rejected, or forgotten. It doesn't bring the rejected parts of the self back into the fold of consciousness. It doesn't erase the internalized disapproval of the parent that is activated when they try to get something for themselves that feels forbidden.

You cannot even heal your disconnection by loving other people or by loving God. You may compensate for your self-hatred by loving others, but you do not heal the breach within yourself. The true corrective lies along a different path. You must start loving *in your partner* those traits, habits, attitudes, and behaviors that give you the most trouble, in fact the very things he or she does that drive you crazy. It could be anything: quickness to anger, tendency toward inertia, constant judgment, drive toward perfection, emphasis on appearances, recourse to grandiosity, or the habit of self-deprecation. On a more mundane level, it could be the need to always (or never) pick up the check, the need to brag about the children, the need to hide behind humor, or the need to always (or never) be busy.

What do your partner's faults have to do with your self-rejection? The answer lies in the mechanism of projection. What you don't like or have rejected in yourself, you tend to project onto others, with the most on-target projections aimed at your partner. In order to continue to relate to the parts of yourself that are missing, you project them onto your partner and relate to them in that form. You can experience the disapproval and dislike you have for yourself by disapproving and disliking those same things in your mate. This sounds far-fetched only because most projections are created in the unconscious. You don't know you're doing it.

However, it's not that you are making all these traits up completely and pasting them onto your partner at random. You're not hallucinating when you think your partner is doing "that thing" again. There is almost always something in your partner that attracts your projections, providing there is something for your projections to stick to. After all, you chose your partner based on your imago, or internalized image of a parent or primary caregiver in the first place. And that means that during the power struggle, your partner really does demonstrate characteristics similar to the ones that injured you when you were young. Those traits really exist to some extent in your partner, and when you encounter them, they are supercharged.

Remember the George and Mary example? Mary was attracted to George, who was loud like her father. As a child she learned to be quiet in order to get along with her dad. She rejected in herself her natural inclination to express herself freely. Now, when George expresses himself freely, she accuses him of being overbearing. It's true that George *is* a talker, but Mary is projecting onto George her own rejected part and the disapproval she feels for it. Her response to George, when he says what he thinks or speaks with emotion, is to feel disapproving. On a gut level, she feels it's a bad thing, just as it was bad when she used to let herself be expressive as a little girl. The more critical Mary is, the more she betrays the extent of her own wounding.

So the key here is to understand, accept, and "love" in your partner the things you hate, because then, in effect, you will be loving them in yourself. This works because your brain doesn't make a distinction between loving yourself and loving the Other. The internal physiology, the chemistry, of loving is the same, no matter who is the object. So when you approach the faults of your partner—or rather, your own *projections* of your partner's faults—with understanding, tolerance, and acceptance, you get a double bonus. You experience understanding, tolerance, and acceptance for yourself as well as for your partner. Through repeated acts of loving acceptance, you gather to yourself all your neglected, abused, and frightening parts. Gradually you are restored to wholeness through the hard work of practicing acceptance.

It's true that partners engaged in this act of accepting are using each other for their own ends. But the use is a positive one. In intimate partnership there is no way to miss the encounter with the missing pieces of the self. Because two partners are also attempting to love in each other what they have rejected in themselves, both of them are restoring themselves to wholeness, and therefore preparing themselves to receive love. They are engaged in a mutual campaign of self-acceptance. Obviously, the relationship has to be the medium of transformation. There is no other way.

Whether the couple is in therapy or not, the power to change resides in the relationship itself. Each partner says: "You can tell me how to heal you," and "I can tell you how to heal me." They are relocating the agency of change away from outside authority and back to the relationship itself.

What You Need to Do

Gaining an overall understanding of how you and your partner are interconnected, for good or ill, is the first step in getting unstuck. Reconceptualizing the root of your relationship problems as self-rejection, and the solution as love of the Other, is primary. But there are other, specific steps you can take to build on your new understanding.

1. **Acknowledge That Your Partner Has Traits That Activate Your Energy and That Are Connected to You in Some Way**

   Get a clear-eyed view of what it is about your partner that bothers you. What traits would you eliminate or exaggerate if you could? Writing these characteristics down will force you to recognize and carefully consider each of your partner's characteristics that are problematic for you.

   Examine your list and know that these same traits are in some way connected to you. They are a mirror of the things you have rejected in yourself. What you make up about your partner (or anyone else) and invest with energy is also true of you. If you want to know who you are below your level of self-awareness or self-concept, then pay attention to how you judge others. The more you're trying to protect yourself from yourself, the more your projections will seem to you to bear no resemblance to yourself and the more you will tell yourself that *you are not like that* in any way. Only when you stop projecting will you know that you've started to become whole.

   Rena knew what she didn't like about Al. He acted as if he was the shepherd and she was the lost little lamb. She couldn't stand the way he needed to know how much she was eating or whether she had managed to keep her food down. But when she thought about what her antipathy to him might have to do with *her,* she made several connections. First, her parents had been overly controlling. Ever since her teens, she had struggled against their desire to direct her life. Second, when she put herself in Al's place, she could see why he might be concerned about her fearfulness and anxiety. He was worried sick and didn't know any other way to cope. Third, and most importantly for this discussion, she had to admit that she herself was something of a control freak. She did everything she could to make the world conform to her preset ideas. Remember that she wasn't going to consider getting married unless her lover conformed to her Prince Charming ideals? When she realized she was, at least in part, projecting her controlling nature onto Al, it helped her realize that improving the situation wasn't going to be as simple as forcing Al to stop doing what he was doing. She also had some work to do.

2. Ask Yourself How These Traits Help Your Partner Function or Survive

All behavior is an attempt to control something or get something done. No one does anything that doesn't help him or her survive. If you don't have this insight into what motivates the behavior in others that you dislike, you might think your partner is just being self-indulgent, careless, thoughtless, or cruel. However, trying to answer, as best you can, what positive purpose the behavior is serving helps you transform your negative attitude into a more compassionate one.

When Stan asked himself what Suzanne got out of being so critical of herself and everybody else, he could see that her criticism arose from a genuine desire to make things better. She desperately wanted to raise good kids, make a beautiful home, and be a good wife. If she voiced criticism, she could clarify for herself what needed improvement. And, he suspected, she wanted to be the first one to pass judgment. She had experienced too many sneak attacks from her mother that ended up making her feel like an idiot. She never wanted to be blindsided by another critical comment as long as she lived. Once Stan realized this, he didn't take Suzanne's criticisms so personally.

3. **Develop Compassion When Your Partner Does Things You Don't Like**
   Value the goal your partner is trying to achieve. You probably still won't like what your partner is doing, and it may still be crucial that the behavior stop or change, but having a more understanding attitude will begin to soften the sharp edge of your judgments— toward your partner and yourself. What you give, you get back. Every time you take a different attitude toward whatever irritates or annoys you, you change your attitude toward yourself.

   Compassion comes from understanding. When Suzanne heard Stan talk about the poverty and violence of his childhood, she could feel how desperately important it was for him to hide from conflict. She cried when she thought about how much her negativity had hurt him. From then on, she reminded herself that even though Stan still had a tendency to withdraw, he really did want to share feelings with her. Suzanne made a real effort to initiate conversations with him softly, especially whenever she wanted to talk to him about something that might be upsetting. He responded by opening up to her more, offering his opinions and listening to hers.

4. **Ask Yourself How You Are Like the Traits You Dislike in Your Partner**
   Assume that your partner's disliked trait corresponds to something in you that was so unsettling, you had to get rid of it in order to feel secure in your important relationships. Can you figure out what your partner's annoying habit has to do with you? Do you have the tendency to do the same thing? Or is that trait so deeply buried that you *never* do the same thing? What can you learn about your missing self? If you can't make a connection, ask your partner for help. Ask your partner what he or she wishes you had more of. And then try to relate the answer to the trait in your partner that bothers you. When you've identified the corresponding characteristic in yourself, ask yourself what purpose this behavior serves for you. How does it help you take care of yourself or function better?

By the time Stan had been married for ten years, he was running a nonstop critical commentary in his head about how dissatisfied Suzanne was. It was only after he'd been in therapy for a while that he realized how dissatisfied and critical *he* had become. It took some effort on his part to develop an "ear" for his own sarcasm and stop himself before he said something negative or cutting. Suzanne had the same kind of realization. She criticized Stan for being unforthcoming, but the truth was that she had trouble telling him what was really on her mind also. She didn't understand at first that all her talking was a smokescreen to keep from revealing her real fears and vulnerabilities. She came to see that maximizing doesn't necessarily translate into communicating important information. Both Stan and Suzanne were surprised at how much they could learn about themselves by examining the characteristics they most despised in each other.

5. **Adopt More of Your Partner's Disliked Traits in a Constructive Way**
Your goals are to stop judging and condemning the traits of your partner that you dislike the most, and see their value, perhaps in a modified form. In this way, you can end the exile of your missing self and reintegrate it back into your conscious self. The best way to do so is to stop demonizing these aspects of your partner and begin making them your own. Every trait, characteristic, or quality is a double-edged sword. It has both positive and negative components, depending on how it's deployed. Take the sword in your hand, turn the negative edge downward and the positive edge toward you. Now find a way to use the positive edge of the blade for the good of yourself and your partner.

For example, if your perception is that your partner steals the limelight, takes over conversations, or appropriates things that belong to others, you might simply think of him as a thief. Now, we are not suggesting that you begin a career in a life of crime by breaking into people's houses! But we do suggest you see how you might have stolen things, including objects, ideas, and emotions, from other people. Or, if you think of your partner as a liar, ask yourself how *you* have been dishonest in *your* relationships.

Al was a blown away when he realized how he really felt about

Rena's involvement with art. He was envious! What he said was that too much of her time and attention was spent away from home, but what he really *felt* was that he was unhappy he didn't have the opportunity to develop his own artistic talents. His parents hadn't supported his creative inclinations, and he had adopted a disdainful attitude toward his own interest in poetry and painting. He could hardly have been more stunned to realize that he didn't want Rena to stop working in her studio; he wanted to join her!

6. **Plan How Both of You Can Attain the Goals You're Trying to Achieve by Exercising the Disliked Traits in a More Constructive Way**

Once you've determined which pieces of yourself have been missing, think about how you can reintegrate them into your daily actions. Ask yourself how you can use the once maligned or neglected attitudes, actions, or feelings to broaden your behavioral repertoire. Sometimes recognizing that you want to manifest more of a particular quality will be enough to reintegrate it, but often you need to do more than just think about it. You must intentionally plan a program of reintegration that involves goals and schedules.

For example, if your partner has not developed her ability to feel anger, how can she begin to use anger in a positive way? Perhaps she could learn to recognize the signs of anger in herself and practice expressing it in a safe environment with her partner. Or, if you have not felt comfortable expressing emotion, how could you put more excitement into your life? Perhaps you could give yourself the task of saying to your partner one true thing a day about your feelings.

Joshua and Anna were able to strengthen their marriage when each of them started to become a little bit more like the other. They stopped shouting at each other from the outer edges of their relationship and met in the middle. For her part, Anna realized that she had a complicated reaction to Joshua's presumption of superiority. At first, she loved it because he made her feel safe. And then she hated it because she felt diminished and stifled. Finally, she vowed to adopt the more positive aspects of his confident attitude for herself. She started assuming that *she* had valid opinions and a right to try to get her needs met. Instead of living to serve the needs of others, she started living more for herself.

Joshua moved in the other direction. He realized what an impossible burden it was to try to always be in charge, always be strong, and always be right. He began to encourage Anna to make more decisions regarding the family. He even asked her opinion about tough questions that arose with his company. The biggest shift occurred for him, however, as he allowed himself to be more emotionally vulnerable. It was very hard for him to tell Anna that he wasn't sure about a decision he'd made, or to admit that his feelings were hurt. But when he did, her caring reaction made him feel better instead of worse. Both of them came to understand that strength is a multifaceted experience, involving competence, confidence, and vulnerability.

The changes you experience by following these six steps will happen because you are giving acceptance and understanding to your partner. Through this act of giving, you will be able to reintegrate the parts of yourself that have been lost to self-rejection. You will knock down your own internal barriers so that new information, feelings, and thoughts can flow through you. When your partner behaves in ways that cause you the most anxiety, you can greet your negative feelings with the countervailing thought that now you can begin to make positive changes. You will move from hatred to understanding to empathy to active reintegration.

It takes a while for the Between to change. But when and how it does has less to do with the number of inner resources you have and more to do with how you *use* what you have. Assume that you already have what it takes inside you, then become focused on achieving your goal—to reconnect with your partner and yourself on a deeper level.

Monitoring the Process

In the course of helping couples through this process of reintegration, we've learned that there are additional ideas that can be helpful.

As you follow the progression of the six steps discussed above, keep in mind the following:

Energy follows attention. You will spend the most time and energy on whatever you allow your attention to rest on. If you spend hours elaborating what your partner does that you hate, that's the part of the process you will put the most energy into. On the other hand, if you spend hours thinking about how to become more compassionate, that's where most of your energy will go. Fortunately, you are more in charge of your attention than you may think. When you find yourself hung up on the negative, exert the mental effort to get unhooked and focus on the positive.

What you think matters. Changing behavior is primarily a mental game. Monitor what you are telling yourself about what you are doing. Just as you can learn to refocus your attention, you can learn to cast your actions in a positive light. Instead of thinking that you are hopelessly stuck, you can tell yourself that your efforts to change make a difference. Also, instead of thinking that your partner is unlikable, you can assume that she is trying to get her unmet needs addressed in the only way she knows how. When you think about it that way, it changes how you feel. It is far easier to soften toward someone whom you perceive is *not* trying to make your life difficult, but who is trying to survive an earlier wound.

Thaw frozen images. All of us carry static "pictures" of our partner's faults around with us in our heads. Especially from times of trauma, there are moments of experience that are freeze-framed, seemingly forever in our memory. The moments of rage and betrayal are etched in stone. Only a subsequent history of safety and pleasurable reconnection can undo this serious damage. But anything short of trauma can be softened by the conscious effort to remember that relationships change and people evolve. The things you are doing to interface with your partner in a new way will cause him or her to behave differently. Be sure your eyes are open to the changes, and your mental pictures are modified as a result.

Pay attention to resistance. There is dynamic energy in resistance. One naturally resists what one feels to be dangerous. This illuminates Freud's contention that fear is always connected to desire. The feeling is, "If I allow myself to have what I want, then the outside world will hurt me." Your fear does not subside just because the fearful conditions that once threatened you are no longer present. Whenever you are presented with something that has been forbidden to you, your wound is activated and you put up the defense you've always used to keep the forbidden desire safely out of your reach. If you can approach softly, you'll have a better chance of not igniting fear. Authoritarian behavior often stirs up resistance, whereas gentleness does not.

Watch for unconscious sabotage. Whether we know it or not, we all have a great stake in keeping things the same and blocking change. It's the seduction of the familiar. We feel we're better off with the evil we know than the evil we don't know. It's even possible for you to think and say that you want to change and still be resistant underneath, below the level of consciousness. Asking the following questions can help you identify such sabotage: "If I wanted to screw this up, what would I do?" Or, "If my partner wanted to screw this up, what would he or she do?" Possible answers can range from, "I, or my partner, would conclude that these ideas are hogwash," to "I, or my partner, wouldn't make an effort to learn to love what we hate in each other." If your answer to these questions matches your or your partner's actual behavior, you've identified hidden resistance that is manifesting itself as sabotage.

Notice and celebrate small changes. Certain individuals are struck down on the road to Damascus, as St. Paul was, and in an instant their old worldview is erased and another is indelibly fixed. But this experience is so uncommon as to be mythic. Mostly, we change slowly by small increments, one baby step at a time. If you only have eyes for the grand, you will miss the small steps that carry you forward. Discussing the process with your partner—for example, sharing your fumbled attempts to express yourself differently and your delight when you succeed—will strengthen your bond and keep you aware that your efforts are making a difference. Since we can't always know the positive effect we are having, there is a certain amount of faith involved in dedicating ourselves to taking those small steps.

Taken together, these suggestions will lead us to an internally quieter, more thoughtful, and more observant role within our relationships. When we are quiet inside, we are not making up stories about the Other. We are simply present to what *is*. If we are always busy constructing our vision of the Other, there is no room for the actual person. How do we stop the noise? We love, give what others need, listen, and validate their point of view. We hold their truth in our hearts and do not distort it or judge it or evaluate it. Only then do we experience inner peace, self-love, and joy.

DISCOVERY

Learning to receive love is a voyage of discovery. Over time you find out things about yourself and your partner that you didn't know before. You refashion your connection to each other so it is both stronger and more flexible. And, you adopt new attitudes toward the things that used to be points of contention. Discovery is both an action and a frame of mind.

Mark and Lynn were stalemated in a battle of resentment that had lasted about twelve years, as long as they'd been married. They assumed they knew everything about each other, inside and out. Yet, here are some examples from incidents that indicate how much they had stopped really trying to communicate. Their comments show how many liberties they took with each other's thoughts and feelings.

> Lynn: *"I didn't tell you my mother had called to ask us to dinner because I knew there was no point. I didn't want you to scold me for dropping everything we had planned just to make her happy—like you say I always do."*

Over another incident she told him: "I knew you'd just blow up if I told you what the teacher said about Jason skipping school."

Mark was guilty of the tendency to make the same kind of presumptions.

> Mark: *"I didn't tell you how I felt about sending money to your brother because I knew itwouldn't do any good. You think I'm too insensitive to care."*

And another time, Mark said: "You always discount my opinion, so what's the point of saying anything?"

This couple had stopped communicating with each other. If they thought they knew what the other would say, there really seemed to be no point in discussing things further. But as a matter of fact, neither of them knew what the other thought or felt or would have done in these situations. Their assumptions were wrong. Mark *would* have gone to dinner at his mother-in-law's, and he *did* want to know what the teacher said about their son, even though the news was bad. Lynn *was* willing to hear Mark's opinions about her brother, if only he had told her. In fact, she *would* have welcomed his thoughts and feelings about a whole range of issues. Each of them had constructed a false persona that stood for the other. They were good at making false assumptions, but they were not good at asking questions.

Mark and Lynn began to change the quality of their Between when they started to approach each other with the respectful caution of friendly acquaintances. That meant sharing information about daily occurrences and starting to ask for input from each other before drawing conclusions. They discovered how much they both hated to be judged and condemned on the basis of false information.

After they had practiced their more tentative, inquiring way of communicating for a while, they were able to recast the comments they made in the examples above.

> Lynn: *"Mom just called and asked us to dinner. I'm not sure how you feel about going. What do you think?"* And, *"Jason's teacher called this afternoon. What she said wasn't pleasant, but we need to talk about it. Is this a good time?"*
>
> Mark: *"I know you're worried about your brother and that you'd like to send him somemoney. I've been thinking about that. Can we talk about it?"* And, *"I would like to tell you how I feel about your discounting my opinions. Can you choose a time that's good for you?"*

Notice how all these statements end with a question that invites further discussion. Notice, too, how different it feels to be asked, invited, and consulted rather than blamed and typecast.

After several months in therapy, Mark and Lynn were able to take a further step. Mark said, "When the therapist asked us if we liked each other well enough now to continue dating if we had the opportunity, we both said, 'No.' That was a wake-up call." They decided, however, that they would treat each other with the same interest and affection as if they *were* dating. They started to reromanticize their relationship, partly by engaging each other in the spirit of inquiry or discovery with questions such as, "How do you feel about this?" "What do you think about this?" "If you were totally in charge, what would you do about such-and-such?"

Lynn summarized what they learned by commenting, "Assume nothing. Find out about everything." This could be a slogan for how to end symbiosis and start the healthy process of becoming individuals, distinct but still held in connection. Mark and Lynn were able to create a new Between that supported a less judgmental environment for the relationship and a less brutal attitude toward themselves.

We've seen that it is possible to reconstruct the relationship you already have along new lines. Couples can use the intimacy, or at least the familiarity, their relationship already affords to become partners in the recovery of their lost selves. As they bring more of themselves into their relationship, those desires, needs, impulses, and inclinations that were once rejected become healed. Instead of trying to relate as ragged and incomplete individuals, they start to become whole. The path toward wholeness is the path toward consciousness. Unconscious behaviors, such as projection and symbiosis, loosen their grip on the relationship, and the two partners have the joy of meeting each other in the moment, without the burden of baggage from the past.

In the next chapter, we'll discuss how Mark and Lynn, and the other three couples we've been following, were able to reconstruct their relationships. There is a mechanism that makes it possible for even estranged couples to know each other on a deep level, end symbiosis, and reconnect through intimacy.

CHAPTER 8

Establishing Contact, Connection, and Communion

If you had told me that we could learn to sit down and talk together about how we really feel, I wouldn't have believed you. But now, we listen to each other and that's brought us much closer.

Physical pain helps us survive. We need to know when our bodies have suffered an injury so we can fix it. But who knew that emotional pain was just as crucial to our survival as physical pain? Recent research suggests that emotional distress is just as important as physical distress in signaling a threat to our safety.

When we get our feelings hurt because we feel excluded from others, our emotional pain registers in the same area of the brain that is activated when we feel physical pain. Apparently, our brains are hardwired to register social disconnection as an emergency that needs our attention. "These findings show how deeply rooted our need is for social connection," says lead researcher Naomi Eisenberger in the news release that accompanied her article in *Science*. "There's something about exclusion from others that's perceived as being as harmful to our survival as something that can physically hurt us, and our body automatically knows this."[1]

This new research confirms one of the most dominant observations of therapy: Human beings need to feel connected to each other. If we aren't, we get sick and sometimes die. But until recently, we could only *observe* that this was true. There was no way to get physical evidence of the extent to which our need for emotional connection is built into our bodies. Now that evidence is beginning to surface.

Our primary psychological task, then, is not to build bridges to other people across the void that separates us. Our task is to keep the "connecting" machinery with which we are born—our connected knowing—in good working order. We must clear away the fears and insecurities that accumulate, rendering our connections inoperative and separating us. As we get rid of this debris and repair the broken lines, we can pull the switch within us that reopens the connecting channels. Our capacity to send and receive information openly and honestly with those we want to be close to can be restored.

The work of understanding your partner's painful history and uncovering the ways it's linked to your own, requires determination, skill, and patience. (Exercises 4, 6, 7, and 9 are designed to engage you and your partner in the process of mutual discovery of your deepest experiences and feelings.) Clearly, what we are describing here is good communication. You can't establish an environment of safety and solicit deeply personal information if your Between is blocked by distrust and defeatism. One or both of you may be so defensive that neither of you can hear what the other is trying to say. Fear can make people deaf. It can limit people to talking, without truly communicating.

If your relationship is at this point—if talking makes you feel more separate and alienated than connected—it's time to learn a new way of talking. You can't learn to love yourself or your partner if, every time you try to communicate, clouds of blame, criticism, or icy silence fill the air. Conversation and discussion must become a medium of bonding, whereby you know you are safe, heard, and understood.

THE IMAGO DIALOGUE

Fortunately, it is possible to start all over—with the same partner. You can learn to communicate, even about contentious issues and secret feelings, whether you were ever able to do this as a couple before or not. You can learn to connect more as you would with a beloved friend, yet with more intimacy. Being "on the same wavelength" with another person as you share ideas and feelings is one of the greatest highs there is: *You tell me something. I respond, and what I say tells you that I understand, and I'm able to add something of value to your original thought. You express this back to me, and I am enhanced by what you've said.* And so on, perhaps for many minutes at a time. Every iteration increases your understanding and adds to your fund of experience, whether you agree with your partner or not! (In addition to the information in this chapter, Exercise 2 will help you and your partner learn how to communicate in this way through Imago Dialogue.)

When we deconstruct this kind of positive communication, what do we find? We don't find a whole lot of unconscious, defensive reactions, but we do find indications that each person is listening to and caring about the other. The dialogue is providing a safe and fertile context for each person to see, hear, and understand the other person, and gain deeper insight into himself or herself in the process. This understanding extends beyond the content of what's being said, down to the *feelings* that convey the emotional truth of what's being said. Both people are paying attention to the words and to the body language that accompany the words. Both are receiving and sending information so continuously that it's hard to tell at any given moment who is receiving what and who is sending what.

In our previous writings, we've referred to this type of dialogue as "Couples' Dialogue," or "Intentional Dialogue." In this book, and from now on, we will use the term "Imago Dialogue," because we don't want to limit the concept in any way. We are seeing applications of Imago Dialogue beyond intimate relationships, including its use in businesses, educational institutions, and other settings where people must interact with each other to achieve mutual goals and solve problems.

There are three elements that are present in the Imago Dialogue when it's working well: mirroring, validating, and empathizing. These are the specific actions the receiver—the one listening—performs in order to make the sender—the one talking—feel safe, heard, and understood. A receiver trained in Imago Dialogue will say things that convey the following messages to the sender:

1. *I am listening so carefully that I can mirror back to you what you've just said.*

   To **mirror,** I exercise my capacities for separate knowing and receiving.

2. *I affirm you and your right to have these feelings and hold these opinions.*

   To **validate,** I exercise my capacities for connected knowing and giving.

3. *I can enter into your world and feel what you are feeling.*

   To **empathize,** I exercise my capacities for connected knowing and giving.

Contact, connection, and communion—all of these levels of connection can be achieved through dialogue that contains the elements of mirroring, validating, and empathizing. Each of them helps to break the fusion of symbiosis. Mirroring is contact, but not necessarily connection. Validation is connection because it cannot be achieved without seeing and knowing the Other as different from the Self. And empathy, which is connection without fusion, leads to communion. All three of these levels of dialogue depend upon the inextricable link that exists between giving and receiving. For example, when you receive me, by mirroring, validating, and empathizing, you are giving to me. I am not able to give to you until you receive me. If we cannot receive, by hearing each other and resonating with each other, then we cannot truly give to each other.

Two partners exchange the roles of receiver and sender during the Imago Dialogue. Since each partner in most dialogues has a chance to be both receiver and sender, the net effect is that the dialogues are an opportunity for both people to have the experience of being accurately heard, validated as worthwhile human beings, and bonded in empathy. Think of how rare and wonderful that is! We seldom have these experiences in our daily discourse. A lot of the time, we can't even be sure that our partners are paying attention to what we're trying to say, much less validating us for saying it or making an effort to look at the world through our eyes. And, we can't be sure we're doing the same for them, either.

Just knowing the three elements that characterize Imago Dialogue will make you a better communicator. But to put these ideas into action if you have a history of defensiveness and misunderstanding with your mate requires a more structured approach to learning the steps. So let's now take some time to explore mirroring, validating, and empathizing more closely.

Mirroring

At first, while you and your partner are learning the mechanics, the Imago Dialogue needs to be practiced in a formal way. It will feel artificial and mechanical in the beginning. When you first start out, there will be false starts, interruptions while you backtrack and try to restate what you've just said, and times when you simply don't get it right. That's okay. This is such a valuable tool that it's worth practicing until it becomes natural. People practiced in dialogue report feeling themselves going from mechanics to craftsmen to artists over time.

It is possible for one partner to use the principles of the Imago Dialogue without the active participation of the other—and still reap significant rewards. But for our purposes now, let's assume that both partners are willing to learn and practice these techniques. Following are six steps describing how to initiate a dialogue and accomplish the task of mirroring. We are assuming that you are the sender and your partner is the receiver:

1. You recognize that you have something you want to share with your partner. Start with something positive, so that dialogue will not be associated only with concerns or frustrations. Tell your partner you want the two of you to set aside time to share some appreciations. Once you have learned the process, you can then use the dialogue to talk about concerns or frustrations. With your partner's input, choose a time when both of you will be receptive and undisturbed.
2. Begin your face-to-face meeting by thanking your partner for his or her willingness to talk with you.
3. State the essence of your message. Make it an "I" message and focus on what you see, hear, think, feel, or desire. And then stop.

4. Your partner mirrors your message back. Mirroring, in this sense, means responding with an accurate paraphrase. If you find that difficult, you can start by mirroring the exact words. The goal is for your partner to repeat your communication without adding or subtracting *anything* else. When you are finished, your partner asks if the mirror was accurate.

5. You say, "Yes, you got it." Or, "No, not quite." If the mirror was not accurate, you repeat your message once again. Your partner then attempts to mirror you again. Repeat Steps 3–5 until your partner mirrors you accurately.

6. After confirmation that the mirror is accurate, your partner asks, "Is there more about that?" The "that" refers to what you were just saying, not to another subject. If there is "more about that," you say it, and your partner attempts to mirror your additional communication accurately. When the mirror is accurate and you have no more you want to say, your partner then says: "Let me see if I got all of that," and he offers a summary of all that he has heard. This is important, because we tend to respond to the last words we hear, forgetting what was said earlier. The summary helps reflect the substance of what you said. Now you are finished with this first stage.

Already, at this point, you've made a big contribution to the quality of your communication. The mirroring step of the Imago Dialogue gives you a total psychological workout. All the major "muscle groups" in your communication repertoire are exercised. You have opened yourselves up to both giving and receiving by taking turns talking and listening. You have had to concentrate on sending a clear message and on truly understanding what was said to you. In addition, both of you are enhanced by your intention to learn more about each other and your ability to speak and listen clearly when you're actively trying. The sender now knows: *I can speak and be heard.* And the receiver now knows: *I can listen and understand.* These are simple realizations, but they have profound implications for bringing you closer together.

Validating

The next stage is for the receiver to validate the sender. This part is a little tricky. Most people think of validating as synonymous with agreeing. That's not what we mean. Whether you agree with what has been said or not does not matter. Of course, if you disagree or are incensed by what your partner has just said, that makes it more difficult for you to validate. But, you can learn to validate in exactly the same way whether your partner has just offered up a pearl of wisdom or a totally disagreeable notion.

It may be helpful to think of the philosophical premise that underlies the act of validation. You are supporting the notion that "truth" is subjective, that every person is entitled to his or her own feelings and point of view, and that your perspective does not issue forth from the center of the universe. The experience that we are the center of the universe is understandable. Each of us experiences the world through our five senses, and we can only see it from our point of view. We call this "centric consciousness," which means our common experience is that each of us is at the "center." But we have to remind ourselves that everyone has this sort of consciousness. Either there are about six and a half billion centers (the current estimate of the world's population), or there is no single center to the universe. In either case, your point of view is not the only one!

Your partner has valid reasons for seeing the world as he or she does. It's not for you or anyone else to dismiss or demean these views or even try to change them. Although the whole dialogue process can be understood as validating, there are specific words and phrases that will convey this message unambiguously. Here are some examples of how to validate after the sender is finished speaking and the receiver has accurately mirrored the message:

- *I get what you are saying, and you make sense.*
- *I can see how you would think about it that way. How it makes sense to you . . .* (summarize what your partner has said).
- *I absolutely see what you are saying and why. It makes sense that you . . .*

- *I can see that you have given this plenty of thought, and I can see what you are saying.*
- *I can see that you have thought about this a great deal and not only do I understand what you are saying, I agree that . . .* (In validation, you can indicate agreement if you in fact do agree.)
- *You are being very clear about how you see it, and you make sense when . . .*
- *I'm glad you went to the trouble of arranging for us to sit down together. When you tell me what you're really thinking, it helps me understand you better. I can see how you think, and what you say makes sense.*
- *I didn't know you thought about it like that, but now that you tell me, I can see how that makes sense.*
- *Before we talked, I had the wrong idea about what was going through your head. Now I can see better where you're coming from.*
- *I am impressed by your argument. It's helpful for me to hear how you are thinking. . . .*
- *I want to* (understand you better, know what's really happening with you, learn more about your childhood, get a sense of what you are really feeling, etc.), *and what you've just said helps me enormously.*

We know that verbal interaction is not the only, or perhaps not even the most important, way we communicate with each other. Every one of the sentences above could be said in a way that conveys the opposite from its intended meaning. Say it with a sneer, and the validating words become a slam. Say it with a lack of conviction, and the message becomes ironic and cynical. Say it with a certain kind of smile, and the "validation" is insincere and mocking.

That's why body language is so important. One of the most effective ways to validate another person is through the signals you send with your body. Use touch, smiling, and gentleness of voice to do some of the work for you. Look into your partner's eyes and *feel* affirming and validating, and then, no matter how you fumble with the words, you will be able to convey validation.

People often find it extremely difficult to validate when they have no experience with it. They may be unaware of ever seeing it done, and may not feel that they have been especially validated by others. Maybe they're right. But it's never too late to learn. And the way to learn is to try it. Practice validating everyone with whom you have a real conversation. If you feel like a fraud at first, so be it. Fake it until you make it. At the very least, you are adding to the courtesy and harmony that exist in the universe.

Empathizing

The last element in the Imago Dialogue involves an internal shift for the receiver. The shift is from hearing what is being said via separate knowing, to resonating with the feelings the sender has about what is being said via connected knowing. The dialogue begins with the receiver connecting through words and ends with the receiver connecting through feelings.

The empathic message is: *You are not alone. Although I recognize that we are separate individuals, and therefore, not symbiotic, I can feel at least some of what you are feeling.* To get a sense of how important empathy is, imagine an interchange where your partner accurately mirrors you, and states your right to have your feelings, but is dead to any empathic understanding of what your experience has been. You would feel as if you were talking to a cyborg or some other robotic contraption with no human sensibilities. The encounter would make you feel alien and alone.

The capacity to empathize is one of the things that makes us fully human. Impairment of this capacity causes a bigger gulf between people than an impairment of language. Two people who speak different languages can still connect through their ability to put themselves in each other's place. Two people who, for one reason or another, cannot speak are still connected through their natural ability to recreate the condition of the other within the imagination. But an individual with no empathy is personally and socially dangerous in his or her isolation.

It is normal to be able to share in other people's experience. We can see how real this capacity is on the physical level when we watch one person after another yawn in what is called "contagious yawning." One person yawns, and pretty soon everyone within sight is doing it. It's so common, we hardly think about the significance of being so in tune that we involuntarily, on a bodily level, recreate each other's experience. Humans are the only living creatures to be so attuned to their fellows on so many levels.

Although the capacity for empathy is natural, there are variations among individuals. It is fortunate that, to a great extent, empathy is something that can be developed. The steps leading to empathic attunement are rather simple: (1) remind yourself that you want to be empathic with your partner at this moment, and (2) allow yourself to imagine what it would be like for you to be having your partner's experiences. The more empathy is practiced, the more second nature it becomes.

After mirroring and validating, the receiver conveys the message, *I am with you.* Hearing this, the sender relaxes. If there were tight muscles or hard edges, they soften. There is no need to be defended or ready for battle. Instead, the sender thinks, *Oh! My partner understands and is sympathetic. I guess I don't need to brace myself for the onslaught or push harder to get my point across. I am being seen and heard. I'm not alone.*

Here are some specific ways to express empathy to your partner:

- *After listening to you, I am feeling your* (sadness, anger, happiness), *and I am feeling* (sad, angry, happy), *too.*
- *When you told me you were feeling* (sad, angry, happy), *I could feel it too.*
- *What you've told me you feel makes sense to me. I am very moved by it.*
- *I'm feeling* (sad, angry, happy) *on your behalf! No wonder you've been preoccupied.*
- *I really feel like I can feel where you're coming from now. Thank you for sharing this with me.*
- *I can imagine that what you've told me makes you feel* (sad, angry, happy). *I'm so glad you told me about it.*
- *I get that you are feeling* (proud of yourself, relieved that it's over, successful), *and I'm celebrating along with you! Way to go!*

More than any other stage in the Imago Dialogue, this is the time when body language is most effective for getting your message across. It is possible to accomplish everything the sentences above are intended to accomplish through just the right gesture. For example, when another person cries along with you, you know you're being received with empathy. As the receiver, there are ways of being *with* another person that supersede whatever words you might come up with. If your intention is to be empathic with your partner, you will be able to convey your compassion, whether you do it with words or with nonverbal signals of solidarity. Your desire to participate in your partner's experience will come through if you genuinely feel it.

Notice that in the Imago Dialogue one person talks or sends, and the other listens or receives. This is the broad outline of what happens. But within each stage, the receiver becomes the sender and the one who has been talking becomes the receiver. This is an accurate reflection of what true intimacy is like—both people are giving and both are receiving continuously. There is no lopsided bump in the smooth flow of a good connection.

Switching Places

It often makes sense for partners to change roles or positions after the person who spoke first has been satisfactorily mirrored, validated, and empathized with. Sometimes, if the content has been draining or highly inflammatory, it is better to suspend the dialogue temporarily and give the receiving partner a chance to take his turn after a recovery interval. If the sharing has been about positives, the receiver also may want to take some time to absorb the gift. But usually the one who was in the receiving position will want to become a sender during the same conversation.

A good way to make the transition smoothly is for the initial sender to ask if there is something the other partner wants to say. If the answer is yes, they switch roles. If the answer is no, then the sender can thank the receiver for listening. They end their dialogue knowing that either of them can initiate a dialogue in the future and they can expect that they will be met by a sincere effort of understanding and caring at that time.

To Dialogue Is to Receive

Just as the "empty" space between planets and stars is not empty at all, but is actually filled with a substance called dark matter, the emptiness between partners is filled with the substance of the Between. The qualities of the relationship are not just "inside" or "outside" each partner, but reside in the relationship itself. Love and spirituality, for example, are generated by the partners together as qualities that help define their connection. So, rather than say that the partners are spiritual, we say that the relationship is spiritual.

One of the most important facts of dialogue is that each partner must be able to receive in order to listen. The inability to listen is always related to how deeply the person is wounded, and therefore self-absorbed, and closed-in. The receiver cannot be self-absorbed or self-centered and still participate in what is designed to be a true interpersonal exchange. Wounds that have been left ignored or untended make it difficult to receive the words, feelings, or viewpoints of others.

To validate and feel empathy, the receiver *must* receive the feelings and viewpoints of the partner who is talking. In other words, the listener must be able to receive the *subjectivity* of the Other. That's one reason that dialogue is an antidote to symbiosis, as well as a way out of the prison of egocentricity. Through dialogue, each partner opens deeply to the other. It is not unusual for one or both partners to cry when they understand that they are being heard and understood, perhaps for the first time.

This means that the sender must also be able to receive the feedback involved in mirroring, validation, and empathic connection in return. It's instructive when we find a case where the sender cannot accept or tolerate the reality of being listened to, when he or she cannot receive being received. There are all kinds of ways to show it. The sender may make any of the following claims: *No, you're not mirroring me right! No, I don't feel like you were really validating me! That's not it. You're not listening.* The sender may tell the receiver that she's not getting it, when, in reality the sender can't allow herself to have the experience of being received.

The whole message of mirroring, validation, and empathy is that the speaker makes sense, is worth listening to, and has a right to his or her feelings. Imagine the internal conflict when someone is not able to receive these measures of esteem and then is confronted with them head-on during dialogue. Depending on the degree of self-rejection, the person will not have permission to be understood. It's true that sometimes the receiver does not receive accurately, but it's also true that sometimes the sender simply can't tolerate the threat when his or her sense of unworthiness is challenged by mirroring, validation, and empathy.

The problem can be compounded when the receiver unconsciously picks up on his partner's resistance and allows himself to be deflected from the task of mirroring, validating, and empathizing. He may make only a halfhearted attempt to get the job done. He may give up and say he just can't do it. The result is exactly the same as if the sender were refusing to let the dialogue in: the sender gets to preserve her internal intolerance of being heard, validated, and empathized with. Although she is probably not conscious of it, she gets to maintain her self-rejection, which includes beliefs such as: *See, no one will ever listen to me! I don't trust my partner to really pay attention and care. It's dangerous to open myself up and be vulnerable. I don't trust people to be authentic with me anyway. I'm not going to take anything from anybody.*

Dialogue can be a reflection of the interlocking patterns of wounds and defenses that characterize the relationship, as both partners replay communication models absorbed from childhood. Since we know it's almost never true that one person suffers from severe self-rejection and the other has none of the same, it's common for both partners to have some trouble with dialogue, at least at first.

One of the common traps is that you can *appear* to be receiving the Other when you're really just going through the motions. For example, Jerry and his wife, Barbara, have been practicing the Imago Dialogue for three years or so. He says, "You have to have a strong intention as well as the outward behaviors. You have to know why you want to dialogue. Something like: I want a better marriage, or I want a better life for me and my children than I ever had presented to me." Otherwise, he says, you can pretend to listen and absorb your spouse's message, but you keep it on a superficial level. Barbara agrees with him: "Dialogue can only be as deep and as rich as the intentions of two people allow it to be. You can do it on a mechanical level and go through the motions, or you can bring depth to it."

In order to be healing, dialogue must be approached with the focused intention of understanding the experience of the Other, and with a charitable heart. A charitable heart is tolerant and forgiving, rather than righteous and vengeful. Repeatedly telling your partner that he or she is doing it wrong will kill the desire to keep trying.

You can now see that the Imago Dialogue is both an indicator of where a couple's communication is blocked by self-rejection, and a means of repairing the damage. It can be used both diagnostically and as a curative as each partner teaches the other how to help and heal. As a result of changing the couple's Between, each partner ends up being changed on the inside as well.

Separate and Connected Knowing

We believe there is another tool that can help clear away the confusion of relationship discord and point the way toward better, stronger connections with each other. If knowledge is power, then how you know what you know has a huge impact on how much power you end up having. We continue our discussion of the theory of separate and connected knowing here because we believe this concept to be both diagnostic and healing for couples who are having trouble achieving a natural balance of giving and receiving.

As we established in the Introduction, the kind of knowing that is strictly cognitive—in the head—we call "separate" knowing, and the kind of knowing that is more holistically integrated throughout the mind and emotions, we call "connected" knowing (see page 9). Everybody employs both methods, but almost everybody tends to favor one way of knowing over the other. We have found that introducing people to these different ways of knowing helps them become aware of their own barriers and limitations at the same time that it clarifies how to overcome them.

"Knowing" is closely related to "receiving," which is why it's relevant to our discussion in this book. Saying that you know something is really saying that you've received information of a certain kind and you've processed it in a certain way.

If you have a "broken receiver," as one of our clients put it, your ability to know is going to be more limited than it would be if you had never experienced self-rejection and the consequent inability to absorb information about your missing self. And if your capacity for receiving love is impaired for all the reasons and in all the ways we've so far discussed, you will have a corresponding restriction in your capacity to know. There are certain things that you will not know, and the things you do know, you will only know in a separate *or* connected way.

Jeff is an example. He grew up in a home with five other siblings and three different stepfathers. He never knew who his biological father was. All three stepfathers were some combination of neglectful and abusive. As a child, he felt his number one concern was to try to stay clear of the violence and chaos in his household. When his own sons became teenagers, his marriage began to fall apart. Through therapy, he realized that his childhood had rendered him emotionally illiterate. There were important aspects and experiences of intimate relationships that he simply had not absorbed or integrated in a way that allowed him to make use of them. He wrote down a long list of things he didn't know. He did not *know*:

- That he could tell and show his sons that he loved them and have it feel natural and comfortable.
- That he could share his negative feelings with his wife, and she would still love him and want to be married to him.
- That differing views and opinions can make a marriage stronger.
- That you can be expressive without being weak.
- That vulnerability is not only universal, but can be a source of strength.
- That it's okay to say you don't know.
- That changing your mind or changing directions in your life can be an indication of strength and not failure.

The interesting thing about this list is that if Jeff had been presented with these sentences in a True or False format, he would have said that every one of these statements was true. The problem is that his "brain" knowing something didn't translate to his "heart" knowing it, too. What he knew using separate knowing, he did not know using connected knowing.

All sophisticated human endeavors require both separate and connected knowing, but they usually emphasize one way of knowing over the other, particularly in certain stages. For example, scientific discovery is built on the separate knowing involved in the scientific method: articulating a premise, testing it through experiment, gathering data, writing a proof, and then repeating the cycle again in order to compare results. What may not be apparent is that the testing of the initial premise, and the connections the researcher makes when confronted with results, almost always involve connected knowing in the form of intuition or imaginative leaps. The history of science is filled with stories of solutions and discoveries that became apparent to the scientist while he was doing something outside the laboratory—dreaming or walking or waiting to board a bus, for example. In other words, the flash of genius came while he was not engaged in the logical, data-based thinking that defines separate knowing.

Unlike science, which at first appears to be an activity of separate knowing, musical performance seems to be wholly an activity of connected knowing. But it, too, really requires both. The musician engages in separate knowing to memorize certain black marks on the page and translate them into playing certain sounds on her instrument. But she calls upon her memories and feelings, or connected knowing, to turn the notes into music. If the music doesn't get beyond the "correct note" level and down to the evocative, imaginative level, we may be impressed by the musician's proficiency, but we are not greatly moved by her music. (Exercise 3 will help you learn more about your skills and deficiencies as a separate and connected knower.)

Separate and Connected Knowing Become Relational Knowing

It's important to say explicitly that both ways of knowing are positive and essential. Separate knowing is not bad, and connected knowing isn't better. Using both makes possible the collaborative construction of knowledge that is more comprehensive than that compiled by using either alone.

Both separate and connected knowing are activated during the Imago Dialogue. The dialogue is composed of the two melodies of separate and connected knowing, which interweave throughout the encounter.[2] Mirroring involves primarily separate knowing on the part of both parties. The sender has information he wants to convey, and the receiver wants to hear it accurately. Validating involves both separate and connected knowing. The receiver is able to leave her self-absorption long enough to understand how the sender's thoughts and feelings make sense to him. And, empathizing involves primarily connected knowing. The receiver moves beyond separate knowing into a place where she can imagine herself to be in the speaker's situation.

We see that dialogue gets its transformative power by moving the two partners away from their positions as separate and toward each other as connected. It begins with the strictly separate knowing of mirroring, moves toward the integration of separate and connected knowing of validation, and finally ends in the communion of shared experience by using connected knowing. Both partners get the chance to speak and to listen, both get the chance to give and receive, and both get the chance to be separate and connected knowers. Through dialogue, they become versed in the kind of comprehensive knowing we call "relational knowing." Become a practitioner of relational knowing, and you become a partner in a conscious relationship.

The Imago Dialogue and relational knowing are at the heart of healing relationships. But there are other specific practices that can help disaffected couples overcome the barriers to giving and receiving love. In the last chapter we shall see how the three couples we've been following, and others, were able to end their isolation from each other and achieve a stronger connection than they had ever had before.

CHAPTER 9

Restoring Life

I regret the time we wasted in being unhappy with each other, but thank heavens we caught it when we did. We still have plenty of time left, and we intend to spend it being happy together and raising our children right.

Gaining and losing make up the essential rhythm of our lives. Over and over again we learn that loss is as integral to our experience as love. People we care about pass on, our hopes and dreams get downsized, and we must adjust to the inevitable disappointments we face at home and work. Besides that, the medium of time in which we live is always passing, every moment departing as soon as it arrives. It's as though we are forever being taught not to hold on too tightly.

In the psychological realm, however, there are some losses we don't have to accept. We do not have to accept that being split is our inevitable fate. We can learn to be the environmentalists of our own souls, working to conserve or reclaim the innate capacities with which we were born. We can do this because we are no longer small and weak and dependent. We don't have to make ourselves less of anything or more of anything in order to stay on the good side of powerful protectors. It no longer serves us well to exile those parts of ourselves that once made others uncomfortable but can lead us into fuller, more satisfying living. We can take steps on our own behalf to regain what we have lost. But we can't do it alone.

As you begin the process of reclaiming your lost self, your best ally is your current partner. You don't have to find someone new to serve as a catalyst for your wholeness. The common assumption is that it takes "new blood" to make a person feel alive again. This assumption is based on the observation that with Harold, for example, you are serious, competent, and responsible. With Sam, you are talkative, creative, and silly. Each of them invites you to explore different corners of your capacity to be human.

Variety of this sort gives spice to our lives, but it also makes us vulnerable to falling in love outside of our original relationship when it gets stale or becomes disappointing. A new lover elicits feelings we haven't recently (if ever) experienced with our partner. We don't know how fascinating and sexy we really are until we see it reflected back in the eyes of a new love. Often we are so hungry to experience the joy of all our feelings and sensations that we are willing to overthrow partners, children, jobs, and respectability just for the promise of it. Seeking completion in this way, though, is very expensive, and often not successful. We do not end up with the fulfillment we wish for—we just end up with a new person and with a different kind of incompleteness.

How much easier and less harmful it is to grow your *existing* relationship beyond its current limitations and into full bloom. A changed relationship with the *same* partner can provide freedom and joy without the wrenching pain of hurting others and starting over. You can have the same benefit you get from being with both Harold and Sam, but you can get it from your current partner. This can happen even when your past experience with your partner has been disappointing.

We are aware that until you actually experience success in re-creating your relationship with your partner, this idea can be a hard sell. When people are unhappy, they can't believe that the people they're blaming for their misery can really turn into their guides and fellow seekers in the search for fulfillment. Change just doesn't seem possible. And it's so much more exciting to imagine a new life with some more perfect mate.

Be assured that the conscious decision to re-engineer your connection together with a willing partner *will*, if consistently maintained, give you the environmental conditions you need to retrain your brain and thus recast your relationship. Developing new habits and communication patterns changes neural wiring and makes it possible for you to think, feel, and do things you've not been able to achieve in the past. You will be able to reconnect to your partner and, in doing so, reclaim your own desires, dreams, and abilities, no matter how long they've been gone or how deeply they've been buried. The same process will simultaneously happen for your partner, and soon you'll discover yourselves to be in the relationship of your dreams.

GOOD PRACTICE

Where do you begin if you and your partner want to recast your relationship so that your connection is safe and loving, you are eager to share with each other, and you are thankful for the refuge your relationship has become? The first step is to understand what the fundamental problem is and how to repair it. The problem is the split self. This trajectory of pain begins with the privacy of parental wounding, travels through the personal and social consequence of self-hatred, and ends with the social devastation now apparent in our culture. The split individual suffers from low self-esteem, and because he can't bear to think of himself as bad, he projects "badness" onto others. If enough people are inflicting their self-hatred onto others, we end up with a society that suffers from a lack of empathy and has a predisposition toward murder and even war. Like algae multiplying in a pond, what starts with a wound in the individual organism grows exponentially to become a universal scourge.

As we discussed in Chapter 7, the most important healing step you can take is to learn to love the parts of your partner that you dislike the most, and thus heal yourself. The problem of the split self starts with wounding in personal relationships, and it must be addressed by healing in personal relationships. Ask yourself what positive goal your partner is trying to achieve with the offending trait. If you find yourself reacting with intensity and repeatedly to your partner's trait, turn your inquiry inward and ask yourself whether it corresponds to a part of you that you have denied, disowned, or lost. If you do find a corresponding trait within you, remember that neither you nor your partner is trying to be annoying and dysfunctional. Both of you are simply trying to get along as best you can. Developing compassion for your wounded self and your partner's wounded self is a prelude to exploring whether there is a better way to meet your needs.

With your understanding of the central role splitting plays in your inability to give and receive love, make a commitment to adopt the following suggestions into your relationship. They come directly from couples who have turned their marriages around, and from our own experience, personally and professionally. You can begin to make these practices part of your relationship right now. They will help you increase both the openness and the safety of your Between. You will learn that it is possible to be your authentic self and be in communion with your partner, without compromising either your freedom or your connection.

Practice Being Receptive

Receiving is both where we begin and where we end. To reach the final goal of being able to receive material, spiritual, and psychological gifts from those who offer them, you must be able to receive in many small ways first. For example, you must be able to accept the suggestions in this book, the feelings and observations your partner offers during an Imago Dialogue, and the continuing stream of feedback from your own mind and body as you retrain your brain and recreate your relationship. In order to learn and change, it is necessary to receive feedback that comes from outside yourself. (Exercises 4 and 6 will help you gain specific knowledge about your ability to receive love.)

Whether the task of receiving is big or small, the process of learning to be open is the same. It needs to be practiced in conscious steps before it becomes integrated into your natural response to life. A safe and effective way to practice receiving is with your partner. Here are seven simple steps:

1. Be alert to feedback. It can come in the form of a compliment, a gift, a valuable suggestion, actual help, or useful information.

2. Pause to take it in.
3. Listen carefully to all of what's being said.
4. Think about it.
5. Feel the love and support behind it.
6. Let your partner know that you've connected with his or her words or action.
7. Voice your thanks.

The key here is remaining conscious of your intention to take in or absorb the content and feelings you are being offered. You have to see it as important that you receive it, give yourself permission to have it, and endure whatever discomfort your unfamiliar openness causes you. If you like, you can imagine a kindly old grandmother gently saying to you afterward, "See, that wasn't so bad, was it?"

Practice the Imago Dialogue

Aside from being willing to be receptive, the most important action you can take toward healing yourself *and* your partner is to integrate dialogue and the spirit of dialogue into your relationship. Doing so transforms troubled relationships into conscious partnerships. The *spirit* of dialogue is the desire to find out about, *to receive,* and be in concert with the inner life of your partner, and the desire to have your partner know *(to give)* and be in concert with yours. One of the joys of dialogue is that, once you and your partner feel safe with each other, your partner will tell you what her wounds are and what she is defending herself against, and vice versa. The *practice* of dialogue means consciously engaging in the three-step process once or twice a week. (See pages 162–165 for details. Also see Exercise 2 for guidance in how to practice dialogue.) The spirit flourishes to the extent the process is practiced. Both the spirit and the practice teach you how to oscillate naturally between being the giver and the receiver.

After you've used this tool for awhile, the quality of all your communications with your partner will improve, whether you're specifically engaged in formal dialogue, or only touching base briefly on the phone. You will become sensitized to your partner as a separate individual with his or her own personal history, personality, and temperament. You will be less inclined to discount or disparage, and more inclined to value, or at least respect, your partner's views and preferences.

Dialogue is the most effective way to make visible what is in your Between and lead you to healing. Through your structured conversations, you not only exchange information, you experience the quality of your connection. If your relationship is strained, reluctant, and blaming—or conversely, smooth and unified—you will know it from your experience of practicing the dialogue. And then, using the same tool of dialogue, you and your partner can take both the small steps and the leaps necessary to heal yourselves and your relationship.

Practice Relational Knowing

One of the primary benefits of dialogue is that it teaches you how to combine separate and connected knowing into the fuller knowing we call relational knowing. (See Exercise 3 for help in learning more about yourself as a separate and connected knower.) In addition to dialogue, there are certain habits of mind that will support the other efforts you are making to become a relational knower.

Ask yourself what your partner's words or behaviors mean. Be a seeker after meaning. Learn to interpret actions within a context of what you now know about your partner's past experiences and current concerns. Is your partner's behavior an anomaly or part of a pattern? Is it out-of-character or in character? What does it forecast about the future (if anything), and how significant is it in light of whatever else has been happening?

Having said all this, we must also add a word of caution: It is possible, and counterproductive to overinterpret. Not everything is meaningful. Some things are, in fact, trivial or accidental. As Freud said, "Sometimes a cigar is just a cigar."

Ask yourself how your partner's words and behaviors relate to you. Your partner is certainly operating in an environment where you are a key factor. But you are not the only factor, and sometimes you are not the most important factor. One of the hallmarks of conscious partnership is that communication is honest and direct. In other words, in a conscious partnership you can usually take things at face value. The words and the emotions are what they appear to be. But when Anna told Joshua she wasn't satisfied with the way he'd constructed the new front walkway, Joshua knew enough to find out more before he reacted. Was she really dissatisfied with the job he'd done, or was she upset about something else, and the walkway was just a handy target?

Joshua had learned that sometimes his wife's words and emotions were affected by or directed at someone or something else besides him, even though she was addressing him. In the case of the disappointing walkway, he was right to double-check. It turned out that Anna was unhappy with *herself* for coming up with a faulty design for him to work from.

As this example shows, if you allow your relationship to teach you about each other, you will become adept at knowing whether what's really important in any given situation is what seems to be happening on the surface of things, or is happening underneath the obvious.

Pay attention to your own physical reactions. Cultivate your own body awareness. Many people have told us that they've discovered they have a kind of "body wisdom" to guide them in confusing situations. Their minds may be filled with arguments and rationales about whether to trust a partner or even stay with a partner, but the body does not lie or prevaricate. Something either feels right or it feels wrong.

One wife described what it was like to come down with a "body allergy" to her husband: "I became 'allergic' to my husband after eight years of living together. I became chronically sick and developed a nervous tic in my face. It all went away when I made the decision to end the marriage. It now strikes me that if I had been aware of the messages my body was sending me, I would have known earlier about the next step on the path for me."

Nurturing body awareness is useful also in your relationship with yourself. It helps keep you honest about who you are and helps you maintain congruence between your inner and outer selves. One husband confessed to a "yearlong stomach ache" during the time he and his wife were doing marriage counseling for others in churches, while their own marriage was falling apart. The strain of presenting himself to audiences as successfully married, while knowing that he really wasn't, literally made him sick to his stomach. It wasn't until the private reality matched the public presentation that he felt well again. After that experience, he learned to use his bodily reactions as well as his cognitive and emotional reactions as important guides in his life.

Practice Eliminating Criticism

There is no place for criticism in intimate relationships. Period. Because your first priority is now establishing and maintaining a safe and loving Between with your partner, your first concern is always what's best for your relationship. Not criticizing is your best bet for establishing a positive environment. So what can you do if you feel the urge to criticize? (See Exercise 5 for a way to counter negativity and increase the positive elements in your relationship.)

The first step is always the same: Stop. Think for a moment or two. Use your separate knowing abilities to assess what is actually happening at this moment. What are the facts? What is the situation you and your partner are in? Then use your connected knowing abilities to take a reading of your emotional environment. Are you exhausted, frustrated, or angry? Is your partner laboring under intense emotions? Are the circumstances volatile or frightening? Maybe your impulse to say something derogatory, nasty, or denigrating is more a function of your emotional state than the actual situation. After you've made a rational assessment of the situation and taken the emotional "temperature," make a conscious decision about when and how you want to respond.

Sometimes you'll decide to say nothing because your comments will do more to fray your connection with your partner than bind you to your partner. Sometimes you'll decide to practice accepting what *is* rather than trying to change it. Simply taking in what's happening is often the best thing you can do. The wisdom of holding your tongue is actually common currency in our culture. It gets expressed in all kinds of ways. Here are a few examples:

- From a pediatrician advising a mother not to worry because her two-year-old is a fussy eater: "Pick your battles. There will be many important issues you will need to confront with your daughter as she grows up. This doesn't have to be one of them." In other words, maybe this issue isn't important enough to disturb the equanimity of the relationship.

- From a calligraphy teacher: "I never comment on a letter when it's done wrong once or twice. But more often than that, I feel it's a pattern that needs to be corrected. Then I say something to the student." In other words, maybe what just happened is a rare or occasional occurrence and doesn't really need to be addressed.
- From an elderly lady out walking her small, fluffy, white dog: "She still isn't completely housebroken. Oh, well. Sometimes you've just got to love 'em the way they are." In the large view, maybe you can live with this annoying trait in your partner because everything else is good.

It is important to know that if you can accept a trait in your partner that you find very irritating and really practice having it be okay, your partner may be able to relax and let go of that behavior completely. For example, one wife complained for years about her husband's arrogance. When she finally got to a place of acceptance, she was surprised at what happened: "I stopped judging. His self-esteem went up, and his arrogance went down. If only I'd known to do that earlier!"

Sometimes, however, you'll decide that your personal integrity, love for your partner, or the desire to strengthen your relationship demands that you bring up your concerns. In this situation, a structured dialogue is best. Going through the steps of requesting a dialogue with your partner, and the requirement that he or she mirror, validate, and empathize with you is a kind of insurance. It ensures that you will have thought through what you want to say and that you know why it will be good for you to say it. And it ensures that your partner will hear and understand your message. If expressing yourself through dialogue seems like too much trouble or like too big a deal, then maybe you should hold off and think further before you say anything.

Sometimes, if you're skilled in human relations, you'll decide to try to influence your partner to do something different without confronting your negative reactions head-on. We are talking here about offering your partner a gentle nudge in another direction. We are not suggesting that you become underhanded or manipulative, but rather proactive in offering improvements or solutions. For example, you might intentionally find an opportunity to model for your partner a better way to handle a difficult situation, or arrange opportunities for both of you to learn new skills by attending a class or reading a book, or take the initiative to bring improvements in the quality of life into your home.

For example, one wife offered to treat her husband to lunch at a new French restaurant and then go clothes shopping with him afterward instead of continually running down the wardrobe choices he made on his own. In another example, one husband brought home a catalog of parenting classes that he and his wife could take together at the local community college instead of harping on her inability to discipline their children.

Only you can decide whether an attack of the critical urge can best be dealt with through your acceptance of things as they are, by a direct dialogue with the goal of affecting a change, or an attempt to add other, better methods to your partner's repertoire of options.

Practice No Judgment

Refusing to judge others is a very large step toward recovering your own wholeness. Every time you summarily pass judgment on someone else, you are demonstrating to yourself and everyone else how low your own self-esteem really is. For reasons we have already discussed, every judgment you make is really an indictment of yourself. *The reasons I give for picking on you show what I have trouble within myself.* If the Between in your relationship is unhealthy, judgment and criticism will grow like noxious weeds, making it impossible to cultivate safety and trust.

Separate and connected knowers both pass judgment in their own ways. Separate knowers collect information, analyze it, and then criticize based on the data. An example would be: "I've watched you make that scaloppini a hundred times. Every time, you put in the garlic and the herbs at the wrong time. I looked it up in the *Joy of Cooking* and it says you're supposed to add them at the end so they don't lose their flavor." On the other hand, connected knowers do not criticize on the basis of actual information. They criticize the image of the other person they've created from their own feelings and experiences: "I know you're trying to show us what a great cook you are. But you're trying to do something that's too hard. Why don't you just stick with something you know how to do?" Both these examples of judging are painful in their own way.

But if both partners understand the need to become less judgmental, they can help each other eliminate this negative element from their conversations. They can develop a language for bringing judgment and criticism to each other's attention if they slip up and indulge in it. Because putting other people (or yourself) down is often ingrained as an unconscious reaction, it can be helpful to have your partner tell you when you're falling into the "dissing" habit again. Think about it this way: When you find yourself tempted to judge, take it as a clue that there's something amiss inside yourself. Follow *that* thread instead of the one that leads to denigrating the other person.

Couples have found lots of different ways to signal to each other that one or both of them has just said something judgmental. One couple taped a sign to their bathroom mirror as a general reminder: "Judgment doesn't live here any more." Other couples have worked to find neutral language to call attention to lapses as they occur. The words can be simple if both partners know what they mean: "That sounded like a judgment. Did I hear that right?" Receiving reminders with good humor helps the change process to move forward easier, too. "Oops. I've done it again, haven't I?" It's also not unusual for couples to get to the point where a certain smile or laugh will be all that's necessary to point out and acknowledge the slip.

One couple worked hard to overcome their habit of using criticism as a medium of humor: "We used to make fun of each other and other people, kind of as a sport. Once we understood how damaging that was, we made an effort to stop. Now, whenever I hear someone else saying something judgmental about someone else, it hurts even though I didn't do it, or I wasn't the one being judged. It feels like a violation."

Practice Optimum Distance

Optimum distance is the best, most appropriate balance of autonomy and closeness in a particular relationship. When neither partner is afraid of being engulfed, abandoned, or obligated, and both of them experience their individual freedom within their connection, then they have found, at least for a little while, their optimum balance. Their connection is strong because they feel like a couple *and* like individuals.

Our yearning to feel connected is universal, no matter how old or how sophisticated we are. All conflict is the result of the actual or threatened rupture of an important connection. We don't outgrow the need, but as we mature, it's possible to learn how to connect in healthier ways than we might have in the past. Developing the ability to maintain a stable but changing balance of autonomy and closeness is the foundation of all successful human relationships.

Since ruptures in connection occur when there is either fusion or distancing, it takes maturity and experience to adjust the balance when one or both partners is feeling smothered or abandoned. The partner who wants more closeness may feel that the connection is under threat and may push for more outward signs of connectedness as reassurance that the bond is still there. The partner who wants more autonomy does not necessarily want less connection; he or she simply finds it more comfortable to be connected when there is more space in which to move and breathe.

Finding the shifting balance of optimum distance in any relationship is an ongoing challenge. People evolve and circumstances change. For example, a wife whose childhood schooled her in how to be independent can learn to accept more togetherness with her husband during her bout of breast cancer. However, just because one partner wants something different doesn't mean the other partner will automatically hop to the new tune. A change like this has to be renegotiated within the relationship.

Practice Re-Imaging Your Partner

How you think about something determines how you feel about it. The words you use make a difference. Consider for a moment how the different explanations below affect your feelings about the husband and wife being described.

First example:

> *Possibility #1: My husband was born selfish, insensitive, and boorish.*
>
> *Possibility #2: My husband was not valued and nurtured as a child, so he has trouble knowing how to listen and support me.*

Second example:

> *Possibility #1: My wife is so demanding. She always has to be the center of attention.*
>
> *Possibility #2: I know my wife has trouble feeling that she is important. The only time she got attention from her parents was when she did something wrong.*

The first explanations in each case are made without any empathic understanding of the partner at all. The behavior is seen and condemned, but there is no knowledge of the early wounding that has led to such behavior. The second explanations take into account the pain the partner has experienced and ensure that the speaker approaches the wounded partner with gentleness and understanding.

If this sounds as though we're making an apology for bad behavior, let's clarify. Excusing bad behavior is not the same as understanding the reasons for bad behavior. Putting moral high ground aside for a moment, the main reason to approach a partner with understanding is because when you *know why* a questionable behavior is triggered, you're more likely to figure out how to affect a positive change. In this sense, gaining an empathic understanding of your partner is a matter of enlightened self-interest. When you know what the wound is, you can help to heal it.

When Will Rogers said he never met a man he didn't like, he was really saying that knowing people draws you into their experiences in a way that increases your sympathetic involvement with them. If you have no knowledge of your partner's formative influences, you will likely have very little feeling for the difficulties and privations he or she has endured or overcome. You will not connect to the reasons for the blunders and inadequacies, and you won't have the pleasure of knowing when your partner has successfully overcome previous limitations. It's like trying to have a full-blown relationship with a plastic doll instead of your real girlfriend. You can't fully love something that isn't real to you.

Practice Re-Romanticizing Your Relationship

Sometimes people think that the best way to maintain romance is to maintain illusions—the illusion that we are perfect, that we are care-free, that whatever happens will be wonderful. But in reality, the best way to maintain romance is to be real and to feel connected. Feelings of attraction, excitement, and adventure don't have to be built on novelty; they can be built on a solid base of everyday caring.

In any relationship that's more than three years old, though, the fires of romance need to be stoked. You have to be aware of the ambient temperature in the room, get up out of your chair, put more wood on the fire, and then tend it, sometimes throughout the night, even when you're tired. And when the woodpile is low, you have to go out and chop more logs for the fire.

Sometimes couples fall into the trap of thinking that romance is optional in a committed relationship, or worse, that it's frivolous. After all, there are so very many pressing concerns in trying to maintain a viable family. It's easy to tend to the urgent and neglect the core. But romance is not something extra that happens naturally in the beginning and then inevitably dies. It's the fuel and the light that makes all the schedules and tasks and duties of committed relationships possible and enjoyable.

By all means, start doing what you can to kindle the fires. *Practice* re-romanticizing your relationship. Say, "I love you." Hug and hold. Help out before you're asked. Speak words of appreciation. Listen completely. Bring home a thoughtful gift. These small actions help. But put your primary effort into sharing, listening, validating, supporting, and empathizing with each other. Do more than make contact. Do more than settle for a connection. Work toward communion. Meet each other where you really *are.*

Remember, when a majority of wives are asked what single thing their husbands can do to improve sexual relations, they answer, "Help more around the house." Anything that strengthens the bond—even changing diapers (maybe *especially* changing diapers)—can be perceived as sexy if it is done in the spirit of loving support.

The Reward: Becoming Relational Partners

Making the changes discussed above will re-engineer your relationship. These changes will turn you into relational partners. You will be able to create a conscious partnership, the essence of which is the free flow of information in the form of thoughts, feelings, wishes, fears, laughter, and body language back and forth between you. (See Exercise 9 to get a better understanding of how you form connections and attachments to other people.)

Here are the benchmarks that define relational partners. Both people can:

- Give love verbally, physically, and emotionally, and receive love naturally and easily
- Communicate clearly by sending messages through dialogue, and listen attentively by hearing messages through dialogue
- Engage in both separate knowing as a detached observer, and connected knowing as an emotionally involved participant

Although giving and receiving love, speaking and listening completely, and engaging in separate and connected knowing are different kinds of functions, we have shown that they are not entirely separate from each other. They are more like related components of an organic system than separate components of a mechanical system. Each is interwoven with the others. If you and your partner can move back and forth from giving to receiving love, this implies that you have regularly engaged in the dialogue process. And if you have engaged in dialogue, then you're able to exercise both separate and connected knowing. You may never have thought about these concepts as such or heard these terms, but if you can give and receive love, you can conclude that you have these skills.

Let's review how this interweaving of giving and receiving, dialogue, and different ways of knowing work together. In dialogue, you begin at the point of separate knowing, become engaged with the fuller experience of connected knowing, and are taught, in the end, what it feels like to participate in the richness of relational knowing. Specifically, to send a clear message, you must be a separate knower. To hear your partner's response when he or she mirrors, validates, or empathizes with you, you must be a connected knower. By the time the dialogue is complete, you've both had the opportunity to be engaged participants, and not just detached observers.

You can see from this progression that there is a correspondence between the role you play in dialogue and the kind of knowing you engage in. The process of shifting between separate and connected knowing as you sustain the different roles in dialogue serves to open both partners up to each other, no matter what the content of their discussion happens to be. To practice dialogue successfully, you have to meet each other in a receptive stance because you will be playing "catch." One of you will throw the ball, and the other will catch it. The catcher will then throw the ball back. The limitation of this metaphor is that the ball is always the same ball, while the message in dialogue is slightly enhanced every time it's sent on.

You will know that you are engaged in relational knowing when you can integrate the facts of separate knowing and the empathic connection of connected knowing into a fuller understanding of who your partner is. To put it simply, you will know what you've always "known," only with greater fullness.

If you cannot give and receive love easily, then either you are not doing dialogue at all, or there is a hitch in the way you're doing it. This has to be the case because learning dialogue and therefore integrating both separate and connected knowing into your functioning *teaches* you how to give and receive love.

While the learning process takes place because of your intention and determination to do things differently, it is successfully accomplished because the new patterns are practiced to the point of becoming embedded as neural changes in your brain. You can't become more "open" merely by making a cognitive decision to be so. You have to reshape your brain and build the neural pathways that allow you to embrace sensory, cognitive, and emotional input from your partner instead of shutting it out. You have to practice receiving until you become receptive. Your capacity for relational knowing must grow on a physiological as well as a cognitive level. Reshaping the brain in this way requires an environment that is safe enough for the learning process to take place. The Imago Dialogue makes this kind of trust possible.

Real Life

The couples whose stories have been used in our profiles are happily married today. Each couple has gone through a period of some years of Imago Relationship Therapy based on the information in this book and our other books. When we asked them what was most helpful to them in reconnecting to each other and developing a conscious marriage, we found that their answers shared some themes in common.

They all said that the most important tool they used was the Imago Dialogue, because it helped them know themselves and each other on a much deeper level. Understanding how their partners had been wounded was key in developing empathy. And knowing each other on this deep level allowed them to escape from the prison of self-absorption and see their partners as separate human beings.

They also talked about how important it was to understand that wounding causes defenses, the most important of which is to shut down their capacity to receive. You cannot develop a conscious partnership unless you feel safe enough to be open, and you cannot be a good partner if you can't receive love. If you can't receive love, you aren't going to be able to give love.

Finally, they all talked about how proud they are of being able to provide a different kind of home environment for their children than was provided for them. They believe that their children will enter adulthood equipped to participate in conscious partnerships of their own. They will know how to speak up for themselves and how to hear others with a compassionate and understanding heart.

Stan and Suzanne

Stan and Suzanne now feel that they have a solid foundation for their marriage. Their solidity rests on the fact that they know so much about each other. Sharing their childhood and early adult experiences has made it possible to trace their relationship problems back to early influences. Suzanne now understands why she was so hard on herself and critical of those around her. She sees that her self-hatred made it difficult to accept Stan's help when he offered it.

Once Stan was able to open up about his childhood, he began to develop empathy for his own story. When he talked about the terror he felt growing up around his father and the pain of his mother's disability and her poverty, he could see why it was hard to let another person get close to him, especially when that person was quite vocal about her complaints.

Suzanne and Stan talked about how much time it took for them to share their private thoughts and feelings with each other. They needed time and lots of practice with dialogue. Suzanne says: "I think about how we dialogued in the beginning and how we do it now. It used to be hard not to just go through the motions. You know, just do the formalities. Then we started really listening to each other, empathizing with each other, and hearing what was so painful and why we were being so reactive."

Stan feels that the Imago Dialogue helped them to see how each piece of their stories fit together and became part of their relationship: "The most important piece for me was being able to draw a straight line across all these issues pertaining to my relationship with Suzanne back to where it started in my childhood. That was the start of my foundation in this marriage."

Connecting to his early wounding was the beginning of Stan's understanding, but what empowered him to change his behavior was becoming intentional in his interaction with Suzanne: "My partner has shared this piece of painful history that I can act counter to, but if I don't bring the intentional, the conscious decision to do something differently, to respond differently, then everything is a waste of time. I'm just shooting blanks."

Suzanne says she's learned to be conscious of the words she uses: "I find I need to be very careful with how I phrase something, because Stan is very susceptible and very sensitive to criticism or what may seem like criticism. Like on *The Simpsons* last night, when Homer was teaching Bart to bat, he said, 'Just concentrate Bart. Focus on nothing but the sound of my criticism.'"

She continues, "I think that 95 percent of people, in relationships, respond from a knee-jerk, reactive place. Working on being more and more intentional and more and more empathic moves you to a deeper place, out of reactivity and into making conscious decisions. I aspire to be a conscious person, a conscious wife, a conscious woman, and a conscious mother."

Stan says, "What motivates the intentionality is wanting a better marriage, and a better life for my children. They are going to benefit from the work Suzanne and I have been doing. Regardless of what frustration or difficulty I have, the end responsibility for making things better lies within me. If I want things to change, I have to get motivated enough, have a strong enough desire, and work hard enough at it."

But he makes a distinction between being responsible for his own happiness and making his own changes, and feeling responsible for the entire success or failure of the marriage: "I will do everything I can to make things better, but I know that Suzanne has to be responsible for her own stuff, too. I used to avoid conflict, but now when Suzanne is vocal, I guess I feel the security to come out and be part of the living energy. When she was colorful and loud, I used to just react. I had many years of building up defenses. Because this process has allowed me to share some things with her I couldn't before, she knows how hard it is for me to stay present. It's still not natural at times, but now, if I do exit, it's for short periods of time. Now I know that if we go to bed upset, we'll get up in the morning and make a joke about it."

They say that they feel they are on a path to wholeness: "We are doing more than just parenting our children, or keeping each other company, or sharing meals together. It feels like we're in something much strong and richer than just our marriage, as we used to know it." They tell a story about walking by their son's school: "He was outside for recess, so he saw us together out for a walk. We came up and watched him play. He waved and smiled. We walked away thinking about what kind of positive effect that would have on a child, where he sees his parents together out for a walk, enjoying each other. We felt good about that."

Stan concludes, "We now have a conscious marriage. We missed some years, but we caught it. Yeah, and now we have the rest of our lives to enjoy it."

Al and Rena

In addition to relationship therapy with an Imago therapist, Rena has been in therapy for her anxiety disorder. Al has participated in Rena's therapy and has learned how to support her as she heals from her illness. They say their biggest challenge was learning how to achieve optimum distance in their relationship. Dialogue helped them construct a connection that made them both feel secure without the fusion of symbiosis.

Al says, "I just remember that her feelings are Rena's thing and it is not for me to control. I have to trust that she can take care of herself. That she is capable of taking care of herself. I need to send that message to her by trusting that she can handle it. I can't let my fears get the best of me."

He says that what he learned about letting go of his need to control Rena's fears helped him let go of the need to control her in other ways. He realized that he came to their marriage with a need for her to conform to his vision of how a wife should behave. He was surprised to learn that what he loved most about Rena—her artistic creativity—was the very trait that kept her from being a traditional wife. This insight made him turn his attention to himself, and his own prejudices and inconsistencies, rather than always focusing on what was wrong with Rena.

Al talks about what it was like to learn to dialogue in the beginning. "Certainly we did try to dialogue. It felt really strange. I can almost recall that feeling of it being so hard and so sort of disciplined. Not feeling at all natural. It seemed so damn contrived and structured. I was afraid that it was going to force out all spontaneity. It was just going to waste all my time. I could not get the concept of validating by saying, 'You make sense to me.' I thought, 'How can you make sense to me when I don't agree with what you're saying?!'" He laughs. "It's hard to say that when you don't like what is being said. Validation is a hard concept. But it's the most important step in dialogue."

Rena says they knew they had to keep practicing the Imago Dialogue: "We would take walks all the time through our neighborhood and we would dialogue on our walks. After a while we got into a pattern of doing it almost every day. Even when we didn't have anything specific or important to dialogue about, we just did it anyway. The more we practiced, the easier it got. I think that we finally learned how to listen to each other because typically we would argue and not really get anything communicated or heard because we would cut each other off and we would start yelling."

She continues, "I think we've really learned how to listen to each other and validate each other's feelings. We kind of do it all the time now informally. Really try to validate what the other one is communicating by saying 'that makes sense to me,' even without having formal dialogue."

Al says, "After dialogue, the second most important thing for me was reimaging my partner as wounded. I had to step up and see myself as a healer. If I could accept my role as a healer and be strong and patient and do these things that Rena was asking of me, I learned that things would begin to change. And I think the shift there was instead of me sitting back and waiting for her to change, I was going to be the first one. We've really gotten into a habit now of being able to talk about our feelings and immediately connecting them to something that happened in childhood."

For Rena, the concept of the imago match was the second vital tool in helping her relationship with Al: "What stuck with me was the idea that we unconsciously choose mates who will react to our wounds, and who will rewound us in the way we were wounded in childhood. We choose this person because we unconsciously want to work through those issues and those hurts. We think that he or she will give us what we are needing. What we work for is being able to heal each other and give each other things that we really never got in childhood, and that we are still wanting. That's been the most important thing for me. Al is always working toward that and really making a lot of changes in order to heal my wounds."

Al says that the result of all their changes is that he can now see Rena as her own person, "with her own ideas and thoughts and feelings, and separate from me. I can now not only validate her difference and her individuality, but I've really come to appreciate it, even if it is different from mine. That was the big change for me in my thinking. I had been raised to think that everybody's supposed to think like me."

Both Al and Rena now think of working on their marriage as a spiritual matter. Al says, "Our relationship is a sacred vehicle. It felt less and less appropriate to go into the small parts of ourselves and wound one another continually. We're surviving and trying to let the love in." And Rena concludes, "Just because there are problems and arguments doesn't mean that it's a bad marriage or a bad relationship. It's a journey that's going to have a lot of ups and downs, but we can get through it."

Joshua and Anna

Joshua and Anna have undergone the biggest observable changes of all three couples. Anna returned to school to get her nursing degree, and Joshua learned of necessity how to support her in her personal goals and pick up more of the slack at home. To let go of the rigid roles they began their marriage with meant they both had to grow beyond the limitations they inherited from their childhoods. Joshua had to understand that he would be stronger as part of a team, and Anna had to understand that she was smart enough and worthy enough to be his teammate.

But according to Joshua, the most important change he made had to do with learning how to just *be*. "The most important thing I did was learn how to relax, to enjoy the moment, to accept that I am good enough without having to perform and achieve all the time."

He credits the Imago Dialogue with allowing him to learn who he really is: "I feel like there's more of me that is available now in our relationship and less of me that is coming from a preconceived idea of what a relationship is supposed to be. There's more of me that is really able to see Anna and all her gifts, shortcomings, and woundings. And, there's more of me to see myself and all my gifts, shortcomings, and woundings. Reimaging Anna as wounded was important, but reimaging myself as wounded was revolutionary. I don't have to be the One and Only. Now, it feels like we truly are on the same team."

Anna adds: "Our relationship is dramatically different than it was before. We're the same people, but there's much more of each of us available. My perception of myself is that I have a lot of tools now to work with. I can be focused on me and not what's wrong with Joshua or what's wrong with us. What I see with Joshua is that he's able to be much more present and I'm able to be much more calm. There seems to be a lot of room for us to work things out and to be okay with letting time go by and not having to power struggle about everything. We definitely have moved through that significant, long, maybe many-year power struggle that we had ongoing in our lives. We're kind of out on the other side now. Not that it's always perfect, but there's a lot more safety. Our relationship now, I would say, is solid and also has elements of freedom and trust that we're still creating."

Joshua and Anna agree that the most helpful change they've been able to make is to be able to call themselves on their own projections. Joshua says, "Our therapist suggested that we develop the habit of saying to ourselves when something significant happens: 'I feel this. . . . I tell myself this. . . . I make myself feel this. . . .'"

Anna explains, "This helped us see how much we were making up about each other that had more to do with our own fears than with the other person. It helped us break the chain of thinking that what we thought was the way the world actually was. We could see how many zillion times we'd done this. We could see how our wounds led us to certain patterns of thinking."

Joshua jumps in, "It was a way to see that I don't always know everything. And that Anna isn't just an extension of me. We both try to be really careful now about making assumptions. To be in relationship with another person I have to respect that they have their center and all of their different parts."

Both Joshua and Anna feel they have softened. Both of them have more patience for themselves, as well as each other. They aren't as harsh as they once were. "We now focus more on the good things, how lucky we are, and how much we have."

One Final Testimony

One of the most appreciative and explicit letters we've ever received from someone who attended an Imago Relationship Therapy workshop and participated in Imago Relationship Therapy counseling was from Burton. Although he and his girlfriend did not stay together, he wrote us a letter one year after their split. He wanted to give us an update on how he was doing, and let us know what he had learned from his relationship failure with his girlfriend. As you will see, he focuses on the characteristics she had that he was first attracted to and then upset with. He underscores how important it is to recognize and address the split in yourself, if you want to create a happy union with someone else.(See Exercise 11 to help you discover which parts of you have been lost and can be reclaimed.) Here is an excerpt from Burton's letter:

> One of the concepts I gleaned from my reading of your works and from the therapy is that we are attracted to the characteristics we see in our partner that we have lost in ourselves. This is where things get interesting. At least to me.
>
> I sat down one evening and made a list of all the things that my girlfriend had that I was attracted to. There were three principal items on my list: (1) She was an artist and creative. (2) She could move and didn't hesitate to do so through dance, yoga, etc. (3) She was "free"—in that before we were dating, she would quit her job, go off and live in India for three months, come back, and then go off to Tibet and live for a month.
>
> I thought about each of these traits and compared them to myself. Curiously, I'm a very creative person (watercolor, stained glass, etc.), but I haven't done anything in more than twenty years. I used to be a very serious dancer, too, but haven't really done anything in more than thirty years. Lastly, if I take a long weekend I feel irresponsible, let alone go anywhere for three months. So, recognizing this, I began a program of action.
>
> First, I completely rebuilt my stained glass studio. Bought

all the tools, set up a worktable, and began a simple trial project. The first day I began cutting glass for practice, just to get the feel of it. I cut and I cut and I cut and about thirty minutes later, I was surprised to find that I was crying. . . . I was crying from the deep sense of comfort and elation at a reunion with an "old friend."

Second, I decided to take a dance class. I have to tell you that this was the equivalent of trying to cut off my own finger. I had such difficulty! But eventually, I did choose a studio and I did enroll in a class. For the first six weeks it was horrible, but by the seventh week, I left the studio with a smile on my face and a bounce in my step that I have never experienced.

The last element of my self-imposed therapy was to take a four-week trip to Chile and Tierra del Fuego last December. I was convinced right up to getting on the plane that this was the most irresponsible thing I'd ever done in my life and I would surely die as a result . . . but I didn't die. At one point, I rolled down the window of my rent-a-car and shouted to the wind, "Look what I'm doing," and then laughed for another ten kilometers or so.

Last, I have to say I'm in a relationship again. It's amazing to me how open and "conscious" it is. I took out the "relationship vision" I wrote last year and was amazed to find that of the twenty-one points I had listed, twenty of them are being met beyond my wildest dreams.

By using your tools and being willing to look at the root causes of my relationship problems, I have resolved some important issues in my life. All because of a relationship "gone wrong."

In gratitude,
Burton

We couldn't say it better ourselves: use your current relationship to uncover your own self-rejection. Love those places in your partner and in yourself that have been demonized, and when you are whole, you will be able to give and receive the love you've always wanted.

APPRECIATION

People who have traveled this healing path often talk about how lucky they are. This is not an accident. Appreciating is the highest form of receiving. Instead of thinking of appreciating as "a nice thing to do," a kind of good idea, we consider it to be psychologically profound. It seems to us that appreciation is the most appropriate response to our true condition in life—which is that we receive with every breath we take. The wonders of the world are there for us to enjoy; they are there for us to connect to in the deepest way. When we do connect, we open the possibility of communion, which is the experience of profound joy in our oneness with life. This is our true nature. (See Exercise 1 for ways to increase your natural capacity for appreciation.)

We remember the first time we absorbed this idea in a connected, knowing way. Everybody knows, of course, that we take in oxygen every time we breathe. This is separate knowing. But when we internally registered the greater implications of this idea, it was life changing. We moved from separate knowing of the facts, to connected knowing through experience, to the relational knowing as the integration of both. Getting the truth of it was different from merely saying the words or having the feelings.

The turning point was listening to a spiritual teacher as he led a small group of us through a breathing exercise: *Breathe out; breathe in. Just be aware that the air is there for you, exactly what you need, when you need it. All you have to do is take it in.* A very simple moment. And, as so often happens, the right kind of moment for enlightenment to break through our dulled perceptions.

The small, everyday experience of breathing opened us up to appreciation at a very deep level. It was one of the things that set us on the course of exploring the role that receiving plays in intimate relationships. We *knew* from then on that we are basically, ontologically, receivers. Our eyes are designed so that we can see. Our ears so we can hear. We don't control, nor are we responsible for the receptive capacities our bodies have. We are given beyond what we've earned and deserved.

When we intentionally extend our capacity for receiving beyond the miracle of our sympathetic nervous systems into those areas we *are* responsible for, we honor the essence of life. Taking in and giving out is the basic rhythm. The more we take in, the more we give out. If something happens to impair our ability to receive love, we need to repair it—for our own sakes, for the sake of our partners and children, and for the sake of the larger world in which we live.

PART III: EXERCISES

All of us have received love throughout our lives, but many of us have blocked the love we've been given. Maybe we've forgotten about some of the love that people have tried to give to us. Maybe we haven't allowed ourselves to experience love emotionally because we are afraid of the obligation, or we don't feel worthy to receive it. Or, maybe we've deflected or rejected love because we have internal prohibitions that prevent us from receiving it.

Part III consists of exercises that will help you regain your capacity to receive the love that is already in your life. The first exercises will help you become more conscious of what you have been given. Then we will invite you to take some assessments of your current capacity to receive love. Along the way, you'll be able to identify where you're having difficulties. Finally, you'll have the opportunity to explore your past relationship with your parents to discover some of the causes of those difficulties. You will learn about how you were wounded and the defenses you developed that interfere with the natural flow of giving and receiving love.

If you want, you can consider these exercises a workshop to be completed after you've finished reading the rest of the book. In that case, you would sit down and do them with your partner, one after the other. Or, you and your partner can do these exercises as they become relevant in the text. In that case, they would be done separately as part of your reading, without paying attention to their order.

The Gift Diary

The purpose of the Gift Diary is to develop a daily consciousness toward receiving love in your life. The first task is to take an inventory of gifts received in your lifetime that have had special meaning to you. Then, you will record the gifts you receive from your partner on a daily basis. Finally, in order to increase your capacity to receive and give love, you will design gifts to be exchanged with your partner in the future.

For the first task, purchase a spiral notebook or some kind of a diary, preferably one that is divided into three sections, and label it "My Gift Diary." Ask your partner to do the same. Remember that receiving is a precondition of true giving.

A. RECEIVING INVENTORY

Label the first part of your diary RECEIVING INVENTORY. Take time to think about what gifts you received in the past that were the most valuable to you. Who gave you these special gifts? How old were you? What did it feel like to receive them?

When you finish making your list, study each entry as a fact. Use your separate knowing to think rationally about the fact of each of these gifts. Then shift to your connected knowing of each gift. Move from your head to your heart, and allow yourself to re-experience the moment you received each one. Be aware of the emotions you felt about each gift and the different levels on which you felt love expressed by receiving the gift. Let yourself spend some time feeling connected to both the gift and the giver of the gift. Savor all the good feelings of the moment.

B. Daily Record

A multitude of gifts we exchange each day can get lost in our busyness and self-absorption. To complete this exercise, you and your partner need to label the second part of your Gift Diary DAILY RECORD. In this part of the diary, you will record three gifts you receive from each other every day, beginning with today. You can note little or big things. Here are some examples: "I appreciate the way you always set the alarm clock correctly." "I appreciate your help with the finances." "I appreciate the fresh towels in the bathroom." "I appreciate your driving me to the airport." "I loved the look you gave me when I brought you hot tea this evening." Talk about the three gifts you each received from the other before you go to bed at night.

After you acknowledge the gift of your partner's love that you received that day, practice moving to another place deep within yourself. Feel your heart opening to your partner's presence in your life and say: "I receive this as a gift, thank you." Let yourself feel the gift. Breathe it in. Hold an image of it in your mind. Move from an abstract separate knowing of your partner's gifts to a connected knowing of your partner's love as you allow yourself to feel the gifts your partner gave and the gift of your partner in your life.

The DAILY RECORD has several purposes. It will help attune your eyes to the gifts each of you may be trying to give to each other, but that you don't receive. It will encourage you to open your hearts and notice the little things you do for your relationship. And, recording your partner's daily gifts will allow you to experiment with moving from separate to connected knowing, by experiencing the gifts in your emotions and by allowing them to be received in every cell of your body.

Share with your partner what it was like for you to receive his or her gift, including all the sensations you experienced. This will help you grow in your capacity to receive. Also, when you notice the three behaviors each day that you value, you are mirroring your partner's efforts. This will encourage your partner to give in ways that have the most meaning for you, and to continue to give gifts to you daily. Remember, receiving love opens your heart *and* empowers your partner to give you even more.

C. DREAM GIFT INVENTORY

Label the last page of your diary MY PARTNER'S DREAM GIFT INVENTORY. In this space you will keep a running list of things you think your partner values receiving. Take some time now to create an initial list.

Now ask your partner to review your list for accuracy, and ask him or her to add what you missed. Review your partner's list and add things he or she missed. Clarify for each "dream gift" the following questions: What time of day, in what setting, and how often would your partner like to receive your gift? The DREAM GIFT INVENTORY will help shift giving in your relationship from unconscious relating, based on what you *think* your partner wants, to conscious relating, based on what you now know your partner wants.

If you give gifts to your partner that he does not mention, ask your partner gently whether he experiences the behavior as a gift. For example, you may enjoy buying a box of candy for your partner from time to time. And while you may be excited to give it, your partner doesn't seem excited about receiving it. Ask your partner if he values getting a box of candy from you. If yes, you will know he is receiving it. So keep doing it, even if he doesn't comment. If he says no, ask him what would seem like a gift to him. Show interest in your partner's feelings and thoughts about what he most values and appreciates. Simply being asked, in and of itself, is likely to be received as a very meaningful gift.

A word of caution: If your partner does not perceive what you are doing as a valuable gift, you could become resentful. If you feel your partner is not receiving something, avoid blaming at all costs. Blaming makes it even more difficult for your partner to open his heart to receive. You need to take the time to ask what would feel like a gift to your partner, rather than become resentful that what you perceive as a valuable gift is not received in the same way by your partner.

You can keep the lists updated by adding hints, things you hear each other say in passing about things you each like—a day with nothing to do, a bright leather jacket, skydiving lessons, breakfast in bed, a trip to the beach, a full hour massage. Be sure to add these hints to your ongoing inventories. These inventories are the key to both your hearts, and if used, will help both of you learn to receive the love you want to give each other.

If you are using these exercises in sequence, you can study the instructions for Exercise 2: The Imago Dialogue next. You can use your experiences from Exercise 1 to practice the dialogue process.

The Imago Dialogue

The Imago Dialogue helps to create safety in your relationship, and safety is a precondition for receiving love. The Imago Dialogue process is the central therapeutic process in Imago Relationship Therapy. Regular practice of this skill will lead to clear communication and deeper emotional connection. It will help you learn how to listen accurately to what your partner is saying, to understand and validate your partner's point of view, and to express empathy for your partner's feelings. By using this tool, you and your partner can learn to create a space between you in which true love can be born.

Before you begin, please review the discussion of the Imago Dialogue in Chapter 8. For a more complete discussion of the Imago Dialogue refer to page 142 in *Getting the Love You Want: A Guide for Couples*.

DIRECTIONS:

1. Choose who will be the sender and the receiver. The one who decides to be the sender should start the dialogue by saying: "I would like to have an Imago Dialogue. Is now okay?" When using this process in your relationship, after this practice session, it is important that the receiver respond as soon as possible. If now is not possible, then set a time when you will be available so your partner will know when he or she will be heard. You should signal your readiness by saying: "I am available now."

2. The sender now talks for a few minutes, sending the message she or he wants the receiver to hear. The message should start with "I" and describe what the sender is thinking or feeling. Remember, in order for the dialogue not to be associated only with concerns and frustrations, start the first dialogue with something positive: an appreciation, something positive your partner did that made you feel loved or a positive trait you appreciate. For this exercise, therefore, the message should be something positive or at least neutral and simple. Example: "I have been thinking about the positive things in our relationship, and I would like to tell you about some of them." If you chose something neutral, you could start with: "I awakened this morning with a sore throat and don't feel like going to work. I think I will stay home." The receiver then mirrors using these suggested sentence stems: "**If I got it,** you awakened with a sore throat, and since you don't feel well, you are thinking you will stay home from work. **Did I get it?**" If the sender indicates he or she felt heard accurately, then the receiver says: "**Is there more about that?**" If the sender has more to say, she or he adds to the message. The receiver continues to mirror and ask "Is there more about that?" until the sender has completed the message. (The question, "Is there more about that," is very important. It helps the sender complete all of his or her thoughts and feelings and prevents the receiver from responding to an incomplete message. And, since it is limited to "more about *that,* it helps the sender limit the message to *one* subject at a time.)

3. When the sender has completed the message, the receiver then summarizes all of the sender's message with this lead-in: "**Let me see if I got all of that. . . .**" When the receiver finishes the summary, he or she should check for accuracy with this question: "**Did I get it all?**" (The summary is important because it helps the receiver understand the sender more deeply and to see the logic in what was said. This helps with validation, which is the next step.) When the sender indicates that the entire message has been heard accurately, you then move to validation, or Step 4.

4. Now the receiver *validates* the sender's message with something like these lead-ins: "**You make sense, because . . .**" or "**It makes sense to me, given that you . . .**" or "**I can see what you are saying. . .** , (example) given that you have a sore throat and feel bad, it makes sense that you are thinking of not going to work." (This response indicates that the receiver understands the logic of what the sender is saying. It is the sender's "truth." The receiver does not have to agree with the sender, but it is essential that they "see" the logic or "truth" of the sender's experience. Since everyone "makes sense," using the phrase ". . . **makes sense . . .**" communicates that the receiver "gets it" and that the sender is not illogical or crazy.) The receiver should check to see if the sender feels validated. If so, then the receiver moves to empathy, the final step.

5. Empathy can be expressed with the following sentence stems: "**I can imagine that you might be feeling . . .** (example) frustrated that you have to miss a day of work." If the sender's report is about the past, the receiver can say: "**I can imagine that you might have felt. . . .**" These lead-ins can be used if the sender has not openly expressed feelings. If the sender has expressed feelings, then the receiver can say: "**I can see that you are feeling. . . .**" (Feelings are best stated using one word, such as angry, sad, upset, happy, and so on. If you use more than one word, such as: "you feel you don't want to go to work," you are probably expressing a thought.) Since one never knows for sure what another person is feeling, it is important to check for accuracy by saying: "**Is that what you are feeling?**" Or, "**Did I get your feeling right?**" If the receiver did not imagine the right feelings or misperceived the expressed feelings, then the sender should again state what he or she is feeling. Also, if the sender shares other feelings that were not picked up by the receiver the first time, the receiver should mirror those feelings and ask: "**Is there more about that feeling?**"

6. When the receiver has gone through all three parts (mirroring, validation, and empathy) then she or he says: "**I would**

like to respond now." Then the receiver becomes the sender and the sender the receiver. The sender (former receiver) may respond to the message he or she heard or the sender may express feelings or thoughts about something from his or her experience.

7. This exercise will feel like an unnatural, cumbersome way of relating, but it is a good way to assure accurate communication. Like learning any new skill, it will be awkward at first, but with practice you will become more artistic and less mechanical. When you have the exercise down pat, you will discover that you do not need to use the structured process all the time. Your communication will become dialogical in spirit. The three steps will be necessary only when you are discussing highly charged subjects, or when communication breaks down. Eventually, you will experience a decrease in reactivity, more emotional safety, and deeper connection.

8. Now use the dialogue process to share what you learned about yourself and your partner by doing Exercise 1. Take turns. The exchange in the Imago Dialogue offers you an opportunity to practice both receiving and giving. Each time you fully listen to your partner, you expand yourself by receiving and you empower your partner to impact you. When you speak, you are giving yourself to your partner and helping them enlarge themselves by taking in your reality. When it's your turn to listen, give your partner your full attention. Mirror what your partner is saying until you get it. Then validate her or his point of view and communicate empathy. You may ask clarifying questions, but do not try to analyze your partner, make interpretations, or express frustrations or criticisms. As you listen, try to visualize your partner's issues with giving and receiving.

The Imago Dialogue helps you develop a new way of knowing, called relational knowing. When you listen accurately to the content of what your partner is saying, you engage in separate knowing. Your partner feels safe with you when you mirror correctly what he or she has said. Then, when you validate your partner's view, you move from your head into your heart, and imagine some of your partner's experience, connecting with your partner's reality. Expressing empathy opens you to an even deeper connectional knowing by allowing you to feel some of your partner's feelings about his or her views, and, at a deeper level, to participate in those feelings. Both separate and connected knowing are necessary for you to really understand your partner, and the dialogue process, done accurately, helps you develop both. You will learn more about separate and connected knowing in Exercise 3.

Learning How You Know

Most of the time we are concerned about *what* we know. Seldom do we consider *how* we know what we know. This exercise is designed to help you learn two ways of knowing, called separate and connected knowing. It will assist you in deciding which best describes how you tend to process information. One way to talk about separate knowing is that it has to do with thinking, learning the facts about things, and knowing them in your head. This is what most people think of when they think about how we know. But connected knowing is an equally valid way of knowing that is just as common; it is simply not talked about as often. Connected knowing has been called "heart knowing." It is a way of relating to the world through intuition and feelings. Connected knowers experience things, events, and persons with their emotions, feeling them in their "hearts." All of us use both kinds of knowing. We were born with the capacity to do both. But most of us have trouble easily accessing both modes of knowing in a balanced way. As a result of our childhood experiences, we come to rely on one kind of knowing at the expense of the other. One becomes dominant and the other becomes recessive.

While the polarity of separate and connected knowing is innate, the degree to which they are out of balance is an adaptation and can be altered. Bringing separate and connected knowing into balance will enhance and deepen your ability to experience life, and will enhance your functioning in all aspects of your life. The achievement of this integration is called, "relational knowing."

For example, you have exaggerated reliance on connected knowing when:

1. You cannot say what you mean succinctly.
2. Your partner/others become impatient with your elaborations.
3. Your partner/others say that you get overly emotional.

You have relied on separate knowing when:

1. You speak clearly, succinctly, and logically, but with little if any affect.
2. You are impatient when your partner/others elaborate their point excessively.
3. Your partner/others say they experience little warmth or empathy from you.

Below is a self-rating scale to access whether or not you see yourself as a separate knower, a connected knower, or a relational knower. Study the examples above carefully and think about how they might apply to you. On the scale below, SK stands for "separate knowing" and CK represents "connected knowing." If you think you are a separate knower, give yourself a rating of 1–4. If you consider yourself a connected knower, also give yourself a rating of 1–4. The closer your rating is to either the left or right side indicates the degree to which you are a separate or connected knower. The closer your rating is to the center, number 5, the closer you are to being a relational knower. If you rate yourself with a 5, you consider yourself a balance of separate and connected knowing, and thus a relational knower.

SK   1   2   3   4   5   4   3   2   1   CK

If you have a partner, ask him/her to rate you and compare your ratings. If you do not have a partner, you might also like to ask a close friend to rate you and compare your ratings.

The exercises that follow will help separate knowers develop their connected knowing skills and connected knowers develop their separate knowing skills. After you have determined which kind of knowing is dominant for you, select the growth process that is appropriate. It will help you develop the balance you need to become a relational knower.

Growth Process for Separate Knowers

PURPOSE: To become a relational knower.

GOAL: To keep your separate knowing skill, but at the same time, increase your connected knowing skill.

STRATEGY: To become more familiar and intimate with your inner world of feelings, images, intuitions, hunches, and body sensations, and to become more curious about and empathic with your inner world and the inner world of others.

PROCESSES:

1. Practice becoming **silent** inside. Use a meditation method to help you focus on your breathing. Allow yourself to experience whatever is going through your mind, then let it go, and return your attention to your breathing. Be aware of your body, note any tension, and then let it go. Note any thoughts and/or images, suspend any judgment, and then, let them go.

2. Practice becoming **present to others.** Use the dialogue process to listen to your partner and others. Create an empty space inside yourself to receive their reality. Simply listen. Place your hand over their heart and experience their body sensations. Release any thoughts, analyses, suggestions, solutions, and judgments, and allow the speaker to be who they are. Become curious about their experiencing; make a space in your consciousness for their reality. Respond with empathy.

3. Practice being **present to your emotional self.** Find a quiet place where you will not be disturbed, and just sit, allowing yourself to be aware of your feelings, images, intuitions, hunches, and body sensations. When thoughts, analyses, suggestions, solutions, or judgments arise, let them go, and go back to experiencing your inner world.

4. Practice **translating action into words and feelings.** The next time you become aware of wanting to take a particular action, such as getting up from your chair, taking a drink, eating, or

going to find your partner, pause first. Rather than proceeding with the action, notice what you are feeling and thinking in connection with your proposed action. Put your feelings and thoughts into words to yourself. Then decide if you want to take the action or not.

5. Practice **expressing your emotions.** Ask your partner for a dialogue. For fifteen minutes, talk about your feelings. Go as deeply into them as you can, suspending any thoughts, analyses, or judgments that you might have. Ask your partner to mirror your feelings. You can also practice expressing your emotions by flooding your partner or a friend with positive feelings you have about them, and/or telling them intensely the positive feeling you have about your relationship. Again, ask your partner or friend to mirror your feelings.

6. Practice **transferring the energy of your mind to your heart.** Find a quiet place, and then imagine your mind in an energy field, radiating energy into your environment. Then shift your focus to your heart, and imagine that your heart generates the same kind of energy radiating out into your environment. If you want, you can visualize your heart encircled with a warm glow that overflows your body and spills out of you.

Growth Process for Connected Knowers

PURPOSE: To become a relational knower.

GOAL: To keep your connected knowing skill, but at the same time increase your separate knowing skill.

STRATEGY: To become more familiar with your thoughts, analytic skills, logical-sequential thinking, ability to solve problems, and to develop your ability to think clearly, to speak succinctly, and to enjoy the external world.

PROCESSES:

1. Practice becoming **silent** inside. Use a meditation method to help you focus on your breathing. Allow yourself to experience

whatever is going through your mind, then let it go, and return your attention to your breathing. Be aware of your body, note any tension, and then let it go. Note any thoughts and/or images, suspend any judgment, and then, let them go.

2. Practice becoming **present to others.** Use the dialogue process to listen to your partner and others. Create an empty space inside yourself to receive their reality. Simply listen. Place your hand over their heart and experience their body sensations. Release any thoughts, analyses, suggestions, solutions, and judgments, and allow the speaker to be who they are. Become curious about their experiencing; make a space in your consciousness for their reality. Respond with empathy.

3. Practice being **present to your rational self.** Find a quiet place where you will not be disturbed, and just sit, allowing yourself to be aware of your thoughts. Let one thought crystallize. Hold the thought in your mind. When a feeling arises, let it go, and go back to experiencing your mind and its thoughts.

4. Practice **finding the thoughts behind your feelings.** Create one succinct thought on any one subject in your mind. Practice becoming less diffuse and more focused with this thought. When feelings, images, intuitions, hunches, and bodily sensations arise, let them go, and return your attention to your thought.

5. Practice **translating feelings into words and action.** Notice the next time you have a strong feeling about your partner or one of your partner's behaviors. Rather than staying in your feeling, initiate a dialogue with your partner. Ask him or her to listen and mirror. Then speak clearly and succinctly—putting a period at the end of each sentence. Next, in the same clear, succinct manner, ask for a behavior you want. Be specific about what you want by making the behavior you want measurable and time limited. Notice how you feel once you have stated what you want.

6. Practice containing **your emotions.** The next time you have a problem that arouses your feelings, instead of staying in your feelings, shift into your thoughts and make a plan for solving the problem.

7. Practice **transferring the energy of your heart to your mind.** Find a quiet place, and then let yourself experience your feelings about your partner, imagining energy circling your heart. Then imagine that energy shifting to your mind, encircling it with a warm glow, and then radiating out toward a problem to be solved. Construct a plan for addressing the problem. Allow yourself to envision yourself carrying out your plan. How does that feel?

Now, as you continue with the exercises, keep in mind how you tend to know and practice both separate and connected knowing with all the new learning that is ahead.

Practice Receiving and Giving

The following tasks are designed to assist you in developing your capacity to receive. Receiving is a prerequisite to giving. Learning to receive enlarges the self and empowers others.

PART 1: RECEIVING SENSORY IMPRESSIONS

When we are wounded in childhood we tend to become self-absorbed and shut down our five senses. We do not take in sensations from our environment. Although we are all dependent upon our environment, self-preoccupation does not allow us to experience the gift of sensation, nor experience the awareness of our dependency.

To reactivate our sensory organs, we need to practice paying attention to the stimuli that come in from our environment. The following is a simple exercise to help facilitate this. The best way to do this exercise is to go outside with your partner and walk around. When you are outside:

1. Just breathe. Be aware only of the air coming in and out through your nostrils. Take a deep breath in and let the air out. Receive the air. Say to yourself: **"I am breathing in the air. It's just there and it's there for me."** Use dialogue to share your experience with your partner. Listen carefully to your partner's words. Let them in and receive them in the same way you took in the air around you. Experience the sensation of receiving your partner's words and emotions.

2. Just see. Look at your environment. Be aware of the images coming in through your eyes. Let them in. Let yourself see the colors of the trees, grass, and flowers; the movement of the birds; and the clouds floating in the sky. Look at your partner. Take in your partner's appearance, the color of his/her eyes, her/his height, and size. Use dialogue to share this experience with each other, letting your partner's words and emotions in.

3. Just touch. Focus only on what you touch. Touch a tree, a blade of grass, a rock, and your partner's skin. Experience the sensations on your fingertips. Let the sensations in. Experience the texture. Use dialogue to share the sensations of touch with each other. Experience the sensation of receiving your partner's words and emotions.

4. Just listen. Using your ears, let in the sounds of your environment. Take in the sound of the wind blowing in the trees, the cars, your partner's voice, and your own breathing. Use dialogue to share your experiences with each other. Be sure to let in the sound of your partner's voice, as well as his or her words and emotions.

5. Just taste. Focus only on the sensations on your tongue. Experience where the taste sensations go in your body. Taste a piece of fruit, taste your own skin, kiss your partner, and taste his or her lips with your tongue. Let only the sensations in, letting any distracting thoughts and feelings go. Use dialogue to share your experience with each other, letting your partner's words and emotions in.

6. Now take the experience one step further. Say aloud: **"I appreciate the air, the images given to my eyes, the sensations of touch, the sounds, and the tastes."** Think of everything in your environment, including your partner, as a gift and experience the joy of receiving.

PART 2: RECEIVING YOUR PARTNER'S REALITY

This part of the exercise will help you become more closely in touch with who your partner really is and help you to pay close attention to what he or she is saying.

1. Find a place where you and your partner can have an uninterrupted dialogue. Ask your partner to talk about his or her experience of letting in sensory sensations. Listen carefully, focusing only on your partner's words, tone of voice, and emotions. Let the words in until you can experience her or his inner world. Let only your partner's words into your consciousness. Let all your own thoughts and feelings go. Focus until you are silent inside.

2. Now change places and talk to your partner about your experience and ask your partner to listen.

3. Now, to deepen your capacity to take in your partner's reality, ask your partner to talk about something that is uncomfortable to him/her in your relationship. Focus. Concentrate. Let your partner's reality be all that is in your mind. Listen until you are silent inside, and aware only of your partner's experience.

4. Say to your partner, "**I appreciate your sharing your reality with me.**"

5. Now switch roles and ask your partner to listen to you and appreciate you in the same way.

Part 3: Receiving a Gift

Remember that receiving expands the self and empowers your partner.

1. Find a place where you and your partner can have an uninterrupted dialogue. Ask your partner to give you something you have never before asked for. It could be a certain kind of kiss, a massage, a physical item, certain words, or an experience—anything you want that you have never asked for. Take your time and think about your deepest desire, the fulfillment of a fantasy, or an unfulfilled yearning. Then, pick one that you'd like to receive today.

2. Be aware of any thoughts, feelings, and physical sensations as you ask, but let them go. Focus only on your asking.

3. Now accept whatever you have asked for. Let any uncomfortable thoughts, feelings, or physical sensations go. Experience yourself receiving.

4. Say to your partner: **"I accept this gift. I appreciate the gift you have given me. It helps me expand myself into a larger person."**

PART 4: GIVING A GIFT

Remember that giving stretches you into new parts of yourself.

1. Ask your partner to set aside some uninterrupted time, and using the dialogue process, ask him or her to ask for something from you that he or she has never asked for.

2. When your partner has asked for the gift, let yourself be aware of any thoughts, feelings, or physical sensations you may have, and then let them go.

3. Stretch into giving your partner what he or she has asked for, no matter how you feel. Focus only on the experience of stretching toward your partner.

4. Say to your partner: **"I appreciate your asking me for what you want. It gives me a chance to grow into a larger, more empowered person."**

Positive Flooding

Practicing mutual positive flooding is another way to develop your ability to receive. It creates more safety and joy in your relationship, opening you and your partner even further to the possibility of receiving.

1. Have your partner sit in a chair and, while walking in a circle around your partner, keep eye contact and say all the positive things you can think of about your partner's physical characteristics, character traits, behaviors you value, and so on. Flood your partner by starting with your voice at its regular volume and then raising it with each of your positive comments. At the end of the flooding, you should be *shouting* positive global expressions of caring to your partner, such as, "You are the most thoughtful husband in the world!" Or, "You are the most wonderful wife in the universe!" Shout these exclamations with a level of intensity equal to your expressions of rage or anger.
2. While you are doing this, be aware of reactions on your partner's face and body.
3. Now, have a dialogue with your partner and ask him or her to talk about how it felt to be positively flooded. Note especially the words you said that were mentally deflected by your partner, those that were let in, and the feelings your partner had with each one.
4. Ask your partner to do the same for you, and repeat the process.

5. Now, list all aspects of yourself that you want your partner to flood. Include what you wanted to hear in your childhood and what you want to hear in the relationship of your dreams.

Physical Characteristics	Character Traits	Behaviors	Global Affirmations

6. Ask your partner to repeat the flooding exercise, using the words you want to hear. Then, share the experience with your partner, using the dialogue process.
7. Now, take your partner's list and repeat the flooding exercise, using the items your partner wants appreciated. Remember to raise your voice as you amplify the list.
8. Ask your partner to share the experience with you, using the dialogue process.

Do this exercise weekly, including the traits you value in each other and the traits you both want valued. Then make it a part of your daily interaction, flooding each other regularly with positive words. This changes chronic negativity into chronic positive flooding. Each time you practice this exercise, you strengthen your ability to give and to receive. Raising your voice while flooding increases the emotional intensity with which you express your positive feelings to your partner. Positive words expressed with intense emotions can overcome any defense your partner may have against giving or receiving love. Your relationship will become safe, and you will continue to grow into your wholeness.

Your "Receiving Quotient" Assessment

Below are fifty questions designed to discover what we are calling your "receiving quotient." Please rank each item with S for "sometimes," O for "often," or N for "rarely" or "never." N items measure your "positive receiving quotient." The combination of S+O items measures your "negative receiving quotient." When you and your partner have completed the assessment, compare your scores.

Exercise your capacity for both separate and connected knowing, as you think about each question. Give yourself time to consider the truth from a factual point of view, and also from a more intuitive, emotional point of view. To get a complete picture of how well you receive, you must call upon your ability to assess your behavior from a separate and connected knowing perspective.

1. _____ Do you feel uncomfortable when someone brags about you?

2. _____ Do you feel critical when someone brags about himself or herself?

3. _____ Do you feel negative toward someone else who is bragged about by another person?

4. _____ Do you feel critical when someone lets himself be bragged about?

5. _____ Do you ever get a gift and feel obligated?

6. _____ Do you ever get gifts and forget you got them?

7. _____ Do you ever devalue the gifts others give you?

8. _____ Do you ever refuse to take gifts?

9. _____ Do you ever deflect compliments when you get them?

10. _____ Do you ever ask for something, get it, and find something wrong with it?

11. _____ Do you ever find yourself mainly remembering only the "bad times"?

12. _____ Do you ever ask for something, get it, and then forget that you asked for it?

13. _____ Do you ever ask for something, get it, and then forget that you got it?

14. _____ Do you ask for the same thing over and over again?

15. _____ Does it ever seem to you that no one wants you to have what you want?

16. _____ Do you ever tell stories of not getting what you asked for?

17. _____ Do you ever say, "I want you to offer it," and when your partner does, you say your partner offered it only because you asked for it?

18. _____ Do you ever feel uncomfortable when another person is getting all the attention?

19. _____ Do you ever feel like "nothing is good enough"?

20. _____ Do you ever feel uncomfortable wanting things for yourself?

21. _____ Do you ever feel uncomfortable with your desires?

22. _____ Do you say you don't want it and then complain about not getting it?

23. _____ Do you see everyone else as having what he or she wants?

24. _____ Do you envy other people having good things you don't have?

25. _____ Do you ever have trouble accepting others' positive valuations of you—your worth, ability?

26. _____ Do you ever see someone else receive something you don't feel he or she deserves?

27. _____ Do you ever feel uncomfortable giving something to yourself?

28. _____ Do you ever feel critical of someone who whines?

29. _____ Do you ever feel critical of someone who is needy?

30. _____ Do you ever feel like a bad person?

31. _____ Do you ever feel worthless?

32. _____ Do you ever feel like a failure?

33. _____ Do you ever feel depression?

34. _____ Do you feel chronic anger at others who are fortunate?

35. _____ Do you ever feel like you put forth a false "good" self and hide your true "bad" self?

36. _____ Do you ever have trouble imagining why others like and accept praise?

37. _____ Do you ever feel critical of people who ask for reassurance?

38. _____ Do you ever feel uncomfortable with people who want nurturing?

39. _____ Do you feel uncomfortable when other people ask for things from you?

40. _____ Do you ever feel like you have nothing to give?

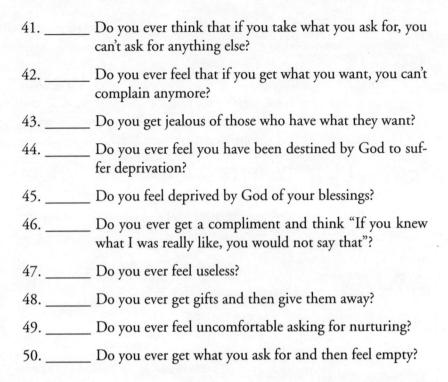

41. _____ Do you ever think that if you take what you ask for, you can't ask for anything else?

42. _____ Do you ever feel that if you get what you want, you can't complain anymore?

43. _____ Do you get jealous of those who have what they want?

44. _____ Do you ever feel you have been destined by God to suffer deprivation?

45. _____ Do you feel deprived by God of your blessings?

46. _____ Do you ever get a compliment and think "If you knew what I was really like, you would not say that"?

47. _____ Do you ever feel useless?

48. _____ Do you ever get gifts and then give them away?

49. _____ Do you ever feel uncomfortable asking for nurturing?

50. _____ Do you ever get what you ask for and then feel empty?

Each item on the list is worth two points for a total of one hundred points. To calculate your "positive receiving quotient," count the items marked N and multiply by two. To calculate your "negative receiving quotient," count the total items marked S and O and multiply by two. If your N number is greater than your S+O number, then your "positive receiving quotient" is higher than your "negative receiving quotient." If your S+O number is higher than your N number, then you have a higher "negative receiving quotient."

Now, ask your partner to take the assessment, and then dialogue with each other about your discoveries. Be sure to note items on your partner's list that are the same and different from yours. You may find that many of the items are different, that one of you is open to receiving and the other more resistant to receiving on the same or different items.

Next, look at all the items marked S+O on both lists and think about how each of you might open your heart to even more receiving. One way you can facilitate your growth is to take each item that you marked with an S or an O and change it to a positive. For example, change, "Do you always feel uncomfortable when someone brags about you?" to "I always feel comfortable when someone brags about me." When you can change all of the sentences above into positive statements, then you have greatly increased your "positive receiving quotient."

You can make a commitment to help each other open your hearts to all the ways of receiving that are indicated on this list. Regardless of your scores, your "negative receiving quotient" indicates an opportunity for growth.

Your "Giving Love" Assessment

Below are fifty questions designed to discover what we are calling your "giving quotient." Please rank each item with S for "sometimes," O for "often," or N for "rarely" or "never." N items measure your "negative giving quotient." The combination of S+O items measures your "positive giving quotient." You and your partner can complete this task separately and then share your answers.

As was true when assessing your receiving quotient in Exercise 6, allow yourself to consider your answers from both a separate and connected knowing perspective.

1. _____ I feel comfortable bragging about someone.

2. _____ I feel positive when someone brags about himself or herself.

3. _____ I feel positive toward someone else who is bragged about by another person.

4. _____ I give gifts without expecting others to feel obligated.

5. _____ I give gifts and do not remember I gave them.

6. _____ I give gifts to people who value them.

7. _____ I accept people who refuse to take my gifts.

8. _____ I give compliments to others easily.

9. _____ I express love easily and freely.

10. _____ I tend to remember only the good times.

11. _____ When I give a gift, I do not expect to be thanked.

12. _____ I express appreciation for the gifts other people give me.

13. _____ I try to give gifts that other people say they want.

14. _____ I give without telling stories about my giving.

15. _____ I like giving anonymous gifts.

16. _____ I feel comfortable when another person is getting all the attention.

17. _____ I give to needy people.

18. _____ I feel comfortable giving to myself.

19. _____ I have a desire to give.

20. _____ I give without complaining.

21. _____ I like seeing other people have what they want.

22. _____ I share the joy of other people who have good things I don't have.

23. _____ I positively affirm the value of other people—their worth, their ability.

24. _____ I feel full inside when I give.

25. _____ I feel comfortable when other people give things to themselves.

26. _____ I believe giving expands me.

27. _____ I feel loving toward people who are needy.

28. _____ I feel like I am a good person.

29. _____ I value myself.

30. _____ I feel like a success.

31. _____ I feel happy most of the time.

32. _____ I celebrate the good fortune of other people.

33. _____ I try to show my best self at all times.

34. _____ I support others who like and want praise.

35. _____ I willingly reassure others who need it or ask for it.

36. _____ I feel comfortable nurturing others.

37. _____ I feel comfortable when others ask me for something.

38. _____ I feel like I have a lot to give.

39. _____ I feel a lot of joy when I give.

40. _____ I give full attention to people who complain.

41. _____ I love it when other people get what they want.

42. _____ I give full attention to people when they are talking to me.

43. _____ I give praise to God for my blessings.

44. _____ I give myself good health care.

45. _____ I like it when someone lets themselves be bragged about.

46. _____ I always feel valuable and useful.

47. _____ I feel blessed to be able to give.

48. _____ I give gifts to persons whom I don't like.

49. _____ I am glad to be alive.

50. _____ I praise God for the gift of life.

Each item on the list is worth two points for a total of one hundred points. Count the total items marked S and O and multiply by two. Then count the items marked N and multiply that number by two. The combination of S+O will give you your "positive giving quotient," your ability to give. Subtract the N number from the S+O number. This will give you your "negative giving quotient," your difficulty with giving. If your N number is greater than your S+O number, then your "negative giving quotient" is higher than your "positive giving quotient." If your S+O number is higher than your N number, then you have a higher "positive giving quotient."

Now, ask your partner to take the assessment, and then begin a dialogue with each other about your discoveries. Be sure to make a note of the items that are the same and different from yours. You may find that many of the items are different, that one of you is open to giving and the other more resistant to giving on the same or different items.

Next, look at all the items marked S+O as a separate knower. These are facts. Now, using connected knowing, think about how you feel about your ability to give. Let yourself experience your ability to give with all your heart. Connect to that part of yourself with appreciation. Then, look at the items marked N and think about how you might change them into giving. Notice them as facts, then let yourself feel whatever you feel about them.

Regardless of your scores, your "negative giving quotient" indicates an opportunity for growth. You can make a commitment to help each other open your hearts to all the ways of giving that are possible on this list. When you can place and S or an O before all the sentences, you have increased your "positive giving quotient."

Your Imago

Our ability to receive and to give is greatly influenced by our childhood relationship with our caretakers. The way they treated themselves was a model of giving and receiving. Most of us unconsciously adopted this model for ourselves and continue to live it out in our significant relationships. In addition to these covert messages, our caretakers also sent us overt messages about giving and receiving. In response to these two sets of messages, we developed our identity by making a series of conscious and unconscious decisions. These include answers to the questions: "Who am I?" "What can I say, do, and feel?" "What kind of person am I?" "What do I deserve?" "What should I do with my life?" "Who are other people?" "How do I relate to them?" "What can I expect as an outcome?" The answers to these questions determine our patterns of receiving and giving to ourselves and to others, and thus influence the quality of our intimate relationships. Although these decisions were not made consciously, we can discover them by looking at our current thoughts, feelings, words, and behaviors.

This exercise is designed to help you construct an image of your primary caretakers as you remember them from childhood with regard to receiving and giving. As such, it will provide you with many clues to your current attitudes toward giving and receiving in your relationships today.

On the chart below or on a separate sheet of paper, make a list of positive and negative words that describe your parents as you recall them.

Mother		Father	
Positive Traits	Negative Traits	Positive Traits	Negative Traits

Now, <u>underline</u> the items below that would apply to your mother (female caretaker) and (circle) those that would apply to your father (male caretaker). If a term applies to both of them underline *and* circle it.

It's okay to want: love, sex, play, fun, intelligence, movement, feelings, nurturing, rest, sleep, education, work, success, happiness, health, food, vacations, spirituality, religious beliefs, touch, laughter, support, warmth, praise, knowledge, your own thoughts, sympathy for others, money, property, recreation, freedom, independence, compliments, negative feelings, hope, orgasms, massages, fear, sadness, anger, grief, happiness, joy, peace, equality, pleasure, musical talent, creativity, artistic talent, faith, doubt, desires, athletic talent, competition, trust, fatigue, education, respect, tolerance, appreciation, gratitude, empathy (add any other words that you wish).

It's okay to receive: love, sex, play, fun, intelligence, movement, feelings, nurturing, rest, sleep, education, work, success, happiness, health, food, vacations, spirituality, religious beliefs, touch, laughter, support, warmth, praise, knowledge, your own thoughts, sympathy for others, money, property, recreation, freedom, independence, compliments, negative feelings, hope, orgasms, massages, fear, sadness, anger, grief, happiness, joy, peace, equality, pleasure, musical talent, creativity, artistic talent, faith, doubt, desires, athletic talent, competition, trust, fatigue, education, respect, tolerance, appreciation, gratitude, empathy (add any other words that you wish).

It's not okay to want: love, sex, play, fun, intelligence, movement, feelings, nurturing, rest, sleep, education, work, success, happiness, health, food, vacations, spirituality, religious beliefs, touch, laughter, support, warmth, praise, knowledge, your own thoughts, sympathy for others, money, property, recreation, freedom, independence, compliments, negative feelings, hope, orgasms, massages, fear, sadness, anger, grief, happiness, joy, peace, equality, pleasure, musical talent, creativity, artistic talent, faith, doubt, desires, athletic talent, competition, trust, fatigue, education, respect, tolerance, appreciation, gratitude, empathy (add any other words that you wish).

It's not okay to receive: love, sex, play, fun, intelligence, movement, feelings, nurturing, rest, sleep, education, work, success, happiness, health, food, vacations, spirituality, religious beliefs, touch, laughter, support, warmth, praise, knowledge, your own thoughts, sympathy for others, money, property, recreation, freedom, independence, compliments, negative feelings, hope, orgasms, massages, fear, sadness, anger, grief, happiness, joy, peace, equality, pleasure, musical talent, creativity, artistic talent, faith, doubt, desires, athletic talent, competition, trust, fatigue, education, respect, tolerance, appreciation, gratitude, empathy (add any other words that you wish).

It's okay to give: love, sex, play, fun, intelligence, movement, feelings, nurturing, rest, sleep, education, work, success, happiness, health, food, vacations, spirituality, religious beliefs, touch, laughter, support, warmth, praise, knowledge, your own thoughts, sympathy for others, money, property, recreation, freedom, independence, compliments, negative feelings, hope, orgasms, massages, fear, sadness, anger, grief, happiness, joy, peace, equality, pleasure, musical talent, creativity, artistic talent, faith, doubt, desires, athletic talent, competition, trust, fatigue, education, respect, tolerance, appreciation, gratitude, empathy (add any other words that you wish).

It's not okay to give: love, sex, play, fun, intelligence, movement, feelings, nurturing, rest, sleep, education, work, success, happiness, health, food, vacations, spirituality, religious beliefs, touch, laughter, support, warmth, praise, knowledge, your own thoughts, sympathy for others, money, property, recreation, freedom, independence, compliments, negative feelings, hope, orgasms, massages, fear, sadness, anger, grief, happiness, joy, peace, equality, pleasure, musical talent, creativity, artistic talent, faith, doubt, desires, athletic talent, competition, trust, fatigue, education, respect, tolerance, appreciation, gratitude, empathy (add any other words that you wish).

Now, using the words you underlined and circled, complete the sentences below as they apply to each caretaker:

Mom (or female caretaker):

> *It's okay to want:*
>
> *It's okay to receive:*
>
> *It's not okay to want:*
>
> *It's not okay to receive:*
>
> *It's okay to give:*
>
> *It's not okay to give:*

Dad (or male caretaker):

> *It's okay to want:*
>
> *It's okay to receive:*
>
> *It's not okay to want:*
>
> *It's not okay to receive:*

It's okay to give:

It's not okay to give:

Now think of these as "messages" you received from your parents about what you could want, receive, and give. Using these messages to you about how to live, study each one and write down what consequences were attached to obedience/disobedience of the negative and positive messages.

If I obeyed the negative messages, then:

If I disobeyed the negative messages, then:

If I obeyed the positive messages, then:

If I disobeyed the positive messages, then:

Next, indicate which messages you obeyed and disobeyed, and indicate the consequences.

The negative messages I obeyed were . . . , and the consequences were . . .

The negative messages I disobeyed were . . . , and the consequences were . . .

The positive messages I obeyed were . . . , and the consequences were . . .

The positive messages I disobeyed were . . . , and the consequences were . . .

Now, given the messages you obeyed, what decisions did you make about:

Who I am:

What I deserve:

What I don't deserve:

Given who I am, what I deserve, and what I don't deserve, I can expect from life that I:

And, given all that, the kind of intimate relationship I will have is:

Now, given the messages you disobeyed, what decisions did you make about:

Who I am:

What I deserve:

What I don't deserve:

Given who I am, what I deserve, and what I don't deserve, I can expect from life that I:

And given all that, the kind of intimate relationship I will have is:

Next,

Which messages are you still obeying?

Which decisions are still active?

What consequences are you still experiencing?

Finally,

Which of the active decisions do you want to change?

What thoughts, behaviors, and feelings would you have to change in order to negate the decisions?

Now, decide what new decisions you will make.

REPEAT THE PROCESS FOR YOU AND YOUR PARTNER

Now you will want to use the process you have completed for your primary caretakers to work out the same kind of results for you and your partner. Start with the beginning of Exercise 8. Based on your experience with your partner, ✓ the words that apply to him or her; X the words that apply to you.

Now, complete the sentences below with messages you think your partner received from his or her caretakers.

My partner feels:

It's okay to want:

It's okay to receive:

It's not okay to want:

It's not okay to receive:

It's okay to give:

It's not okay to give:

Then, review the list again, and this time, complete the sentences with messages **your partner sends to you.**

In my relationship with my partner, it's okay for me to want:

In my relationship with my partner, it's okay for me to receive:

In my relationship with my partner, it's not okay for me to want:

In my relationship with my partner, it's not okay for me to receive:

In my relationship with my partner, it's okay for me to give:

In my relationship with my partner, it's not okay for me to give:

Review the list once again, and this time complete the sentences with messages **you send to your partner.**

In my relationship with my partner, it's okay to want from me:

In my relationship with my partner, it's okay to receive from me:

In my relationship with my partner, it's not okay to want from me:

In my relationship with my partner, it's not okay to receive from me:

In my relationship with my partner, it's okay to give to me:

In my relationship with my partner, it's not okay to give to me:

These messages indicate what prohibitions and permissions around receiving and giving exist in your relationship.

Now using the dialogue process, talk with your partner about the messages you both received from your parents. (For a full discussion of the Imago Dialogue, see Chapter 8, pages 162–171.) It's important to recognize that you and your partner will no doubt have different perspectives on some of these issues. Engaging in the Imago Dialogue will help you both clarify where your perspectives are different and where they are similar.

Next, dialogue about the messages you give to each other about giving and receiving. Then, write down the messages you wish you had heard from your parents, the messages you want to hear from your partner, and the new permissions you will give to yourself. Using dialogue, share them with your partner.

The results of this exercise will give both you and your partner insights into the origins of messages you have received from your respective primary caretakers as children, as well as ways in which those messages continue to have life within your relationship. You can use these insights to identify and discuss through dialogue your barriers to giving and receiving love.

Intimacy

PART I: BARRIERS TO INTIMACY

Many of us fear the love we need. These fears, rooted in childhood wounds, show up in partnerships as barriers to intimacy and connection and interfere with our ability to receive and to give love. Identifying these fears, honoring them, and creating a conscious partnership for mutual healing is the path to wholeness and real love.

The categories below refer to normal developmental stages in children. When a child's developmental needs are not supported in a particular state, the child develops a wound that manifests as a fear in intimate partnerships. Read through the categories and their corresponding fears carefully and select those fears that apply to the way you feel in your intimate relationships, which can include your partnership, family relationships, and close friendships. Review your selections and circle the one fear that you feel most often. Your choice will reveal how you may have been wounded in childhood and point to what needs to change in order for healing to begin.

1. Attachment

    1a. I am sometimes afraid that my partner does not want me, and that he or she might reject me and leave me.

    1b. I am sometimes afraid of being abandoned, and that if I take time for myself, I will lose my relationship.

2. Exploration

2a. I am sometimes afraid of being smothered, absorbed, or humiliated by my partner.

2b. I sometimes become afraid when my partner is unreliable—when he or she is sometimes there and sometimes not there for me.

3. Identity

3a. I am sometimes afraid of being shamed for being who I am and losing my partner's love.

3b. I am sometimes afraid that if I give in to my partner, I will become invisible and lose my partner's love.

4. Competence

4a. I sometimes fear being seen as a failure, and that I have to prove my worth or risk losing my partner's approval and love.

4b. I am sometimes afraid that if I am seen as aggressive, successful, competent, and powerful, I might lose my partner's love and acceptance.

5. Concern

5a. I am sometimes afraid that my partner does not see me as an equal and/or does not like me and does not want to be with me.

5b. I am sometimes afraid that if I show my partner that I have needs and express them, my partner will exclude me.

6. Intimacy

6a. I am sometimes afraid that my partner wants to control me and I will not be free to express myself without being criticized.

6b. I am sometimes afraid that I will not have my partner's

approval because I am different from my partner and other people.

PART II: PATH TO INTIMACY

This section will help you figure out how to go from fear to growth and healing by identifying the following:

- your relationship wound
- your relationship defense
- your character structure
- your relationship growth challenge
- your partner's profile

You and your partner can work through this section separately. When you have completed it, ask your partner for a dialogue. Share your discoveries and ask your partner to share his or her discoveries also. Make a commitment to journey on the path toward intimacy together, stretching toward growth, and helping to heal each other's wounds.

1. Attachment

If you selected either 1a or 1b: Your main wound was in the attachment stage of development, birth through eighteen months. In addition to food, what babies need most to survive are physical and emotional contact, and a reliable source of love and comfort. When babies do not get that consistent nurturing, they either become excessively clingy, or excessively detached.

If you selected 1a:

Your Relationship Wound: Fear of rejection, and loss of self through contact with your partner.

Your Relationship Defense: Avoider. You tend to be detached and avoid social interaction. As an avoider, you probably fear too many feelings and chaos, and think contact will lead to rejection. This could be due to inadequate care during the age of attachment from birth through eighteen months. You might feel like you have no right to exist, and then withdraw and engage in obsessive thinking to attend to your needs. An avoidant or detached adult will believe: "I will be hurt if I initiate contact with you."

Your Character Structure: Minimizer. You tend to hold your emotions inside, inhibit general expressiveness toward others, and devalue expressiveness in yourself and others.

Your Relationship Growth Challenge. Detached adults must learn to claim their right to *be,* and maintain connection, especially with their partners, by initiating emotional and physical contact, expressing feelings, and increasing body awareness and sensory contact with their environment.

Your Partner's Profile: Clinger.

If you selected 1b:

Your Relationship Wound. Fear of loss of self if you lose contact with your partner.

Your Relationship Defense: Clinger. You tend to cling to your partner and give him or her little breathing room. Your parents' inconsistent nurturing after your birth through eighteen months may have left you with a voracious appetite for connection and love. When conflicts arrive, you instinctually heighten demands to get your needs met, and you refuse to negotiate until you give in altogether. As an adult, a clinger will hold the following belief in relationship: "I am safe if I hold onto you."

Your Character Structure: Maximizer. You tend to exaggerate your emotions and general expressiveness toward others, and to overvalue expressiveness in yourself and others.

Your Relationship Growth Challenge. Clingers must learn to focus on letting go, do things on their own, and negotiate while maintaining connection—especially within their partnerships.

Your Partner's Profile: Avoider.

2. Exploration

If you selected either 2a or 2b: Your main wound was in the exploration stage of development, eighteen months through three years. A toddler mostly needs support and encouragement to explore his or her environment. When a child does not get the support and encouragement, the child tends to be overly isolated or overly pursuing.

If you selected 2a:

> **Your Relationship Wound:** Fear of being smothered and losing self by merging with partner.
>
> **Your Relationship Defense: Isolator.** You tend to isolate yourself and protect your privacy. It seems that your parents prevented you from exploring the world to the degree you desired. Love left you feeling smothered and humiliated, so you distanced yourself from loved ones. You wish to demand freedom, but are afraid of losing relationships. Thus, you resort to passive-aggressive tactics and suppress your rage. As an adult, an isolator will believe about relationships: "I can't say no and be loved, so I won't ask for anything."
>
> **Your Character Structure: Minimizer.** You tend to withhold your emotions and general expressiveness toward others, and to devalue expressiveness in yourself and others.
>
> **Your Relationship Growth Challenge.** Isolators must focus on initiating closeness, sharing feelings, increasing time together, and integrating the negative and positive traits of their partners.
>
> **Your Partner's Profile: Pursuer.**

If you selected 2b:

> **Your Relationship Wound.** Fear of neglect and loss of your partner.

Your Relationship Defense: Pursuer. You tend to pursue your partner, invade his or her privacy, and act dependent. Wounded by caretakers who weren't always there when you returned from explorations, you equate independence with being abandoned. You may think that you can't count on anyone when you need support. You see your partner as distant and self-absorbed, and may frequently voice complaints, criticism, and fears when facing conflicts. You pursue, but then withdraw. A pursuer will have the belief: "If I act independent, you will abandon me."

Your Character Structure: Maximizer. You tend to exaggerate your emotions and general expressiveness toward others, and to overvalue expressiveness in yourself and others.

Your Growth Challenge. Pursuers must learn to initiate separateness, develop outside interests, accept their partners, and integrate the positive and negative traits of their partners.

Your Partner's Profile: Isolator.

3. Identity

If you selected either 3a or 3b: Your main wound was in the identity stage, ages three through four. When a young child is trying on new identities, the parent needs to mirror and validate whoever the child is being at the moment. When this supportive and safe atmosphere doesn't exist, the child becomes either a rigid controller or an invisible person with diffuse boundaries.

If you selected 3a:

Relationship Wound. Fear of shame and loss of partner's love if you lose self-control or fail.

Your Relationship Defense: Rigid Controller. You attempt to control and manage your partner and others. Your childhood was likely full of discipline, rules, and shame, limiting your ability to form an identity that expressed all of you. In turn, you believe that you can't be yourself and be accepted. You feel compelled to take charge and lay down the law, though you don't enjoy it. You fear embarrassment due to your partner's nebulous desires, and can't bear the chaos, vulnerability, and passivity he or she brings to the relationship. As an adult, the rigid controller will believe about relationships: "I'll be safe if I stay in control."

Your Character Structure: Minimizer. You tend to withhold your emotions and general expressiveness toward others, and to devalue expressiveness in yourself and others.

Your Growth Challenge. Rigid controllers must focus on relaxing their control, mirroring their partners' thoughts and feelings, and becoming more flexible and sensitive.

Your Partner's Profile: Compliant Diffuser.

If you selected 3b:

Your Relationship Wound. Fear of being ignored and becoming invisible, and therefore losing your partner's love.

Your Relationship Defense: Compliant Diffuser. You tend to be unclear and indirect. Alternately fearing invisibility and self-assertion, you adopt passive-aggressive methods to get the attention you secretly desire, and seek love by pleasing others. You resent your partner's control of the relationship, but are at a loss to make any suggestions. You exaggerate your emotions defiantly, and then become self-effacing and compliant. The invisible person with diffuse boundaries will have the following belief as an adult: "I'll be loved if I go along and please others."

Your Character Structure: Maximizer. You tend to exaggerate your emotions and general expressiveness toward others, and to overvalue expressiveness in yourself and others.

Your Growth Challenge. People with diffuse boundaries must learn to assert themselves, set boundaries for themselves, and respect the boundaries of others—especially within their partnerships.

Partner's Profile: Rigid Controller.

4. Competence

If you selected either 4a or 4b: Your main wound was in the competence stage of development, ages four through seven. At this stage, a child needs continued nurturing, plus warm and consistent praise for his or her efforts to master new skills. When this praise is not forthcoming, the child becomes either overly competitive or overly compromising.

If you selected 4a:

> **Your Relationship Wound.** Fear of being dominated by your partner and loss of love if you fail.
>
> **Your Relationship Defense: Compulsive Competitor.** You tend to compete with everyone, including your partner, and you want to win. Your caretakers probably placed larger expectations on you than you were prepared to handle. They made you feel that you had to be perfect, and you became afraid that failure would result in loss of all love. You compete with your partners, but their weak and manipulative tactics frustrate you to no end. You put them down ruthlessly and then feel guilty about it. The overly competitive child, as an adult, develops this belief about relationships: "I'll be loved if I am the best."
>
> **Character Structure: Minimizer.** You tend to withhold your emotions and general expressiveness toward others, and to devalue expressiveness in yourself and others.
>
> **Your Growth Challenge.** People who are competitors must focus on accepting their competence and becoming cooperative, and mirroring and valuing their partners' efforts.
>
> **Your Partner's Profile: Manipulative Compromiser.**

If you selected 4b:

> **Your Relationship Defense: Manipulative Compromiser.** You tend to devalue yourself, withhold your opinions, and compromise. You may think your partner is never satisfied and doesn't

respect your contributions to the relationship. It's hard to get the respect you desire, because you naturally adopt a compromising role, thinking goodness and cooperation lead to love. Your partner's more aggressive nature makes you feel helpless and resentful, so you resort to manipulation to get your needs met. The overly compromising child has this belief as an adult: "I'll be loved if I am good and cooperative."

Your Relationship Wound. Fear of being aggressive and powerful, because engaging in rivalry will lead to the loss of your partner's approval.

Your Character Structure: Maximizer. You tend to exaggerate your emotions and general expressiveness toward others, and to overvalue expressiveness in yourself and others.

Your Growth Challenge. Compromisers must learn to be direct, express power, develop competence, and praise their partner's success.

Your Partner's Profile: Compulsive Competitor.

5. Concern

If you selected either 5a or 5b: Your main wound occurred in the concern stage, ages seven through twelve. The older child needs wisdom and guidance from parents, but also the space and time to integrate the connection with his or her peers. If this does not happen, the child can become either an excessive loner or an excessive caretaker.

If you selected 5a:

Your Relationship Wound. You fear being rejected by your partner and ostracized by your peers.

Your Relationship Defense: Loner. You tend to withdraw and, when hurt, to refuse nurturing; and you tend to exclude others. You may believe that you're truly unlovable and fear the agony that closeness will arouse. Your partners, however, seek you out and try to intrude on your lonely world. You might avoid them and reject their overtures, but you must confront the pain of self-exile in order to escape depression and loneliness. As an adult, the loner believes about relationships: "I'll be hurt if I try to be too close."

Your Character Structure: Minimizer. You tend to withhold your emotions and general expressiveness toward others, and to devalue expressiveness in yourself and others.

Your Growth Challenge. Loners must learn to become inclusive, develop same-sex friends, and enjoy socializing by sharing feelings and thoughts with others, especially their partners.

Your Partner's Profile: Sacrificial Caretaker.

If you selected 5b:

Your Relationship Wound. You fear rejection or exclusion if you express your needs.

Your Relationship Defense: Sacrificial Caretaker. You tend to serve others and meet their needs, while denying and ignoring your own. Loved ones who rejected your gestures of concern hurt you. You still find yourself with partners who exclude you from the essential part of their lives and fail to reciprocate your love. This leads to resentment and depression as you struggle to meet their needs. The caretaker believes: "I'll be loved if I meet your needs."

Your Character Structure: Maximizer. You tend to exaggerate your emotions and general expressiveness toward others, and to overvalue expressiveness in yourself and others.

Your Growth Challenge. Caretakers must learn to express their needs to their partners and others, practice self-care, respect their partners' privacy, and take time to be alone.

Your Partner's Profile: Loner.

6. Intimacy

If you selected either 6a or 6b: Your main wound occurred in the intimacy stage, ages twelve through eighteen. The teenager needs to be surrounded by a family where people regularly share feelings and thoughts, and communication is natural. When this does not happen, the teenager can become either a rebel or a conformist.

If you selected 6a:

Your Relationship Wound. Fear of losing personal freedom and being controlled by your partner and others.

Your Relationship Defense: Rebel. You tend to challenge instructions, rebel against authority, and act out your feelings: Fearing oppression and conformity all around, you recall parents who didn't let you break the rules. You may think no one trusts you, and that growing up equals selling out. Your partners are generally self-righteous followers who tire of your flamboyant outbursts. You want everyone on your side, but can't trust anyone who's nice to you. Rebels, as adults, share this belief about relationships: "I'll be controlled if I give up dissent."

Your Character Structure: Minimizer. You tend to withhold your emotions and general expressiveness toward others, and to devalue expressiveness in yourself and others.

Your Growth Challenge. Rebels need to maintain their identities, and be responsible and learn to trust others, especially their partners.

Your Partner's Profile: Conformist.

If you selected 6b:

Your Relationship Wound. Fear that if you are different and express your uniqueness, you will lose your partner's approval and the approval of others.

Your Relationship Defense: Conformist. You try to be like others by always being agreeable and avoiding risks. Wounded in the stage of intimacy, you fear disapproval and being different. You believe you have to be good and hold things together in order to survive. The childish rebelliousness of your partners threatens the stability and normalcy you crave, but their freedom and zealousness attract you. Nevertheless, you rely on condescending and reactive behavior to place boundaries around the relationship. Conformists, as adults, believe this about relationships: "I have to hold things together."

Your Character Structure: Maximizer. You tend to exaggerate your emotions and general expressiveness toward others, and to overvalue expressiveness in yourself and others.

Your Growth Challenge. Conformists need to experiment with being different from others, take more risks, and develop their identities—especially within their partnerships.

Your Partner's Profile: Rebel.

As you read through the definitions of relationship wounds and their effects, you probably noticed that childhood wounds lead to the development of either maximizing or minimizing tendencies in adulthood, and that maximizers and minimizers tend to pair with each other.

Maximizers tend to exaggerate their energy, escalate their feelings, express intense emotions, and confuse their feelings with facts. When you ask maximizers what they think, they will tell you what they feel. Minimizers tend to diminish their energy by holding onto their feelings and showing little emotion. They are mainly interested in facts rather than feelings. When you ask minimizers what they feel, they will tell you what they think. Both maximizing and minimizing are survival tactics that have become habitual.

Everyone has elements of both maximizing and minimizing within them, since holding energy in and expressing energy outwardly are natural forms of defense. In early life, either maximizing or minimizing becomes dominant and habitual because it is effective in creating a feeling of safety. The imbalance, however, is ineffective in adult intimate partnerships because it creates a sense of danger, and thus fear, in the other partner. This results in a rupture of connection.

The most effective way partners can facilitate healing for each other is to become more like the other, especially, more like the part that they dislike in their partner. This means that maximizers need to learn to contain their energy, to minimize, and minimizers need to express their energy more, to maximize. It is a core change, one that is difficult and often takes a long time, depending upon the depth of the wound and the rigidity of the defense. However, it is the greatest opportunity we have to promote healing in our intimate relationships.

Becoming Whole Again

All children are born whole and have natural talents and impulses that express who they are. As a result of praise from caretakers, children develop some aspects of themselves, such as creativity, musical talent, or curiosity. However, other self-aspects, such as athletic skills or intuition, are ignored by caretakers and thus not developed. When caretakers criticize talents and impulses, such as sexual curiosity, abstract thinking, or assertiveness, children take the same attitude toward those self-aspects as their caretakers. They see those aspects as bad and dissociate from them in order to survive. But ignored or criticized talents and impulses do not disappear; they are simply rejected and pushed out of awareness. They do not fit into one's self-concept. This creates a "split" in the self, which can be recognized as a sense of emptiness accompanied by unspecific longings, and is the source of self-hatred and low self-esteem.

The ignored and criticized talents and impulses simply lie dormant. Since they are split off and repressed, they do not receive input and they do not express themselves, because they are unavailable for communication with the conscious part of ourselves. In other words, these aspects of the self can neither give nor receive. They are blocked. In addition, when parts of us are blocked, relational knowing is split into separate and connected knowing. For example, if our thinking is blocked, we tend to know things emotionally. If our emotions are blocked, we tend to know things in our minds, but not in our emotions.

In order to become whole again, to be able to receive, give, and engage in relational knowing, we must become aware of talents and traits we possess that do not fit our concept of ourselves, and integrate them. Only then can we truly receive, give, and know with our minds and hearts.

Some blocked impulses and traits may be considered by you and others to be positive. These are called "disowned" traits. But other blocked impulses and traits will appear to you and others as negative or undesirable. These are called "denied" traits. For instance, you may not think of yourself as "creative" or "soft" (disowned), or "distant" or "critical"(denied). But those who know you well, such as your partner, friends, or family members, may have already observed and reported these traits to you. Since the major characteristic of a disowned or denied self-trait is its invisibility to you and its visibility to other people in your environment, any association of such a trait with yourself may produce discomfort and/or your denial.

The way you can know whether a positive or negative trait is descriptive of some disowned or denied aspect of yourself is if more than one other person has reported it to you, and if your emotional reaction and denial of the trait is strong. These are clear signs that the trait describes some aspect of you which others have seen exhibited in a behavior. Since the trait describes some aspect of yourself, your denial of it amounts to an emotional rejection of that aspect of yourself.

The fate of rejected self-traits is self-hatred, which underlies low self-esteem. Another fate of these criticized talents and impulses may be their conversion into compensatory traits. For instance, a person who has denied his or her sexual curiosity may become a crusader against pornography or become a "prude." Or early childhood possessiveness, which is labeled "stingy" by caretakers and thus rejected by the child as a desirable trait, may show up in adult life as "frugality."

On the other hand, rejected self-traits may be projected onto others via adoration or criticism. For instance, we may adore musical talent in others or criticize their intelligence as "eggheadedness." The rejected trait or undeveloped talent is projected most often onto persons who are emotionally close to us. Commonly, we project onto our partners and our children. There is some behavior in our partner or our child which is activated by some behavior in us that attracts the projected trait. The paradox here is that emotionally we are relieved of the trait and at the same time we are able to create a relationship to it. In this way we experience an unconscious and spurious wholeness.

These projections, however, have consequences for our relationship with our partner and others. For example, we may adore a talent we think our partner has, insist that he or she develop it, and disown it in ourselves. Or, we may ignore it as our caretakers did ours. When we project a rejected self-trait onto our partners, we criticize them for having it, expect our partners to admit they have it, and then try to eradicate it. Our partners, then, become the victims of an ancient interaction between our caretakers and us.

DISCOVERING REJECTED ASPECTS OF YOURSELF

To free your partner from your own history and avoid involving him or her in unresolved issues from your own childhood, it is important that you know, admit you have, and become willing to change traits that are inconsistent with your concept of yourself. Then you will be able to relate to your partner as a subject-person, rather than a mirror of rejected aspects of yourself.

To discover rejected aspects of yourself, take a blank sheet of paper and draw a large circle that covers most of the page. Now divide the circle horizontally. Place a plus sign on top of the circle and a minus sign below it.

POSITIVE TRAITS +

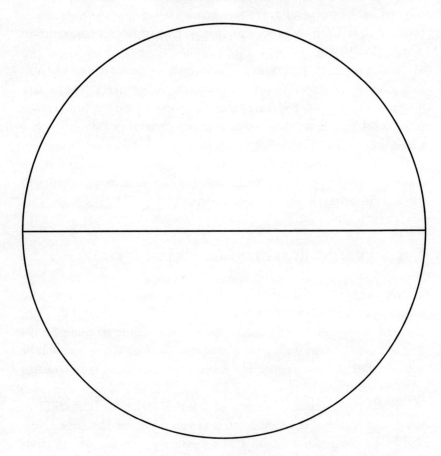

NEGATIVE TRAITS –

In the circle, above the horizontal line, list the positive adjectives that describe your caretakers, partner, any ex-partners, the traits you admire or adore in any opposite-sex person(s), and the traits you admire or adore in any person.

In the circle below the horizontal line, list negative adjectives that you assign to your caretakers, partner, any ex-partners, the traits you dislike or despise in any opposite sex person(s), and the traits you dislike or despise in any person.

Now study the circle carefully. The top circle suggests positive traits that you may possess, but disown. In some context in childhood, you decided not to develop certain traits that most people would value as positive, but that represented a danger to you. The traits listed below the horizontal line suggest negative self-traits that you may possess, but deny. In childhood you used behaviors that had survival value to you, but that were rejected as "bad" by your caretakers. The combination of these disowned positive traits and denied negative traits suggests a description of your rejected self.

To deepen and add validation to this process, select three to five persons who know you well and ask them to make a list of adjectives that they think describes you and/or their experience of you. Ask them to hold nothing back and to put a plus sign (+) or a minus sign (–) beside each trait.

Next, take all the positive and negative traits from your circle and from all the lists your loved ones compiled for you, and enter them in the chart below, or make a similar one on a separate piece of paper. Put positive and negative traits in the appropriate columns. The final chart will be a refined and accurate description of your disowned and denied self-traits.

CHARACTER TRAITS LIST

Column A—Positive Traits	Column B—Negative Traits

Now rank each item on both lists from one to five, with one being the trait that you think is most unlike you and five being the trait that is most like you.

Then, pick five traits from both columns that have the ranking closest to one and put them on the chart below according to the categories. The trait *least* descriptive of you is #1, #2 is less descriptive, #3 is somewhat descriptive, #4 is somewhat more descriptive, and #5 is most descriptive.

When you finish this question, you will have identified a total of ten traits, five positive and five negative.

Ranking	Positive Traits (Column A)	Negative Traits (Column B)
1. Least Descriptive	_____	_____
2. Less Descriptive	_____	_____
3. Somewhat Descriptive	_____	_____
4. Somewhat More Descriptive	_____	_____
5. Most Descriptive	_____	_____

You must own these traits to become whole and to make any significant changes that will influence your relationship with your partner. As you own, integrate, and change these traits, your imago will change and your relationship with your partner will improve.

PERSONAL GROWTH PLAN

This exercise will help you integrate the disowned and denied traits you have uncovered, helping you to overcome your split. Please follow the instructions below. Move the five traits under column A, Positive Traits, in the chart on page 264 to the appropriate column in the chart below.

A

Positive Traits	Potential Traits	Behavioral Expression	D

Then move the traits under column B, Negative Traits, in the chart on page 264 to the appropriate column in the chart below.

B

Negative Traits	Potential Traits	Behavioral Expression	D

The traits in column A represent positive potential you possess that other people already see, but which you may have denied. You need to claim and integrate these traits into your self-concept. You can do this by changing the name of a positive trait that may feel like too much of a stretch into a potential trait that you want to develop. You can list potential traits in the space provided for all five positive traits, if necessary. Then, design a behavior that expresses the positive or potential trait in interpersonal transactions. The behavior should be positive, concrete, specific, and quantified. Use the space provided and record behavioral expressions for each of the five positive or potential traits. Next, rank the behaviors one to five with one as most difficult, in Column D.

For instance, if one of the traits is "creative," you can keep that word or choose a similar word, such as "insightful." If you keep "creative," you can express it behaviorally as follows: "I will write poetry at least once each week for the next six months."

Now change the five traits in Column B into traits that for you would be positive and desirable. Changing to an opposite trait is okay, if that is the new trait you want to develop. Use the space provided to record behavioral expressions for each of the five positive or opposite traits. Next, rank the behaviors one to five, with one as most difficult, in Column D.

For instance, if you listed "stingy" as a trait, then you can change it into "prudent" and express it behaviorally as follows: "I will establish a savings plan that will enable me to save steadily over the next twelve months."

You can use the example below as your guide.

Ranking	Positive Traits (Column A)	Negative Traits (Column B)
1. Least Descriptive	creative	stingy
2. Less Descriptive	intuitive	distant
3. Somewhat Descriptive	adventurous	arrogant
4. Somewhat More Descriptive	warm	suspicious
5. Most Descriptive	intelligent	rigid

SAMPLE PERSONAL GROWTH PLAN

A

Positive Traits	Potential Traits	Behavioral Expression	D
Creative	Insightful	I will share my new ideas daily.	1
Intuitive	Perceptive	I will express a perception I've had to my partner once a week.	2
Adventurous	Bold	I will take a risk each day.	3
Warm	Intimate	I will express my deepest feelings with my partner once a week.	4
Intelligent	Intelligent	I will take one course a quarter in an effort to finish my college degree.	5

B

Negative Traits	Potential Traits	Behavioral Expression	D
Stingy	Frugal	I will make careful decisions daily about spending my money.	1
Distant	Boundaried	I will protect the time we plan for relaxation each weekend.	2
Arrogant	Proud	I will positively flood our relationship once a week.	3
Suspicious	Watchful	I will help double-check that we have positive energy in our relationship daily.	4
Rigid	Reliable	When you call, I will come.	5

Thinking about and writing this exercise is a practice in separate knowing. Putting this exercise into practice requires becoming more of a connected knower, and thus moving toward relational knowing. Sharing and receiving feedback and support from each other will increase your ability to receive and to give.

When you complete the written exercise, ask your partner for a dialogue and share your growth plan. Ask your partner to share his or her growth plan with you. Then develop the new traits by practicing the behavior expressions regularly. Each week, pick a trait and practice it. The more whole you are, the more you are able to receive the love in your life, too.

Discovering Your
Hidden Potential

We are born whole. In that original state, we can take in and send information with our minds, feel and express our emotions, interact with our environment through our five senses, and move our muscles in all sorts of ways. We call these the "four functions of the self": thinking, feeling, sensing, and moving. These functions are all connected and work together seamlessly. And, through them, we are connected to everything—other people, our environment, the universe, and to that from which it all originated and is sustained.

For most of us, however, this wholeness and connectedness is short-lived. To develop and sustain our connection with our selves, and our environment, we need attuned and supportive caretakers, as well as peers. We are relationally dependent. But we have not evolved enough yet as a species to rear our children without rupturing their connection to themselves and everything else, in small and large ways. Our caretakers, unconsciously and with the best of intentions, assist or impede the development of our four functions of self to their full potential by the messages they give us.

For instance, our caretakers may tell us it is okay to think or they may ignore, deflect, or criticize our thinking. They may honor our feelings and thus confirm their validity, or they may tell us not to feel at all or to feel only certain feelings. Some caretakers encourage the use of our senses and show us how to look at flowers, smell their aroma, listen to music, develop our taste buds, and touch our bodies.

Others ignore educating our senses and sometimes deflect or devalue our sensory curiosity. Some caretakers encourage us to move our muscles, to dance, or be athletic, while others tell us not to move, not to dance, and not to run into things.

The functions that are impeded or ignored by our caretakers fail to develop and are lost to our awareness, but they do not disappear as a potential. Their loss in childhood results in a split in the self that we call the "lost self." These lost traits were functional in your selection of your partner, and they can be recovered within your relationship.

Unlike the disowned self-traits and the denied self-traits, which are visible to others, the "lost self" is not only out of our awareness, it is also out of the awareness of others. Thus, we can neither receive input nor express these missing functions in our relationships because those channels of relating are not open for giving and receiving. Their loss also interferes with relational knowing, and depending upon which functions are missing, we become either predominantly separate or connected knowers.

RECOVERING THE LOST SELF

This exercise is designed to help you identify and recover your "lost self" in your relationship. Your partner can help you in this process. In the columns on page 272, record the positive and negative messages you received from your caretakers about each aspect of yourself listed in each column. Study the examples below before you start. They will guide you in doing the exercise.

EXAMPLES:

THINKING: Statements from caretakers:

You don't need to go to school.

You think you are so smart.

Message: Don't think.

I am so impressed at your clear thinking about that.

I really like your idea. Could I hear more?

Message: It's okay to think, to use your mind.

FEELING: Statements from caretakers:

You are so emotional.

Don't show your anger around here.

Message: Don't feel (or feel certain feelings).

So you are feeling sad right now.

Tell me about your anger.

Message: It's okay to feel your feelings.

SENSING: Statements from caretakers:

Don't waste your time listening to music.

Wanting hugs is silly.

Message: Don't experience your senses.

I'm glad you like hugs.

Look at the beautiful sunrise.

You seem to hear the melody in the music.

Message: It's okay to use all of your senses

MOVING: Statements from caretakers:

Don't climb or run so much.

Don't sing at the dinner table.

You are always wiggling.

Message: Don't move your muscles.

I like the way you are dancing.

You can really run fast.

Your body is so agile.

Message: It's okay to move your body.

CORE SELF   (Your real self): Statements from caretakers:

Don't be.

Don't.

Don't be you.

Don't want things.

Message: Don't exist.

It's okay to be.

It's okay to be you.

It's okay to be all of who you are.

Message: It's okay to exist.

Thinking	Feeling	Sensing	Moving	Core Self

Use the chart above to record the messages you received from your care-takers. Identify the positive messages with a + sign and the negative messages with a – sign. Count the total number of positive messages you received about each function and the total number of negative messages you received about each one. See the sample below.

An example of how Joshua would fill out this chart. As you remember from Joshua's story, he was born to parents who were deeply religious and conventional in their view of the family. When he was young, Joshua's father died, leaving Joshua with the desire to follow in his father's footsteps as a "perfect man." When Joshua became a teenager, he suffered a lot of guilt and confusion over his normal sexual feelings. In the absence of real information, he concluded that his sexual urges were a punishment for his moral failings. He could never shake the feeling that God was watching everything he did and judging him according to His set of black-and-white rules for moral purity.

This is how Joshua might fill out the chart below. It is a strong example because the messages Joshua received as a child were unusually clear-cut. Some things were mandated, while others were forbidden. His parents and their community worked from a preconceived template of how their children should be.

Thinking	Feeling	Sensing	Moving	Core Self
Don't think for yourself –	Don't have forbidden feelings –	Don't touch –	Don't dance or indulge in individual expression through your body –	It's not safe to reveal who you really are –
Don't be intuitive –	Don't be vulnerable –	Don't be sexual –	Do be physically strong +	Become like an idealized version of your father +
Do be assertive in promoting our views +	Be judgmental –	Don't drink or watch TV –	Do be athletic +	
Do well in your school-work +	Do have Christian feelings toward others +	Do enjoy the beauty of our worship +		
		Do appreciate the beauty of other cultures +		

Now, on a separate sheet of paper, draw a circle and divide it horizontally and vertically. Write the word **thinking** in one section, the word **feeling** in the next, the word **sensing** in the next, and the word **moving** in the last, and then in the center write **core self**, which refers to you, your existence.

On the diagram, record the number of negative and positive messages you received for each function. Study your negative messages for each function and black out your estimate of the percentage of that function you feel was repressed in your childhood.

The sections of the circle which you black out as repressed functions constitute your "lost self." These functions were rejected by your caretakers and thus by you. The remaining white space reflects the percent of that function that was not repressed.

You can see from Joshua's example that he emerged from childhood with a large part of himself lost to his consciousness. He grew up in a repressive atmosphere where his individuality was discouraged and his conformity to community standards was promoted.

When you fill out this chart for yourself, you will discover which parts of yourself you rejected under pressure from your caretakers. In most intimate relationships, the functions you rejected in yourself are the opposite of those rejected by your partner in him- or herself as a result of his or her caretakers' messages. This means that what is missing in you is developed in your partner. Because the functions that

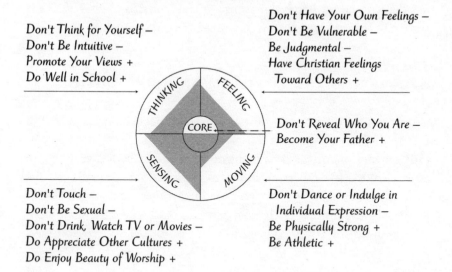

JOSHUA'S
LOST SELF-FUNCTIONS

Don't Think for Yourself –
Don't Be Intuitive –
Promote Your Views +
Do Well in School +

Don't Have Your Own Feelings –
Don't Be Vulnerable –
Be Judgmental –
Have Christian Feelings
Toward Others +

Don't Reveal Who You Are –
Become Your Father +

Don't Touch –
Don't Be Sexual –
Don't Drink, Watch TV or Movies –
Do Appreciate Other Cultures +
Do Enjoy Beauty of Worship +

Don't Dance or Indulge in
Individual Expression –
Be Physically Strong +
Be Athletic +

are "on-line" in your partner are "off-line" in you, you will tend to reject those functions in your partner because your caretakers forbade them in you. In other words, you will take the same negative attitude toward those functions in your partner that your caretakers took toward them in you. You will ask your partner, through criticism and devaluation, to sacrifice those same parts that you surrendered in order to survive in your family. (If you have children, you may find yourself asking your children to inhibit or repress aspects of themselves similar to the ones you were asked to inhibit or repress.)

On the other hand, you may have been initially attracted to that part of your partner that you were asked to repress, those areas that in your partner are naturally open and alive. But later, those parts of your partner may arouse concerns in you, and you may then initiate limitation or repression. If you were asked by your caretakers, for example, to inhibit your thinking, you will be attracted to a person whose thinking function is fully expressive and alive. But in your relationship, you will no doubt ask him or her to limit, inhibit, or repress his or her thinking. You will do this unconsciously, even though you may want your partner to be free in the areas in which you were inhibited. You cannot give your partner the permission you were denied, for your unconscious will prevent it. Since the function was denied you for survival reasons, your unconscious will repeat the same task for the same reason in your current relationship.

RECOVERING THE LOST SELF IN RELATIONSHIP

Repeat the Recovering the Lost Self exercise beginning on page 272 as it applies to your partner. Think about the statements you make to your partner about his or her freedom to think, to feel feelings, to experience the five senses, to move, to be his or her core self. Use the same chart of statements that you used for yourself.

Now draw another circle on a new page and repeat the same steps you followed for yourself, beginning on page 274. When you have

Thinking	Feeling	Sensing	Moving	Core Self

finished, you will have a picture of the parts of your partner that you may be unconsciously or consciously attempting to inhibit. This will result in conflict or acquiescence. If your partner acquiesces, those parts will be lost to his/her consciousness and become part of his/her "lost self." Becoming conscious of these messages will enable you to support all the functions of your partner.

To recover *your* "lost self," ask your partner to help you develop the undeveloped parts of yourself. Study each function in your partner that is missing in you and ask your partner to help you develop that function. You can use your partner as a model to learn how to think, feel, experience all your senses, and move your muscles. You may not develop your function in the same way as your partner, however. For example, your partner may be good at thinking and express it as a philosopher, while you might choose to develop your thinking by becoming a businessperson or a biologist.

When your partner offers help to develop a function, or if you choose to develop it on your own, develop your separate knowing by receiving it with your mind and then let yourself feel it in your whole being. Let it be real in your imagination and feelings, and then express it in behavior. In this way, you will develop your ability to receive and to give, and at the same time balance separate knowing and connected knowing into relational knowing.

To complete this exercise, convert all the negative messages about your four functions of self and your core self into positive ones. For instance, convert a "don't be" message to your core self into "it's okay to exist." Convert a "don't move" message to your muscles into "it's okay to move my body." Convert a "don't be sexual" message to your senses into "it's okay to be sexual." Convert a "don't feel" message to your emotions into "it's okay to feel all my feelings." Convert a "don't think" message to your mind into "it's okay to think all my thoughts." You might ask your partner to say these positive messages to you. Receive them, think, feel, touch, and act on them, and absorb them into your being. When you complete them all, you will be whole again. You will be able to give and receive in new ways in your relationship, and relate to your environment with both channels of knowing.

Afterword

There are periods in the life of a marriage when things are fragile. You scrutinize every little gesture and action to see whether the signs point toward your staying together or splitting up. For us that time came right after we decided to give our marriage one more year before we either renewed our vows or divorced.

During those early weeks we felt we had entered a world of signs and portents. In addition to using our rational skills to improve our relationship, we found ourselves searching for personal meaning among the detritus of everyday life. Everything said either "stay" or "leave."

One evening we found ourselves in a bookstore picking up a large book on relationships and astrology. We looked up the horoscope for our marriage. Given our birth signs, it cautioned us to "achieve freedom from negativity," and "stop the unrelenting scrutiny of each other." We were shocked. It was as if the authors had followed us around taking notes. The simple and direct advice was helpful, and we followed it. We decided to establish the ritual of flooding each other with positive words daily. We became super-aware of keeping our Between safe. Both of these resolutions meant getting the negativity out of our relationship. This leap into the positive turned out to be transforming.

We aren't saying you should put this book down and take up astrology. The point is that it can be life-changing to read a book so on the mark that it seems written just for you. We hope you have found something in this book that strikes you that way. We want you to know that relationships follow certain courses that can be known and understood. Once you identify where you are in the pattern, you can follow the reliable path toward healing.

Our message, too, is simple and direct: *Learn to receive the gifts that are everywhere around you.* Life itself is a gift! We have learned this on a deep, personal, connected-knowing level. Every breath we take, every color we see, every sound we hear, every taste we experience comes to us without our asking. Learn to accept praise and appreciation from others, see the serendipities of life as moments of grace, and love all aspects of yourself as wonderful. When you can do that, emptiness will disappear, longing will be assuaged, and you will become a true giver. This is the best way to heal your deepest wounds and your intimate relationships.

On a professional level, the concept of receiving love has been a linchpin in our understanding of many things outside the complexities of partnership. What we've learned about intimate relationships can be applied to the hurting society in which we live. We see applications of the personal to the public everywhere. We can't read a newspaper, attend a meeting, or discuss world events without wanting to use Imago Relationship Therapy tools and concepts to clarify the underlying dynamic or improve communication.

We admit to a certain amount of bias. There is no doubt that our work has shaped the way we see things. When you're a hammer, everything looks like a nail, and when you're involved in Imago Relationship Therapy, everything looks as though it can be understood in terms of relationship. Here are some of the conclusions we've reached that we would like to continue to explore:

Every couple who creates a conscious marriage is making a significant contribution toward the common social good. For a long time, we've observed that couples who complete the Imago Relationship Therapy process tend to become social activists. They don't necessarily march in parades or join social organizations (although some do!), but they become involved in improving the world in lots of simple ways. They coach Little League, recycle their trash, become better parents, and take better care of their neighborhoods. One couple began to pick up garbage along their various local highways. Another planted trees in an empty lot. Still another couple began to care for abandoned cats and dogs.

They knew what it was like to feel connected to each other, to experience empathy, and as a consequence, they felt more connected to all of life. When they were no longer split inside, they did not experience cracks and fissures in their relationship to things outside themselves. They felt more at home in the wider world. Charity really does being at home. Happy couples make better citizens and call for a better world. Conscious marriages turn partners into conscious parents. The brains of new babies and children are shaped by the quality of their parents' relationship. Children who are the products of conscious parenting are healthier, more creative, and more productive. They will want to live in a better world and will be willing to work to create it.

What would happen if every couple became conscious and replaced negativity with kindness and care? What would happen if they parented their children with attunement, neither invading nor neglecting them?

Here is what would *not* happen.

- We would *not* have a 50 percent divorce rate each year—affecting one million marriages.[1]
- Over one million children each year would *not* lose their homes and one of their parents.[2]
- 63 percent of youth suicides would *not* occur.[3]
- 90 percent of children who run away and become homeless would *not* run away.[4]
- 85 percent of children with behavior problems would *not* have behavior problems.[5]
- 71 percent of high school students who currently drop out would *not* drop out.[6]
- 85 percent of youths in prison would *not* act out their anger in society.[7]
- 50 percent of single, teen motherhood would *not* occur.[8]
- Nearly $3 billion annually would *not* need to be spent on alcohol and drug abuse recovery programs.[9]
- Nearly $1.2 billion annually would *not* need to be spent on obesity.[10]
- 30 million people would *not* be raised in poverty.[11]
- Over $9 billion would *not* have to be spent on the foster care of children.[12]

- $25 billion annually would *not* have to be spent on the criminal justice system.[13]
- $150 billion would *not* be spent on mental health services.[14]

This does not include the cost to the environment of people living on the earth without empathy for nature in all its forms, nor does it include the savings possible from improved physical health worldwide. Many of our most lethal diseases are related to stress, and happy relationships provide a defense against stress-related illnesses.

Instead of trying to fix the social ills of poverty, violence, addiction, and abuse *after* they've occurred, we could focus on improving the relationships that are the most determinative for every individual from the beginning. We could put more emphasis on upriver prevention, so that we don't have to keep losing the battle of downriver cleanup.

We believe the *only* way to clean up the river of life is to go upriver and transform all intimate partnerships, and then parenting. Heal the splits in the individual, the couple, and the family, and then our social fabric will not be so split and torn. Social programs and government projects will not succeed in creating a just and peaceful society when all they can do is try to react to the ruptured connections of family life. This is why our mission and the mission of the Imago Relationship Therapy community is to transform the world, one couple at a time.

Dialogue can be adapted to a broader range of social, economic, and political relationships. Imagine that the principles of dialogue governed the standard of information sharing among political leaders of different countries, business owners and trade unions, business people at all levels, different ethnic and racial groups, divorcing parents, and students and teachers, among others.

In Israel, an Imago Relationship therapist and a researcher have been teaching Imago Dialogue to preschool children. When we visited their school, we saw videotapes of the children mirroring each other. We were moved to tears when we heard a five-year-old boy say to his playmate: "So you don't like it when I play with your toys? That makes sense." Then the two kids hugged each other. The researcher and the therapist told us that the children insist on being mirrored, and they love it. There was no conflict in the classroom. The adults administering this program told us that they have come to the conclusion that dialogue is the natural language of children, and thus of human beings. Unfortunately, in childhood, we surrender this inborn voice of dialogue.

Consider what life would be like if we were all accustomed to interacting like this: "*You have my full attention as I listen to you and try to understand your point of view. What you are telling me is valid. I can enter into your worldview. I know you will do the same for me.*" It may sound too good to be true, for just as Gandhi reputedly said about Christianity, "It's a great idea. Too bad nobody's ever tried it." But the Imago Dialogue is easier to try than Christianity. We are not proselytizing for a philosophy or a religion. We want to give people the tools they need to communicate better and connect empathically. We believe that this one change would go further than any other to end depression, anger, and all forms of self-abuse—the sources of violence in our world.

We know that people can be taught to dialogue fairly quickly. Yes, it takes practice to become good at it, but it is not out of the reach of anyone who wants to learn how. Dialogue is already being used in some nonprofit organizations. People tell us that it's easier to come to true consensus this way. The process of expressing and absorbing different points of view takes longer, but the organization is stronger and decisions are more secure when dialogue is part of the group culture.

The concepts of separate, connected, and relational knowing can make important contributions to our information culture. The idea that we can expand our capacity to receive and process information from outside ourselves is one of the most exciting ideas to come out of our work on this book. The capacity to receive depends upon developing the capacity for relational knowing. We have seen how couples are able to open to each other when they become aware that there are ways to enlarge their restricted understanding of each other into something much bigger. They are able to overcome the limits of an overreliance on either separate or connected knowing and achieve the balance of comprehensive understanding we call relational knowing. Information is power. Information is currency. Information is energy. It makes sense to pay attention to epistemology, to *how* we know what we know, as well as the content we are trying to understand.

We want to explore how these ideas can be applied outside the confines of personal relationships. What if entire organizations were able to understand diverse or foreign points of view and become more humanitarian and more effective because of it? What if the wisdom that comes from relational knowing were to become more characteristic of the institutions that define our society? Perhaps we could end all forms of violence, including war.

There is a new archetype of partnership evolving in our culture. Marriage is alive and well, but the form of marriage is changing, as all forms do when they no longer fulfill their originating purpose. The personal marriage, which is dominant today, focuses on meeting personal needs at the expense of the relationship. This is the marriage that is being abandoned by more than 50 percent of couples every year. The lesson our culture is learning very painfully is that it does not work to be self-centered, to look out only for yourself. We are by nature relational creatures and connection is our essence. Although we cannot actually lose our connections, we can lose our awareness of them. And when we feel disconnected, we not only suffer, but we inflict suffering on others.

The marriage of the future will become a partnership where the focus is no longer on the individuals involved, but on the relationship itself. For the first time in history, marriage will be healing, because it will restore wholeness and transform society. The partnership marriage will be characterized by commitment, dialogue, the absence of negativity, and the increase of appreciation, empathy, and kindness. Monologue will be replaced by dialogue, symbiosis with differentiation, and conflict with connection. The current question is, "How can this marriage meet my needs?" The new question will be, "What does our *relationship* need?"

Our own experience has taught us that marriage can be the birth of love, even after it feels as if love has gone. We try to stay connected to each other now, even when we argue or are apart. And, every night before we fall asleep, we whisper our vows to each other again in the darkness. We don't ever want to forget how close we came to losing each other.

That is our story, but you have your own. Don't settle for the *idea* of healing through love. Don't mistake the intellectualization for the experience. Take hold of love for yourself. Don't rest until you experience in every cell of your being what it means to partake of the joy of a connected relationship and the generosity of life. Take in the breath, light, water, and earth that are your true inheritance. Be a receiver first and then be a giver. That's the joy and the power of putting your relationship first.

Notes

Introduction

1. Dostoevsky explores the idea that God cannot ever be totally encompassed by the human mind alone, that comprehension must come through the gateway of wisdom and love. See, for example, Fyodor Dostoevsky, *The Brothers Karamazov* (New York: Modern Library, 1996), pp. 261–62.
2. Harville Hendrix, *Getting the Love You Want* (New York: HarperCollins, 2001).
3. Harville Hendrix, *Keeping the Love You Find* (New York: Pocket Books, 1992).
4. Harville Hendrix and Helen LaKelly Hunt, *Giving the Love that Heals* (New York: Pocket Books, 1997).
5. Couplehood has changed form over historical time, and each form has served a specific social purpose. The first form of couplehood was the "pair bond" of hunter-gatherer societies that lasted until 10,000 years ago. Although they were not marriages in a legal sense, they were durable unions of males and females for the purpose of procreation and survival. There is no historical record for the origins of marriage as a legal institution, but it is generally assumed that it began with agrarian cultures. These unions, determined by parents, were what we refer to as "arranged marriages." This form of marriage replaced the instability and chaos of the pair bond with order and stability. Its purpose was to ensure the transmission of property and to enhance social stability. Parallel with the rise of the concept of property, wives and children were perceived as property of the husband and father. This form of marriage, which we call the "social marriage," existed until the rise of eighteenth-century democracies in the Western world wherein a new form, "marriage by choice," arose. Freedom from monarchy and hierarchal rule allowed persons to select their own marital partners based on romantic attraction.

    We interpret the mutual experience of romantic attraction as an indication of a match between an inner representation of the parents, the imago, and the character traits of the attractive partner, thus creating an "imago match." We call this the "personal marriage," the purpose of which was personal need satisfaction rather than economic and social stability. This type of marriage was inherently unstable, thus initiating another historical period of chaos. The model began to dissolve in the middle of the twentieth century with the rise of the divorce rate. In our view, it is being replaced with what we call the "partnership marriage," in which the focus is on the needs of the partnership rather than on personal needs. In our view, this shift from the personal to the relational, for the first time in history, gives marriage transformational power for persons and society, thus heralding the beginning of a new age of stability.

6. Ontology is a philosophical inquiry into the nature of reality. The term is derived from the Greek word for "being," *ontos,* and the Greek word *logos,* which means "word" in English. Literally, ontology refers to the "discourse about reality." Essentially, it is an inquiry into what there is that stands behind and accounts for everything.

7. Epistemology is another philosophical mode of inquiry that asks, how can we know what is, and what is the nature of knowledge? Essentially, it addresses the question: "How do we know what we know?" Historically, epistemology has posited two modes of knowing: the objective, or rational, and the subjective, or intuitive. Objective knowing is related to science and the discovery of "facts," and intuitive knowing is associated with creativity and the arts. In the Western world, the former has been more valued than the latter. In Imago epistemology, we translate these two traditional ways of understanding the knowing process as "separate" and "connected" knowing. We give both equal value and integrate them with the concept of "relational" knowing, which we see as crucial in the process of understanding and change in intimate partnership.

8. Daniel J. Siegel, *The Developing Mind* (New York: The Guilford Press, 1999). This is a comprehensive statement of the influence of interpersonal experience on neurobiological development.

9. Mary Field Belenky, Blythe McVicker Clinchy, Nancy Ruth Goldberger, and Jill Mattuck Tarule, *Women's Ways of Knowing* (New York: Basic Books, 1986).

10. Although each person is both a separate and connected knower, with one mode dominant and the other recessive, each couple is complementary. One partner is more a separate knower and the other more a connected knower. Since this can be a source of misunderstanding and conflict, it helps couples to understand and accept each other's way of acquiring and processing information. Since therapists also have both modes of knowing, with one recessive and one dominant, they need to learn about themselves. Some therapists are more intuitive than logical and vice versa, and thus may unconsciously ally themselves with the client whose mode of knowing mirrors his or her own.

Chapter 1: Nothing's Ever Good Enough

1. We use the term "receiving deficiency" as an answer to the question: "Why do people reject compliments?" We have noticed in ourselves a tendency to deflect compliments offered at our seminars. We have also noticed others deflecting our compliments. As our interest in the question grew, we became aware of the general phenomenon that most people tend to deflect or reject compliments. In addition, we noticed a tendency in most people to diminish or reject positive things in their lives, but an equal willingness to accept the negative.

2. We made the discovery of the reason why people erect barriers to receiving in a couple's therapy session. At first, the male partner was resistant to responding to his partner's request for statements of appreciation expressed in a warm tone of voice. After understanding that his partner's desire was connected to a deficit of warmth in childhood, he agreed to praise her as she requested. She coached him to praise her just the way she wanted, and he did. She agreed he did it perfectly, and it seemed to me he was behaving just as she wished. But, no matter what, she found something wrong with his praise. When I asked her to relax and imagine receiving the praise, she became visibly upset and started crying. When I coached her to regress into childhood memories and report what triggered her feelings, she reported hearing her mother's voice saying she wanted too much and was not worth loving. She recalled making a decision never to ask for anything and rejected her desires for warm appreciation. As we processed her experience, she connected her husband's coldness to this previously unconscious memory.

    Imago Relationship Therapy posits that partners in an adult intimate relationship are, in important ways, mirrors of their caretakers. Thus, the original desire is reactivated, and partners try again to get what they did not get in childhood. But their partner responds as the caretaker did and this recreates the original frustration. However, the desire, which originally was free of conflict, is now contaminated by the caretaker's rejection, a rejection with which the child identified. Furthermore, an injunction from the parent is now attached to it, which to the child consciousness means that the desire is bad, and it is bad to have this desire. And, if she violates the caretaker's injunction, the inner parent might abandon her and she would die. Therefore, no matter what her partner did, she could not accept it because that would violate the parental injunction in her unconscious. It follows that she had to find something wrong with her partner's best efforts in order to stay alive. Until she could dismantle this inner drama from childhood, she had to remain deprived.

    Sigmund Freud accounted for this phenomenon with the concept of the superego. In psychoanalytic theory, which he developed, all conflict was a function of intra-psychic dynamics. For him, these dynamics consisted of interactions between the id and the superego mediated by the ego. The superego that disapproved of id impulses, such as the desire for pleasurable praise and other pleasures, was a psychic structure, not just a memory, whose function was to prevent id impulses from inappropriate expression in order to protect the individual from social censure and protect society from the expression of libidinal impulses.

The only other book I have seen on receiving deficits is James R. Scroggs' *Letting Love In* (Englewood Cliffs, NJ: Prentice-Hall, 1978). Scroggs assigns the inability to let love in to having not been loved in childhood.

Chapter 2: Three Marriages Gone Wrong

1. Martin Buber, *I and Thou* (New York: Simon & Schuster, 1996). Buber's intention was to describe the hyphen, or what we call the Between. His classic phrase is that "all life is meeting." But most readings of the book focus on the I and the Thou. His intention was to give ontological status to relationship. This was so revolutionary at the time he wrote it that his intention was overlooked by an intellectual climate that focused on the individual.
2. Buber's focus on relationship was an expression of a new paradigm for understanding human experience. This paradigm is reflected in Imago Relationship Therapy. Relationship and intersubjectivity have been a major focus in psychoanalysis in the last twenty-five years. For more on this development, see George E. Atwood and Robert D. Stolorow, *Structures of Subjectivity* (Hillsdale, NJ: The Analytic Press, 1984), and Stephen A. Mitchell and Lewis Aron, *Relational Psychoanalysis* (Hillsdale, NJ: The Analytic Press, 1999).
3. The concept of "empty mind" is described in D. T. Zuzuke, *An Introduction to Zen Buddhism* (New York: Grove Press, 1966).
4. For a discussion of contemplative prayer, see Thomas Merton, *Contemplative Prayer* (New York: Doubleday, 1996).

Chapter 3: The Unconscious Connection

1. For a more in-depth discussion of the stages of relationship, see the first book on Imago Relationship Therapy, *Getting the Love You Want*.
2. For reference to the Chinese symbol for opportunity, see Eberhard Wolfram, *A Dictionary of Chinese Symbols* (New York: Routledge and Kegan Paul, 1986).
3. The situation is actually more complicated. A child not only reacts to an intrusive or neglectful parent, he also identifies with them. In addition, every child has both types of parents, and he learns both types of defenses. One defense is primary and the other is secondary. The primary defense is a

response to the parent with whom the child experienced the most injury, and the secondary defense with the parent who was less active in wounding. In adult intimate relationships, partners use their primary defense when they experience their partner behaving in a way that was criticized by a parent. On the other hand, when their partners criticize them in a way that activates unconscious memories of their caretakers, their wounds are reactivated, and they respond to their partners with the defense they used with their parents. In other words, when one partner is intrusive, the other partner feels like a child and will withdraw and diminish any response. When one partner is neglectful, the other partner will exaggerate any response. On the other hand, when someone feels as if a partner is acting like a child, the other will behave toward the partner by being intrusive or neglectful, re-enacting the way the person was treated by his or her caretakers. In all cases, each of us is capable of both defenses, because we all possess both wounds.

4. Sigmund Freud first used the concept of projection in a letter to his friend Fleiss in 1895. (Sigmund Freud, "Extracts from the Fleiss Papers," 1895, reprinted in *The Complete Psychological Works of Sigmund Freud* [London: Hogarth Press, 1953–74, Vol. 1] p. 207, and developed in his essay, "The Unconscious" [in the same publication, Vol. 4, pp. 159–215]). Essentially, it refers to an unconscious process by which one represses painful mental content—thoughts, emotions, intentions—and assigns them to others, and then criticizes others for possessing them. This is a common experience in committed relationships. For an excellent research-oriented book that builds on Freud and develops a broader view of projection, including how parents project onto their children, see James Halpern and Ilsa Halpern, *Projections* (New York: Putnam, 1983), pp. 37–55.

5. Technically speaking, symbiosis is the mutual dependency of two life forms upon each other for their mutual welfare. An example is the white heron sitting on a cow's back feasting on the ticks. The heron gets dinner, and the cow gets rid of bloodsuckers! In schools of psychoanalytic developmental psychology that focus on intra-psychic dynamics, symbiosis refers to the fusion of the newborn infant with the mother. They posit that the infant has no awareness of its boundaries and experiences a transient and necessary oneness with her caretaker. An infant's first developmental task is to emerge from this cocoon-like existence by differentiating from its mother. (See Margaret Mahler, *On Human Symbiosis and the Vicissitudes of Individuation* [New York: International Universities Press, 1968].) This theory is challenged by the social-psychological view that an infant is innately social at birth and that the first developmental task is to become attached to the caretaker. (See Daniel Stern, *The Interpersonal World of the Child* [New York: Basic Books, 1985].) In this relational model, which we support, symbiosis is not the natural state of the infant, but a result of an early relational injury around attachment. The emotional pain of a stressful bonding process activates the infant's sur-

vival fears, producing an absolute state of self-absorption. In this self-absorbed state, nothing exists except the infant's subjectivity, and that subjectivity becomes the infant's world. This exaggerates our natural concentric perception—the fact that all of us experience ourselves as the center—so much that our experience becomes absolute.

The infantile psychosis that Mahler thought was the natural state of the child is, in fact, relationally created, and because it is so widespread, it becomes both a personal and social disease. If this condition is not relieved by positive experiences, the capacity of the infant/child to experience his perspective as relative will be lost. In adulthood, she will operate on the assumption of sameness: that the world is the way she sees it, that the way she sees it is the right way, and that all persons see it that way—or they are wrong and may even be bad. Difference is difficult to tolerate, and the subjectivity of others is almost impossible to conceive. This makes intimate relationships difficult for many and impossible for some. In this absolutist state, empathy and tolerance, a precondition for all positive relating and two necessities for a humane society's civilization, will be missing. Symbiosis is the culprit in all couples conflict, and the inability to accept Otherness is the source of all human struggles, including war.

6. While men tend to be minimizers and women maximizers, these defenses are relationally determined, not gender determined, and men and women have both possibilities. In every person, one is dominant and the other recessive. The fact that minimizing is the dominant defense of most men and maximizing the dominant defense of most women is a function of the socialization process. Although we are in a new, transgender age, men still are asked to contain or repress their emotions, so they act them out in sports and war. Women are allowed to express their emotions, but they are not asked or required to develop their minds; consequently, they have fluid boundaries and difficulty containing emotions. However, in all homes, children learn to defend themselves based on what will work in their family, or what their caretakers support as appropriate behavior. Thus some women learn from experience or are asked (usually unconsciously) to minimize their energy, and vice versa for some men. In our experience, 80 percent of men and 20 percent of women are minimizers, and 20 percent of men and 80 percent of women are maximizers. But we also feel these ratios are changing as men and women are becoming more and more freed from traditional roles. For the first essay on these defenses, see Sigmund Freud, "The Neuro-psychoses of Defense," (1894) *Standard Edition*, Vol. 3, pp. 43–68.

Chapter 4: The Childhood Roots of Self-Rejection

1. Splitting is a technical term that refers to a distortion in the self as a result of suppression and repression of certain aspects of the self. The dynamics of suppression and repression are a defense against experiencing parts of the

self—wishes, thoughts, behaviors, and body parts such as the genitals, and so on—that have been rejected in some way by one's caretakers. In psychological literature, splitting is considered pathological and is at the core of personality disorders. In this book, we use the term to refer to a nonpathological state, which is less severe and more common. We call this state "ruptured connection" and assign its source to unattuned parenting. Since we have not evolved enough as a species to know how to parent children without emotional injury, we believe this is a universal condition. For more information on splitting, see Philip Manfield, *Split Self, Split Object* (Northvale, NJ: John Aronson, 1992). Although Manfield's book focuses on pathological states, it enables the reader to see that pathological states are exaggerations of a general condition. For more information see also J. Breuer and Sigmund Freud, "Studies on Hysteria," (1893–1895) *Standard Edition*, Vol. 2, pp. 268–70.

Chapter 5: Rejecting Self/Rejecting Love

1. To my knowledge there is no psychological literature on the concept of connection as we use it in Imago Relationship Therapy. Most theories about relationships talk about attachment, bonding, and empathic communion; in psychoanalysis, relationship is conceptualized as transference or countertransference. Relational analysis talks about an authentic relationship between analyst and analysand that comes close. But connection is more than attachment, bonding, emphatic communion, transference, countertransference, or an authentic therapeutic relationship. These are developmental tasks and therapeutic tasks, and our success with them in childhood or adult therapy determines our awareness or lack of awareness of our essential connection. When these exist, our defenses relax, and we open to connection as our essence. But when we talk about "connection," we are referring to a philosophical view of life that considers all life to be connected—whether we can see it or understand how to prove it. The best source we've found for understanding connection as our essential state is quantum physics, which posits that the universe is an unbroken wholeness. (See David Bohm and B. J. Hiley, *The Undivided Universe* (New York: Routledge, 1993.) Everything is connected, all the way up and all the way down, and at the highest level of consciousness, and we are aware of this cosmic unity and our intrinsic connection to it. (See Danah Zohar, *The Quantum Self* [New York: William Morrow, 1990]. For a fascinating and systematic statement of the oneness of the universe and our connection to it see Dean Radin, *The Conscious Universe* [San Francisco: HarperEdge, 1997], pp. 266–67. See also Menas Kafatos and Robert Nadeau, *The Conscious Universe* [New York: Springer-Verlag, 1990].)

   Connection is essentially energetic. It can be experienced. When we are connected, we feel an energetic pulse and the experience of joyful aliveness.

When two people connect, everyone in the context experiences energy. This frequently happens in the dialogue between couples, either in private or in public workshops. When it happens publicly, everyone in the room feels the surge of energy, like a ripple effect. At that moment, we are one with Everything; it is a spiritual experience.

Chapter 6: The Science of Relationships

1. Louis J. Cozolino, *The Neuroscience of Psychotherapy* (New York: W.W. Norton, 2002). This is a basic text on the neurosciences in psychotherapy. While the focus is on the development of the brain and its repair, the references to interpersonal factors are extensive.
2. Stephen A. Mitchell and Margaret Black, *Freud and Beyond* (New York: Basic Books, 1995), pp. 1–22. In the chapter "Freud and the Psychoanalytic Tradition," Mitchell and Black give a brilliant summary of Freud's struggle with the polarity of the intra-psychic and the interpersonal. With reference to the therapy process, they clarify Freud's method as scientific, detached, and clinical and compare it with his awareness of the power of the transference relationship as a healing alliance.
3. Daniel J. Siegel, *The Developing Mind* (New York: Guilford Press, 1999), pp. 276–337. Most of the material we present about developments in neuroscience and neurobiology are taken from this excellent book. It is among the definitive works that establish the interpersonal nature of neuro-physiological development.
4. Martin H. Teicher et al., "Preliminary evidence for abnormal cortical development in physically and sexually abused children using EEG coherence and MRI," in *Annals of the New York Academy of Sciences 821,* pp. 160–75. Teicher and his associates are renowned for their research on the effect of emotional, physical, and sexual abuse on the brain. Their research proves the impact of interpersonal experience on the neurological system.
5. Cozolino, p. 309.
6. Siegel, p. 41.
7. Siegel, p. 13.
8. Teicher.
9. Siegel, pp. 276–300.
10. Cozolino, p. 3.

Chapter 7: Learning to Receive

1. Daniel J. Siegel, *The Developing Mind* (New York: Guilford Press, 1999), pp. 321–24.

Chapter 8: Establishing Contact, Connection, and Communion

1. N. Eisenberger, M. Lieberman, and K. Williams, "Does Rejection Hurt? An MRI Study of Social Exclusion," *Science 10,* Oct 2003; 302: 290–92.

2. All therapies have a conscious or unconscious epistemology. And they can be distinguished by their implicit or explicit employment of separate and connected knowing. In classical psychoanalysis, the analyst assumed an objective stance while listening to the free associations of the client and then reported his interpretation to the client with the intention of provoking emotional insight. When successful, the effect evoked connected knowing in the client. (See Stephen A. Mitchell and Margaret Black, *Freud and Beyond* [New York: Basic Books, 1995], pp. 1–22.) Relational psychoanalysis, beginning in the 1970s, abandoned the objective stance of classical analysis and developed a conscious epistemology of connected knowing. (See Mitchell and Black, *Freud and Beyond*, pp. 229–53, and Robert Stolorow, George Atwood, and Bernard Brandchaft, *The Intersubjective Perspective* [Englewood, NJ: Jason Aronson, 1994], pp. 43–53.)

   Until our encounter with feminist theory, Imago Relationship Therapy focused on ontology and human nature. As a result of the influence of feminist research on the knowing process, Imago Relationship Therapy has adopted separate and connected knowing as its epistemology. We have found that the healing process is deepened when the therapist alternates between separate and connected knowing. We have also discovered that the dialogue process contains both modes of knowing. The integration of the two into relational knowing makes it possible for clients to transform cognitive knowledge about the Imago Relationship Therapy process into effective behavior.

Afterword

1. U.S. Census Bureau, 2000
2. Ibid.
3. U.S. Department of Health and Human Services, Administration for Children and Families, 1999.
4. Ibid.
5. Ibid.
6. Ibid.
7. Ibid.
8. Ibid.
9. Lewin Group, "The Economic Costs of Alcohol and Drug Abuse in the United States," National Institute on Drug Abuse, Table 7.6, 1992.

10. Center on Aging Society, Institute for Health Care Research and Policy, Georgetown University, "Childhood Obesity: A Lifelong Threat to Health," March 2002.
11. USDA, "The Food Stamp Program," 1999.
12. Roseanna Bess, Jacob Leos-Urbel, and Robert Green, U.S. Department of Health and Human Services, Administration for Children and Families, "National Clearing House on Child Abuse and Neglect," 2001.
13. Lewin Group, loc cit.
14. National Alliance for the Mentally Ill, "Facts and Figures about Mental Illness," 1999.

Index

About Imago Relationship Therapy

Imago Relationship Therapy is a process that helps couples use their relationship for healing and growth. Its goal is to help intimate partners understand that the unconscious purpose of committed couplehood is to finish childhood and shows them how to transform inevitable conflict into connection, thereby creating the relationship of their dreams. The Imago process is taught by over 2,000 therapists in more than twenty countries and is practiced by millions of couples worldwide.

If you are couple and want to consult an Imago therapist;

If you and your partner are interested in belonging to an international couples organization called Imago Couples International;

If you are a clinical professional and want certified training in Imago Relationship Therapy;

If you would like training as an Imago educator;

If you would like to teach the Imago process for Churches: Couplehood as a Spiritual Path;

If you would like information on couples and singles workshops, seminars, other books, audio and video tapes: Please go to *www.imagorelationships.org,* or call +1-800-729-1121.